Reviewers and readers respond to *Virtually Eliminated* and *Terminal Logic,* also by Jefferson Scott

"This exciting, fast-paced techno-thriller is set in the near future, as the cyberrevolution continues to change how people live. *Virtually Eliminated* is a well-told tale of repentance and of good versus evil."—*Bookstore Journal*

"I love *Virtually Eliminated*. It is great to read a techno-thriller that is not crude, vulgar, or otherwise blasphemous. The book is also very convicting. I know the struggle to keep my career and hobbies (also computer related) balanced with my commitment to my family and my Lord."—via the Internet

"I finished *Terminal Logic* and immediately headed to my Christian bookstore for *Virtually Eliminated*. Great writing and morals. It is nice to see a view of the future that does not take everything to the techno-extreme. Jefferson Scott does a fine job of advancing technology in many areas while keeping the human element in balance."—Long Island, New York

"*Terminal Logic* is a well-done fantasy that includes high drama built on the premise of accelerated technology. I raced through the final pages."—*CBA Marketplace*

"*Virtually Eliminated* is a great novel. A+ on a book well done! *Terminal Logic* is on my list for future purchases. If it is as good as *Virtually Eliminated*, it will be well worth my time. I hope to read more by Jefferson Scott in the future."—via the Internet

"*Virtually Eliminated* is fabulous! I really enjoyed the final showdown with Patriot on the BattleMech field. I look forward to grabbing the second book in the series (and the third when it comes out)."—via the Internet

"*Terminal Logic* combines nicely plotted suspense, the obvious fruits of research and expertise, and a very consciously Christian protagonist."—*Fort Worth Star-Telegram*

"I really enjoyed *Virtually Eliminated* and *Terminal Logic*. It's nice to see techno-thrillers from a Christian author. I look forward to reading the third book and hopefully many more after that."—via the Internet

"I've read more techno-thrillers than I can remember. Some are so sketchy it's a chore to follow the story and some are so overwritten it's a bore to wade through. Jefferson Scott's books walk the fine line right down the middle. They are well thought-out and extremely believable."—via the Internet

"*Virtually Eliminated* is quite the page-turner. My thanks (and blame) to Jefferson Scott for much lost sleep while reading this novel."—Kennesaw, Georgia

"Jefferson Scott has extrapolated modern technology and created a not-so-distant world that is all too believable. Uncomfortably so, for us near-technophobes. *Virtually Eliminated* will make you think even as it expands your imagination and takes you on a roller coaster ride of tension."—*Dusk & Dawn*

"*Virtually Eliminated* is a great read! Jefferson Scott has captured the world of cyberspace perfectly, and the plot keeps you guessing until the end."—via the Internet

"*Virtually Eliminated* is a very good Christian thriller. Scott's strongest points are story/character development, suspenseful pacing, and believable dialogue. If you like techno-thrillers, then this is a book for you. I am looking forward to reading *Terminal Logic*."—Fort Worth

"*Virtually Eliminated* deftly blends page-turner excitement with serious spiritual issues. Warning! Don't read this book if you are unwilling to face your own addictions and life choices. *Virtually Eliminated* is a real page-turner and, quite possibly, a life-changing experience. A great first novel from a very promising author."—via the Internet

FATAL DEFECT

FATAL DEFECT

A GENETIC THRILLER

JEFFERSON SCOTT

Multnomah Publishers *Sisters, Oregon*

FATAL DEFECT
published by Multnomah Publishers, Inc.

© 1998 by Jeff Gerke
International Standard Book Number: 1-57673-452-8

Cover photographs © 1998 by Peter Dazeley/Tony Stoné Images
Designed by Kirk DauPonce

Scripture quotations are from:
The Holy Bible, New International Version
© 1973, 1984 by International Bible Society,
used by permission of Zondervan Publishing House

Multnomah and the colophon are trademarks of
Multnomah Publishers, Inc.
Multnomah is registered in the U.S. Patent and Trademark Office.

Printed in the United States of America

For information:
MULTNOMAH PUBLISHERS, INC.
POST OFFICE BOX 1720
SISTERS, OREGON 97759

Library of Congress Cataloging-in-Publication Data

Scott, Jefferson.
    Fatal defect / by Jefferson Scott.
    p. cm.
    ISBN 1-57673-452-8 (alk. paper)
    I. Title.
    PS3569.C6356F38 1998
    813'.54—dc21   98–18027
                            CIP

98 99 00 01 02 03 04 — 10 9 8 7 6 5 4 3 2 1

To my grandmom, Sally Gerke,

Whose legacy to me is an insatiable thirst for learning

And the tendency to talk to the occasional tree.

Acknowledgments

I would like to thank the following people for their assistance in the creation of this book.

Proofreaders: Brian Walker, John and Anne Gerke, Reba Hill, and Sue King.

Genetics/biotech: Dr. Karl J. Roberts and John Ross. General science: Bryan Bradford. Satellite communications: Rich White. Military: Jack Horton. Thanks also to an unnamed information operations specialist.

Thanks as always to my editor, Rod Morris. Special thanks to my wife, my daughter, and my Lord.

PROLOGUE

wo chimpanzees. Five gibbons, a couple of baboons, one rhesus monkey. Ten lab rats thrown in for good measure. All wandering around together in a sealed, glass-walled chamber.

On the other side of the glass wall, Dr. Oscar Redding sat staring at the computer monitor before him. His mind was far away. He was thinking of Gabriel, the first patient who'd responded to his then-radical gene therapy. People always remembered the groundbreaking achievements—and the tragic failures—but Redding remembered the children. Gabriel had been six back then. So small, but full of life. His chopped hair and brown freckles. And this terrifying disease locked in every cell of his body. Redding sighed. To be able to be back there again.

John Lipscombe, GeneSys's chief administrator, bustled in from the observation room next door. "He's all set."

Redding rolled his chair heavily to the console. He handed a wireless microphone to Lipscombe, who took it with the slickness of a circus barker.

"Mr. Fashir," Lipscombe said into the microphone, "let me give you a little information on what you're about to see. In every chromosome there are sections of DNA called transposons, whose function is not yet known. Scientists have learned that it's possible to join these genetic elements together, creating new genes. Many of these new genes produce enzymes, as genes usually do. You may know, Mr. Fashir, that while most enzymes produced by an organism are essential, some enzymes that may be created using transposons can actually be poisonous to the host.

"In other words, Mr. Fashir, it is possible to take pieces of a person's own DNA and join them together into something that will kill him instantly. Observe."

Redding was staring at the rhesus monkey, who was screeching at a baboon that had wandered too close. How many lab animals had Redding killed over the years? It came with the territory. If the formula you were testing was wrong, it was better to kill a rat than a human. But that wasn't the case here. This wasn't a test. This was a demonstration.

A rapping on his console brought him back to the moment. "Any time, Doctor," Lipscombe said.

Redding reached for the button on his keyboard that would release the fine spray into the chamber, then sat back with a sigh and rubbed his forehead. He could feel Lipscombe's impatience beside him.

"Oscar," Lipscombe said, "what are you waiting for?"

"John, I think the test is too big. Let's demonstrate the toxin with the rats only."

Lipscombe leaned forward. "Oscar, this man has come a long way to see this test. He's rightfully upset because of how long it's taken your department to make his product."

"My department? You know very well—"

"Oscar, this is no different from any other animal test you've done for GeneSys over the years. Just push the button and this man will get on the plane and go away."

"No, John," Redding said. "Don't say this is no different from anything else I've done. You always tell me that. You've made it very clear to me every step of the way that the next thing is no worse than the thing before. And so I've come, step by step, further away from where I started. From where I want to be. And now I...I've lost my way, John."

Lipscombe pushed the button for him. "The mist you see, Mr. Fashir," he said into the microphone, "is a chemical compound we've developed which will trigger the synthesis of transposons into new genes. As soon as the compound is absorbed through the skin or inhaled, the process begins."

The floor of the animal chamber was suddenly thick with dead bodies. A gibbon was still twitching, but the rest were inert.

Lipscombe all but clapped his hands. He made an effort to keep the excitement out of his voice. "The effect, as you can see, is nearly instantaneous. It works like a nerve gas, but without any observable chemical signatures. There is absolutely no risk of contagion. And it's 100 percent lethal. The best part, Mr. Fashir, is that it's absolutely untraceable. It's the perfect terror weapon."

The door to the control room opened abruptly. A Middle Eastern man walked in, surveyed the room, then strode up to Lipscombe, who stepped back involuntarily.

"For this you say I should wait these many weeks?" the man said with a light accent.

Lipscombe gestured to the death chamber. "Did you see how quickly it worked?"

"This is not acceptable."

"Not acceptable?" Lipscombe asked. "I'm terribly sorry, Mr. Fashir. What do you find—"

"They felt nothing," Fashir said. "The beasts felt no pain."

"I assure you," Lipscombe said, sputtering, "they did feel tremendous pain. Didn't they, Dr. Redding? Tell him what pain they were in."

"They felt no pain," Redding said. "The gene produces a lethal toxin that acts instantly, too quickly for pain to register. They died mercifully."

"This is unacceptable," Fashir repeated.

"You would prefer they died in pain?" Redding asked him. In the corner of his eye he saw Lipscombe trying to warn him about something.

"Yes. This is what I would prefer. Great suffering prolonged for hours, followed by wasting, agonized death." Fashir turned to Lipscombe. "This is what I have paid for."

"And this is what you will get," Lipscombe said. "We guarantee satisfaction; not to worry." He put his hand on the client's arm, but it was shrugged off. "Dr. Redding will get to work on it right away, won't you, Doctor?"

"What you want," Redding said to Fashir, "is something more like a disease: Ebola or anthrax. Am I right?"

"Yes. Something that causes great pain and death. A wasting disease. HIV2, perhaps. Yet it must not spread. Can you do this?"

"It is a trivial procedure. An undergrad could do it. We'll engineer a recombinant form of rabies, I think. That should meet your needs."

"They will die like dogs?" Fashir said. "Excellent."

"But I will not do it," Redding said.

"What?" Lipscombe said.

"I won't do it, John. Not for you, not for him, not for all the money in the world. This is a weapon of mass terror and I won't be a part of it." Redding saw something in Lipscombe's eyes. "It *is* different from what I've done before, John. Don't even say it. What I've done here," he gestured toward the death chamber behind him, "was the last straw. Frankly I'm glad it failed to please. I'll destroy the records immediately. I'm finished with it."

"Excuse us, Mr. Fashir." Lipscombe said. He pulled Redding aside. "What are you doing?"

"I'm quitting, John." Redding saw a mental image of Gabriel and thought he'd be pleased with the decision.

"No, you're not." Lipscombe said. He was quiet a moment before continuing in a low, measured tone. "Oscar, GeneSys owns you. Mortimer McCall owns you. In a moment we'll take a look at the contract you signed. You're McCall's until 2010, when the option to renew is his alone.

"Think about it, Oscar," Lipscombe continued. "You don't belong anywhere else. The scientific community hasn't forgotten the children your 'therapy' killed. I'll make sure the press and the FBI are reminded if you leave. Your career is dead everywhere but here. But look at what Mr. McCall gives you, Oscar. He gives you money and facilities for you to continue your research so more children don't have to die. Who else is going to give you a chance, Oscar?"

Redding looked at Lipscombe with murder on his mind, and an idea came to him. He turned back to Fashir.

"I've decided what you want," Redding said. "Not rabies, but botulism. It kills in eighteen to thirty-six hours, so victims have time to suffer. And suffer they will. It affects the central nervous system, interrupting nerve impulses, but the mind continues to function normally. They will be fully aware of their distress. Incapacity progresses from difficulty in walking, swallowing, seeing, and speaking, to violent convulsions, and ultimately to paralysis of the respiratory muscles, suffocation, and death.

"It can be delivered with the same kind of mist that we've used here. It won't spread because the aerosol carrier cannot survive long in sunlight. If you like, I'll put a project leader on it today. It shouldn't take more than a week to ten days."

"That," Fashir said, smiling, "is acceptable."

"So happy to please you," Redding said.

For days afterward, try as he might, Oscar Redding could not conjure up the image of a little boy named Gabriel.

PART ONE

If there's a market for it, someone's going to do it.
Ted Koppel
Speaking about questionable biotech procedures
Nightline, April 1997

CHAPTER ONE

than Hamilton put the picture book aside. His daughter was asleep on his shoulder. Finally. Wysiwyg their cat was nestled in his lap. His watch told him it was past two, early on the morning of June 22, 2007. Katie needed to be back in her bed and Ethan needed to grab some sleep. Nevertheless he didn't get up just yet. Having his daughter asleep on his shoulder these days was rare. It was worth a few minutes more, just to soak it in. He stroked her blond hair and marveled at the delicate beauty of her face.

An insistent vibration at his hip put an end to his moment of paternal bliss. Ethan stood carefully and tucked the three-year-old back in her bed. He switched the pager off and headed into the hallway. He paused there, listening for contraband TV signals emanating from Jordan's room. Satisfied, Ethan passed the master bedroom where his wife, Kaye, was sleeping, and walked down the metal spiral staircase. Thirty seconds and two banged toes later, Ethan Hamilton descended into his underground game room.

"Penny," he said to the ceiling, "flame on."

A woman's alto voice issued from hidden speakers. "Reactivating previous configuration."

Cooling fans whirred, monitors set in the black walls popped on, storage drives clicked, overhead lights brightened.

Ethan's game room was his refuge, his inner sanctum. It expressed his personality perfectly: aesthetically plain but equipped with awesome horsepower. The underground chamber was about the size of a master bedroom. The only pieces of furniture were a table with two black swivel stools pushed underneath. Computer monitors and keyboards punctuated the black paneling all around. One wall was completely taken up by a huge flat-screen monitor.

There were no decorations, per se—no nooks with potpourri or pressed flowers. But four posters were on display, one on each of four narrow doors set at the corners of the room. One poster showed Luke Skywalker on Tatooine, another showed the Army's A1M4 Main Battle Tank, another showed a portrait of Falcon's Grove Castle (from a virtual world created by Ethan), and the fourth showed the dashing figure of Marvin the Martian. These doors led to the holiest of holies: Ethan's virtual reality gaming cockpits.

Ethan faced the giant screen, which had popped on. The monitor displayed more than twenty computer-generated figures staring at him from a plain virtual room. A wire-grid floor stretched to the artificial horizon. Each person in the "room" was dressed distinctively. Several wore the uniforms representing the four military branches. One wore a Bogey trench coat. One had a red FBI cap on. Two looked like rocket scientists and several looked like archetypal nerds. Where a virtual face should be, each figure had real video of the person's actual face. It was an eerie effect, made more so if the person moved around at all.

This was Ethan's multiagency counter-cyberterrorist team. President Rand Connor had created the team less than a year ago and established Ethan as its first director. There were thirteen member agencies in the U.S. intelligence community, more than half of whom were from the Department of Defense. Each agency had assigned two agents to the pilot program. Congress had outdone itself designing an especially unwieldy title for the little group: Joint Intelligence Detail, Information Operations and Counter-Cyberterrorism, Provisional, or JIDIOC-P.

"Good morning, sportsfans," Ethan said. "What's the situation?"

The only female in the group, a pretty Asian woman in an Army uniform, answered. "Operation Hydra is set to go, Director. Delta Force is approaching the target."

"Very good, Major Lee," Ethan said. "All right then. Let's go around the horn." Ethan looked at the left-most figure, a Marine in dress blues, saber and all. "Major Fontana?"

Fontana's real face bobbed slightly in the space allocated for it atop his virtual body. "Sir, Third Combat Engineer Battalion, First Marine Division is in position in Denver and standing by."

"Good," Ethan said. "What's the status on the delivery boys?"

The figure with the red FBI cap spoke up. "Denver PD's got 'em passing north of Mile High Mall. That's about ten minutes out."

Ethan nodded at the camera inset in his wall. "All right. Dean, is your man in place?"

"Yes, sir," the figure in the trench coat said.

"Did you tell him when he joined the CIA that he'd be mopping the floor of a mental institution?" Ethan asked.

"We all do our part to clean up the world, Director."

"Ha, ha," Ethan said. "Are we getting video from him?"

"I'll punch it up."

On the virtual wall behind Ethan's team a moving image of a concrete hallway appeared. Every now and then a mop entered at the bottom of the frame, held by strong black hands.

"Good," Ethan said. "Department of Energy, you guys ready?"

One of the rocket scientists gave a cybernetic thumbs-up. "Piece of pie."

Ethan shifted. "You're sure your ray gun is going to work, Earl? This is the only part of this whole thing I'm nervous about."

"Boss, DoE's been doing this since the sixties. It's not a problem."

"You're just going to point that microwave gun at the bad guy and he's going to turn into a vegetable?" Ethan asked.

"Well, Brainiac," Earl Hatfield said, calling Ethan by his code name, "let's just say he'll be extremely susceptible to suggestions."

"Okay," Ethan said. "Just don't point it at Agent Coakley by mistake." He took a deep breath and prayed for the hundredth time that God would hold this whole house of cards he'd constructed together, at least for the duration of this operation, code named Operation Hydra.

"Not to worry, Director," the CIA figure said. "This is the best-trained janitor in all of Colorado. These guys aren't going to know what hit them, even if DoE blows it."

"Hey," Hatfield said.

"Cool it, you two," Ethan said quickly. "All right, the institution's taken care of for now. What about you, Gary? Is the Air Force ready?"

"One hundred percent, sir," Captain Gary Reinke said. "AWACS is in position over the target. Electromagnetic pulse is charged, just waiting for you to give the word."

"Good," Ethan said. "You're sure the pulse won't interfere with Delta Force or the plane they're jumping from?"

"As long as the grunts know how to follow orders."

"Excuse me?" the other Army figure said. His freckled, Richie Cunningham face wagged in the face spot. "Did the fly-boy call those warriors 'grunts'?"

The female Army figure intervened. "That's enough, Mr. Barnes."

"But he—"

Even in cyberspace Ethan could see the look Major Lee gave

him. "I said that's enough. We've got enough going against us here as it is. Don't add anything."

"Yes, ma'am."

Ethan sighed. He'd been told when he took this job that the single largest problem he would face as JIDIOC-P's director would be territorialism. President Connor had warned him about it. Mike Gillette had warned him about it. Even his son Jordan had warned him about it. The military people didn't want to work with the civilians, and vice versa. The Navy didn't want to work with the Army, the FBI didn't want to work with the CIA, and nobody wanted to work with the more academic organizations such as the National Imagery & Mapping Agency. A common enemy was what they needed. Something to bond them together. Ethan was hoping it would happen through Operation Hydra.

The FBI agent said, "Delivery's passing Claremont. Four minutes out."

"Thanks, Max," Ethan said.

"I only meant," the Air Force figure said, "that if the Delta Force units took off all their electronic equipment, as per their briefing, they'll be safe from the EMP. The MC-130's electronics have special shielding."

"Okay," Ethan said. "Let's finish up. NSA, Sai, you guys ready?"

"Just waiting on you, boss," Sai Cho said.

"Max," Ethan said, "how's my man Gillette doing?"

"He's fine," Max answered. "His team's in place outside the Manning warehouse."

"Good."

"He told me to give you a message," Max said.

"Shoot."

"He said to tell you he's ready to bust another door down for you."

Ethan smiled. "Just tell him to try the doorknob first. His shoulder can't have that many more busted doors left in it."

"I'll tell him."

Ethan scanned the faces. "Anybody else have anything?"

A Navy officer raised a virtual hand.

"Go ahead, Commander Dunbar."

"Just an old sailor's sour gut about this op, sir."

"Can you be more specific?"

"Is it too late to call the whole thing off?"

"Yes, Commander, it's too late. Unless you've got a very good reason."

"KISS, sir."

"Excuse me?" Ethan said.

"Keep it simple, stupid."

Ethan pursed his lips. "You think we've got too many things going?"

"By about 2,000 percent, sir. Ever hear of a little fiasco called Desert One? Carter's plan to save the Iranian hostages. And that was only trying to coordinate branches of the professional military. Why can't—" He cut himself off.

"Don't stop now," Ethan said. "Say it."

"Well, sir, why can't you just let each agency and branch do their own thing in their own way? You're gonna end up getting men killed trying to give everybody a piece of the action. Believe me, sir, we don't care if another agency gets the credit."

Ethan scanned the real-video faces. He saw assent reflected in several. He was conscious of all the elements they had, literally, up in the air. Every second they delayed made Commander Dunbar's prediction closer to self-fulfilling prophecy.

Ethan noticed, belatedly, a new element to the virtual room: a surveillance camera icon mounted on the wall. It meant the director of Central Intelligence, Roy Pickett, nominally Ethan's superior, was tuned in. Roy was probably eating this up, Ethan thought.

"Glad you could join us, Roy," Ethan said.

"Wouldn't miss it, buddy," he said in his tenor voice. A virtual pane appeared on the left wall of the artificial room. It was a live feed from Pickett's location. It showed his chubby face and sly eyes. "Hello, everybody."

The team members answered cordially.

"Say, Ethan…" Pickett said. "I'm a little confused. General Lowe tells me you pulled a Delta Force unit out from under his nose. Would you like to explain yourself?"

Ethan paused a moment to let the Holy Spirit remove the caustic words that came to his tongue. "Sure, Director Pickett. But I'm wondering if maybe we could find another time for it? How about I call you in the morning?"

"I'm sure sorry, buddy, but I'm afraid that isn't good enough. I need you to tell me now."

Ethan rubbed his face. "Max," he said to the FBI agent, "what's the status of the delivery?"

"Denver PD estimates two minutes, Director."

"All right, Roy," Ethan said. "How about a one-and-a-half-minute briefing?"

The director of Central Intelligence shrugged.

Ethan sighed and prayed for a good way to explain it. "Okay, Director. How about this? Do you watch much pro football?"

Pickett sniffed. "Only the world champion Redskins."

"Okay, imagine a football team. All of us, Delta Force included, are offensive players about to run a play. Everybody on the field has a task, right? Some of the tasks are very different from one another. The receiver running his route has a far different job from the lineman blocking. These tasks happen in different places on the playing field. But everybody's working for the same goal. If everything goes right, we move the ball a long way down the field. If too many parts, or even one crucial part, break down, we suffer a loss. With me so far, Roy?"

Pickett smirked. "If you'd come up through the ranks of any intelligence agency, you'd know that you don't—how should I say it?—you don't run a flea flicker when a quarterback sneak would work just as well."

Ethan ignored it. "Your Agent Coakley is in Denver, along

with the DoE and the Marines, to take care of the bombers. They're like the offensive line blocking the rush. The FBI strike team will take out the enemy's computer component, and General Lowe's Delta Force unit will neutralize the enemy's military arm. They're like receivers taking the linebackers out of the play. The Air Force's electromagnetic pulse will knock out the militia's electronics—like the quarterback's pump fake that freezes the secondary. And the NSA's code breakers will get me into the enemy's central computers, like the fullback's block that springs the halfback through to pay dirt."

Ethan was pleased with the analogy. It helped even him think about the complexities of Operation Hydra more clearly.

"Look," he said to his team, "I know this is the first time we've attempted anything this big before. And I know you're not sure it's going to work. It being nighttime doesn't help many of you, I know. I see as well as you do that any number of things might go wrong. But look, all I know is we need each other. Not one of your agencies could bring to bear everything we've got going in Hydra. The bad guys are breaking all the old molds, so we'd better, too."

Ethan gestured over his shoulder, as if the enemy were standing right behind him. "These people are monsters; they blow up babies and old people. But they're also professionals. Now, you military people correct me if I'm wrong, but as I understand it, you only get the element of surprise once. Once they find out we're on to them, they're going to disappear in a cloud of smoke."

How, Ethan asked himself, had he gotten here? How was it that a virtual reality programmer from Texas came to be sending commandos into battle and CIA agents into harm's way? Ethan knew that others were wondering the same thing. His eyes flicked to Roy Pickett's plump face.

"This op," Ethan said, "Operation Hydra, is the only way we can grab everybody we need to get. This is exactly the kind of thing this team was put together to do. If it works, we'll have pulled off the biggest victory for the American intelligence community since…well, I don't know that stuff. But the biggest victory in a long time."

Ethan cringed. Not exactly a Patton-like ending to his speech.

Max's face looked down. It was a strange effect, since his body remained perfectly upright. "Boss, Denver PD says the delivery's on the block. About thirty seconds now."

"Okay, everybody," Ethan said. "This is it. What do you say? Do we go on with Hydra or do we scrub?" He scanned their faces. No one said anything. "All right then. I expect each one of you to hit this with everything he's got. Let's make it work." He turned toward his VR cockpit but then paused at the door. "We're going ahead with it, Director."

"Sure, buddy, don't let me stand in your way."

Ethan ducked into a cockpit. He slid into his vinyl gunner's chair. His hands were trembling. Icy sweat shot down his ribs. *O Father,* he prayed silently, *please make this work.* As he powered up his cockpit for his upcoming gambit in cyberspace, a word kept buzzing around in his head like a mosquito.

Buddy.

"'Don't let me stand in your way'?"

Director Roy Pickett looked at his aide across his desk. "Did you like that?"

The aide, a wispy-haired young man named Colin Bates, nodded. "Nice touch."

"I am DCI, you know. I do want them to succeed."

Bates spread his hands. "What'd I say?"

"Just shut up, will you? It will look very bad on all of us if Hydra goes wrong. Not to mention the lives at risk."

"Mm-hmm." Bates turned his gaze to the wall of monitors displaying Operation Hydra. "One day I'm going to have to ask you what this poor schmuck did to deserve your wrath."

"Oh," Pickett said with a tired sigh, "it's not him so much." He shook his head. "One day you'll understand, my son."

"When I'm old and cranky like you."

"Exactly. Now shut up."

CHAPTER TWO

Special Agent Mike Gillette had no intention of busting this door down. Mostly because it was steel. But also because he'd promised Liz he wouldn't play superhero for at least the first year of their marriage. He didn't know what it was that made him expendable after twelve months, but he wasn't about to argue.

He'd been in Phoenix for ten days now, waiting for Operation Hydra to begin. Elements of the FBI strike team he now commanded had been on stakeout duty at this warehouse for six weeks. Inside the warehouse across from them, a band of computer experts, so-called cyberterrorists, maintained the electronic security for the people blowing up long-term care facilities across America. It was thought these hackers actually sent the detonation signals themselves. Tonight they were going down.

Gillette shook his head. It was a brave new world. Cyberterrorists. Remote-controlled bombs. The FBI working with the CIA, and all of them working with the DoD, DoE, NSA, and the rest of the Mouseketeers. Maybe the strangest of all was that Ethan Hamilton was in charge of the whole shootin' match. Him being all buddy-buddy with the President and all.

He had to hand it to Ethan for conceiving Hydra, though. Nobody on the inside would've come up with it, that's for certain.

And Ethan was right: the black hats were jumping fences left and right, blowing away old ways of doing things. The Iranians were working with the IRA, the KGB was working with the Mafia, and every major corporation had a corps of ex-hackers (some of them not so "ex") on the payroll to guard their electronic gateways. If the white hats wanted to keep up, they were going to have to give up their tried and true ways, too.

But where Gillette might've settled for the occasional coinvestigation with military intelligence, for example, Ethan went whole hog. Operation Hydra was the perfect example. So complex as to make the head swim—utilizing ten out of thirteen agencies in the American intelligence community. Gillette was sure Ethan would've used the other three if he could've figured out how. To Gillette—and several others he'd heard talking—it seemed designed to fail.

Yet there was something to be said for making the solution fit the problem. In this case, the enemy they faced was multifaceted. If Ethan's conclusions were correct, there were three major factions working together: an antigovernment militia group, this band of computer mercenaries, and representatives from good old American big business. Maybe a multiagency interdiction effort made sense, after all.

The particular militia group involved, Canton People's Militia, was thought to be responsible for the destruction of several long-term care facilities around the nation: nursing homes, cancer wings, and one neonatal ICU unit. Captured communications revealed that they thought people who needed long-term care were unacceptable burdens to society. CPM had been infiltrated two months ago by an FBI agent.

The cyberterrorists, who called themselves the White Company, had been contracted by someone (Ethan thought he knew who) to bring an information warfare element to the cause. They kept prying eyes away from the militia's private computers and also primed targets for destruction by remotely dismantling computer defenses. The biggest service they provided, however—according to Ethan Hamilton's best theory, anyway—was keeping hidden the identities of the real bankrollers of the CPM bombing spree.

Gillette spun his white Stetson on his hand. The possibility of a sugar daddy behind these bombings was, in his mind, the best argument for a harebrained idea like Operation Hydra. The FBI could take these cyberterrorists down fine and might even take the Canton People's Militia without creating another Waco. But if that happened and there truly was a silent partner behind these bombings, he, she, or they would simply find another group willing to do the dirty work. Better to use specialists at every level, and better to hit them all at once.

Gillette preferred his role in Operation Hydra to Ethan's. Ethan, who had assured Gillette he knew who the real villain in these bombings was, tonight had to get inside that suspected company's computers and find proof. Without getting caught or breaking a plethora of laws, of course. The problem was that the targeted computers were guarded by the White Company.

That's where Gillette's strike team came in. JIDIOC-P agents had traced CPM data packets to this warehouse in Phoenix. The FBI stakeout had confirmed that people were going in and out of the place daily, though it was supposed to be vacant. A spy camera they'd planted showed banks of computer equipment inside. Gillette's group was to hit the building like lightning, preventing the White Company from locking Ethan out of the target computers. Assuming he was right about the target, of course.

There was also the little matter of remotely disarming the bomb that was about to be planted in Colorado. If Gillette's group failed to do that, hundreds of long-term care mental patients—and three government agents—would die.

It all made him sick. In fact, things were making him sick all the time now. The things that used to make him angry now just made him sad. Maybe he was getting world-weary. He'd seen it happen often enough in law enforcement. You spend enough time elbow to elbow with the scum of America and it slowly begins to rot your gut.

He thought the transfer to Ethan's counter-cyberterrorism unit would be a welcome change. He thought crime fighting would seem more clinical if he only saw the bad guys on a computer screen. But inevitably every investigation had to culminate with a down-and-dirty arrest. And, he had to admit, he was too much of a doer to let someone else do it all. So here he was, about to get neck deep in human scum again.

Gillette wasn't ready to tell anyone yet, but more and more often his thoughts had been turning to God. Maybe it was spending so much time with Ethan that was doing it to him. Maybe it was burnout. Maybe it was being newly married and suddenly respectable. Maybe it was something else.

He looked on the floor beside him where an FBI agent was watching a camera monitor. It was a wide-angle fisheye showing the inside of the warehouse. Rows of computers lined tables radiating out from a central area. Young men hunched over their keyboards late at night, weaving their illegal magic like wizards casting enchantments.

The NSA had broken the encryption protecting the computers Ethan was going to infiltrate. If Gillette's team took out the active defenses represented by the White Company, the remaining passive defenses would crumble under the expert code breakers' craft.

It was truly a multiheaded beast they were going after. As much as he tried to avoid it, Mike Gillette began seeing the need for a multiheaded beast to kill it. Operation Hydra.

Gillette heard a connection open. He pressed a finger to his earpiece.

"Mike?" It was Max Cobb, the other FBI agent on Ethan's team.

"Go ahead, Max." With his other hand Gillette unholstered his pistol.

"Stand by, Mike. Thirty seconds or less."

"Check." Gillette placed his cowboy hat on the dusty floor and pulled his night-vision goggles on. He looked around. There was no way to tell it wasn't bright daylight outside—he saw color, shadows, and distance. The green tones of older low-light gear had been replaced by a computer-enhanced palette. Though it was vastly better than the pea-soup feeling of older goggles, it always made Gillette feel as though he were in a cartoon.

"Max, tell those Delta Force grunts not to shoot our guy at the CPM compound, will you?"

"They know, Mike," Max said.

"They better." Gillette turned to his strike team. "Okay, cowboys, mount up."

"Put me in, Penny."

Ethan's game room computer answered: "Initiating GlobeNet interface."

He emerged on a simulated platform overlooking a large metropolis at sunset. This was GlobeNet, the 3-D successor to the Internet. It appeared as a stylized city, like a map of Disneyland. Artificial buildings of all shapes and designs crowded inside a circular wall of rock. It always looked to Ethan as if the city were inside the ring of a volcano. Tunnels cut into the walls all around, leading to other areas within GlobeNet. The sky was always burnt orange, as if GlobeNet was ever on the verge of night.

Ethan piloted his virtual craft toward the target company's online storefront.

Five large flat-screen computer monitors wrapped around him like panes of a windshield. Ethan's cockpits were designed to simulate any kind of single-seater vehicle—P-51, X-Wing, BattleMech, submersible—whatever. The GlobeNet cityscape sped by outside the "windows."

He sat in a swiveling gunner's chair with black segmented cushions. A joystick met his hand at the end of the right armrest and a throttle met his hand at the end of the left. The charcoal-colored console at his lap was rigged with a recessed keyboard, a tiny monochrome monitor (the combat command frequency, or CCF), and one small joystick. Columns of lighted buttons covered every available surface above and between the windshield "panes." When Ethan shut the door behind him, the cockpit lights turned to battle-ready red. It was a computer gamer's dream come true.

In 2007, GlobeNet was 3-D. In order to navigate the depths of cyberspace, one had to use virtual reality gear. The most prevalent setup was a pair of lightweight goggles and some kind of movement device, either a special joystick or a slip-on glove. A more expensive and thus less common approach was the VR cockpit.

A primary benefit of the goggles-and-glove approach was the sensation of total immersion in the artificial world. But that was exactly what Ethan wanted to avoid. The cockpit interface gave him a sense of being once removed, as if he were in some kind of vehicle which was itself in cyberspace. Ethan had once struggled with distinguishing the line between real and virtual, so he appreciated the psychological distance.

There was one other method of accessing GlobeNet: direct cerebral connection. As far as Ethan knew, only one person had ever used that method. But that was another story.

He slowed to a hover just outside the target company's virtual storefront. On a row of conservative-looking buildings, this one looked the most conservative of all. A brick edifice twelve stories tall. Metal fire escapes zigzagged down both sides; a cubical digital clock rotated on the roof. It spoke of boring but stable respectability.

Ethan reached for a toggle switch over his head but then hesitated. He was at the threshold of either the biggest disaster of his fledgling intelligence career or the biggest conquest. He was as sure as he could be that there was, inside the virtual building before him, evidence linking this company to the long-term care bombing spree that had outraged America. Well, he was mostly sure.

He looked up at the letters spelling out the company's name: Bundt/Alliance Life Insurance Company. If the American public discovered that a respected insurance company was behind a string of terrorist atrocities, that company would soon cease to exist. So he'd better be right.

Ethan was convinced that at least one executive from Bundt/Alliance Life was behind the bombing spree. He suspected there were more within the company. He also suspected there were collaborators at some of the other major insurance companies. It made a grisly kind of sense. If significant numbers of these "burdens to society" were eliminated, insurance companies wouldn't have to pay for their maintenance. Think of the savings they could pass on to their customers. But as yet there was no proof.

Ethan toggled the switch to send a message to his whole team. "Greetings, sports fans, this is Brainiac. I'm in position. Is everybody ready?"

Multiple versions of "Yes."

"What's the status on our delivery, Max?"

The FBI agent's face appeared in the black-and-white CCF. "They're picking the lock now."

"All right," Ethan said. "Listen up, things are about to get crazy. We're at the line of scrimmage and the quarterback's calling the count. When Max tells us the delivery's through the door, Delta Force will jump and the Air Force will pulse the CPM compound. That will be the snap. Everybody can move then.

"Mike's team can hit the White Company, Agent Coakley and the Denver PD can take on the bombers, and the NSA can go to work on the Bundt/Alliance Life encryption. When they're through, I'll go in and see about ferreting out our still-hypothetical silent partner. If all goes well, the whole thing will be over in thirty minutes, we'll have a short debriefing back here, and we can all go back to our mundane lives. And no more bombs in long-term care centers. That, my friends, would be a touchdown." Ethan liked that speech better. "I know you all will do great. Okay, Max, give us the word."

"Stand by…" Max said. "Okay, Denver PD says the delivery's inside. Repeat, they're in."

"Okay," Ethan said with more courage than he felt. "Major Lee, tell Delta Force to go."

"Yes, sir." A moment later Lee gave a thumbs-up. "They're away."

"Very well," Ethan said. "Attention, everyone. Operation Hydra is go, go, go."

"Sarge? Hey, Sarge?"

Dwayne Cabot scowled at him. "What?" he hissed.

The skinny teenager sidled up to him in the darkened back hallway of the Denver Home for the Emotionally Fatigued. "Sarge, I just lost contact with HQ."

Cabot glared at the buck private the Canton People's Militia had assigned him. "Wiley, you sure you got that thing plugged in?"

Private Wiley fiddled with the radio on his belt. He checked the connection to his earpiece. "I think so, Sarge." He banged the radio against his thigh.

Cabot stopped Wiley's hand and pushed him into the shadows. Down the slick hallway he thought he'd heard something. "Forget the radio, Wiley. Dead battery."

"No, sir, Sarge. I changed it before we left."

Cabot grabbed Wiley's throat. "Then it's gremlins, you pig-eyed slop-for-brains. It's tech stuff. Let the techs figure it out later. We don't need it. We'll plant the charge and extract."

Unable to speak, Wiley nodded.

Cabot led them down the hallway. He'd heard something again.

Andy Culbertson opened a vidphone window on his monitor to call his girlfriend. Well, virtually his girlfriend. Her real boyfriend had started behaving again—the pig—so Cindy felt obliged to spend time with him. Andy wanted to know if she was back from her date yet. It was two in the morning, for crying out loud. "I'd better not be interrupting anything, either," he said quietly.

The vidphone window came up black, the Indianapolis phone system's "Temporarily Out Of Service" message floating in the display.

"Hey."

Charlie Potts leaned over from the station beside Andy's. "What's wrong?"

"My phone's dead. Is yours?"

He checked. "Nope. Mine's fine."

Andy stared at his monitor. "Hmm. Oh, well. I'll try again later."

A man in his forties strode down the carpeted workstation silently, the only sound the rustling of his habitual windbreaker. John Hawkwood. He had the ability to make people nervous just by walking by. Hawkwood descended the three stairs from the so-called battle bridge to Radial 3 and came to stand between Andy and Charlie. "What is it?"

"Nothing, Mr. Hawkwood, sir," Andy said, swiveling quickly back to his computer.

"What were you talking about?"

"His phone's dead, sir," Charlie said.

Hawkwood leaned over Andy's keyboard and called up a vidphone window. Temporarily Out Of Service. Hawkwood cursed softly. "Move."

Andy leaped out of the chair. Hawkwood sat down and

typed. "It's all right," Andy said. "You don't have to fix it. I don't have anybody I need to call right now."

Hawkwood didn't answer. He keyed an intercom button on Andy's console. "Rainulf, flush NLI-22G for me."

"Yes, sir," said the voice on the intercom.

Andy looked at Charlie. Others on Radial 3 were beginning to take notice. A pimply-faced kid came down from the battle bridge. "Mr. Hawkwood?" The intercom beeped. Hawkwood held up a finger to the newcomer.

"Go ahead, Rainulf," Hawkwood said.

"Sir, it looks like a router failure at either Kennedale or Cheyenne."

"Okay," Hawkwood said. "Tell you what, send a sparkler down the shaft anyway, will you?"

"Yes, sir."

Hawkwood switched the intercom off. He stood from the chair and turned to go.

Andy called him. "Mr. Hawkwood, sir? Did you just send a sparkler-bot on a public phone line? Won't it knock out a few thousand phones?"

Hawkwood turned easily. "No more than two or three thousand. They'll lose GlobeNet and 911 for about five minutes." He smiled. "Don't worry, junior. It's not a big thing. See, there's a tiny chance that this little phone outage could be the beginning of an IOps attack."

Andy's eyes got wide. IOps stood for Information Operations—electronic warfare. "Sir, I'm sorry."

"For what?"

"I..."

"You didn't do anything, kid. If there was somebody trying to crawl up your phone line, the sparkler took him out." Hawkwood pointed a narrow finger at Andy's nose. "Better paranoid than Polaroid. Remember that."

"Yes, sir." Andy wasn't sure what that meant. Maybe Polaroid referred to a police photographer's picture of your dead body. Hawkwood's paranoia was legendary.

Instead of returning to the battle bridge, Hawkwood stood just behind Andy's chair to speak with the pimply-faced kid. "What is it, Count Christoffer?" He said it with a mock German accent.

"Oh, it's nothing, Mr. Hawkwood, sir. I mean, I'm sure it's nothing. I wondered if you'd take a look at something, though."

"Sure thing." They began walking back to the battle bridge.

Andy turned to his monitor to get back to work. He had just laid his hands on the keyboard when he heard Hawkwood shout.

"What! How long ago?"

Andy couldn't hear Christoffer's reply, but he heard Hawkwood clearly.

"Blow it. Now! Detonate!" Hawkwood ran to a terminal at the center of the battle bridge.

Christoffer trailed him, his voice rising. "But the guys are still in there."

Hawkwood struck the computer monitor with the palm of his hand and cursed. "We're cut off."

Andy stood, sucked inward with the other technicians by Hawkwood's energy. On the battle bridge platform, too, the officers of the White Company gathered around their leader dumbly.

Hawkwood saw them. "What are you doing? We're cut off! Find a way to restore contact with Denver! As soon as you do, detonate."

People stumbled over each other to get back to their posts. Andy heard Christoffer's nervous voice. "But our guys! They'll be blown to bits."

Hawkwood shoved him backward, and Christoffer fell out of sight. "Don't you get it?" Hawkwood shouted over him. "We're under attack. If we don't blow this thing now, we're all dead!"

He never got over the scream. The way the wind pummeled his ears as he fell through the air at 110 miles an hour. That was good. If he ever got accustomed to it, he might forget to pull his ripcord. He had another ninety seconds to free-fall—ninety-two if he wanted to die.

This was Lieutenant Phillip Bartlett's seventh combat HALO jump. Of this he was positive. He'd lost count of regular drops. He'd jumped out of so many aircraft into so many war zones with Delta Force that they all blurred together. Add unnumbered insertions by other means and his life began to appear as one big antiterrorist op. But High Altitude, Low Opening jumps, because of their adrenaline rush, stood out.

In a HALO jump, the team leaps out of a cargo plane— usually an MC-130 turboprop, but sometimes a modified 727—at extremely high altitude, 14,000 feet or so. Most often at night. They free-fall the entire distance, deploying parachutes at literally the last moment. The advantages are obvious: a team can jump out of a plane so far away from the target that it appears to be innocent air traffic; they do not appear on radar; they hit the target silently, all at once, and with the element of surprise.

If anyone misjudges, he hits the target physically.

Bartlett could've sworn he felt the Air Force's electromagnetic pulse sweep over him. Two miles below, he saw the lights at the Canton People's Militia compound go out. He sneered. Were those chumps in for a surprise.

He eyeballed his men in the air around him. His EMP-shielded night-vision goggles let him see them perfectly, as if it were a bright blue morning jump. He stifled the urge to order them to link up in a ring.

He checked the old-style altimeter on his wrist. The dial spiraled down crazily. A glance at the horizon told him that the EMP had taken out power at the only other structure in the area, an automatic gas well a mile and a half away. Somebody was going to have to get out of bed to fix that. Tough.

An electromagnetic pulse, or EMP, was normally only generated by atmospheric ionization during the explosion of a nuclear weapon. An EMP severely damaged electronic equipment, including communications systems, as nuclear pioneers discovered the hard way. It wasn't long before someone realized the military potential of such a phenomenon. Now it was used as a preemptive strike weapon by armed forces all over the world.

Bartlett felt the air getting warmer. He looked down. He could see the CPM compound structures clearly now. His passive infrared overlay revealed someone sitting out on the porch having a smoke. Bartlett hand-signaled his men to spread out and prepare to pull chutes.

This was going to be fun.

CHAPTER THREE

Sergeant Cabot sneaked a peek around the corner. The hallway was empty. Of course. Why wouldn't it be? Even at a mental institution—his officer training made him say it again, this time nicely—even at a place like the Denver Home for the Emotionally Fatigued, no one would be likely to be up at this hour of the morning. Still, he thought he'd heard something. But all he saw was a dimly lit nurse's station and a wheeled mop bucket.

"Come on, Wiley," Cabot said.

He judged the nurse's station to be as good a place as any to set the charge, so he took it out of his satchel and walked over. He placed it on the counter and armed it. The LED began counting down 360 seconds.

"Let's make tracks, kid." But Wiley wasn't with him. "Private, get over here." Cabot went back down the hall they'd come from.

Wiley was standing in the middle of the dark hallway, staring into space, his mouth slack. Cabot had seen the look before in people who watched too much television. He knocked on the kid's forehead. "Hello, anybody home?"

Wiley's eyes focused on him. The voice that came from his mouth made the hair on Cabot's neck stand up. "Do you hear the angels?"

"Kid, you freakin' on me?" Cabot hadn't thought before about how the rooms around him were filled with crazy people. Maybe it was a disease, after all. Maybe Wiley had contracted it. Maybe he was giving it to him.

The floor spun under him. Cabot steadied himself against the wall. Then he thought, just for a moment, that maybe he did hear light, angelic singing. His head dropped to a comfortable angle to listen.

Something tugged at his mind. There was some reason why he shouldn't be standing around listening to angels. With great effort he lifted his eyes toward the way he'd come. A figure stepped into the concrete hallway, coming toward him. How nice, he thought, for an angel to come see him here.

It made perfect sense to him that the angel would be carrying a mop.

The abandoned Manning Freightways warehouse had five regular entrances and one roof door. Mike Gillette's team was poised at all six spots. Tiny explosive charges waited above every lock. He'd given the go-ahead two minutes ago. Twenty FBI agents watched twenty hyperaccurate wristwatches count down.

They'd rehearsed this strike in virtual reality, thanks to Ethan Hamilton's computers, Manning blueprints, and the spy camera. Every detail had been worked out, not the least of which was how not to shoot other FBI agents by mistake. When they entered the well-lit warehouse, the night-vision goggles would adjust instantly.

The only variables were the men inside. How would they react? Did they have concealed weapons? Were there security systems no hidden camera could detect? The White Company didn't strike anyone as fools. Who knew what insidious traps might be lying in wait?

Gillette's watch hit zero. Six plastic explosive charges detonated simultaneously. The FBI strike team poured in the doors with the familiarity of people entering their own living rooms. Two snipers entered from the roof and quickly drew a bead on those below. Gillette and his team charged toward the computer tables shouting, pistols leveled at the men at their computers.

"FBI! Move away from the computers. Now, now, now!"

Vince Dreyer sat at the bench cleaning assault rifles. He loved the smell of gun oil, the cool black metal in his hands, the decisive sound of bolt action and loading mechanisms, the quiet click of a hammer falling. Whatever he might think about the members of the Canton People's Militia, Vince was almost going to be sorry when this mission was over.

He looked around the aluminum building. Phillips and Sagamore were asleep in front of the tube. Doc was out front with the radio, having a smoke. The diesel generator chugged away in its shed. From time to time Vince could hear ol' Morris's mantra from down the hall. Two sentries walked the perimeter with their dogs. Everybody else was asleep. A typical night at the CPM compound.

Typical except that two of their number were out in Colorado right now planting a bomb in a place full of innocent people. No, Vince wouldn't be sorry for this mission to be over, after all. Here he was, an FBI agent inside an enemy camp, and he couldn't do a thing to stop them. He even had to help them.

He looked at the gun barrel in his hands. Would it be used to kill someone tomorrow? A mother and child, perhaps. Because Doc Castle and his troops—or whoever it was they were working for—decided they sucked down too much aid money.

Vince wished his superiors would get their rears in gear and shut these vigilantes down. How much evidence did they need, anyway? True, he hadn't been able to find out who CPM's employer was. But that was beginning to matter to Vince less and less as the mission protracted.

Vince felt his stomach lurch. His vision dimmed. His hearing seemed to fade. He thought he was going to pass out. *Must be the strain,* he thought. *And maybe Santos's chili.* Oh well, it was time to get some sleep anyway.

Someone swore. "What the—"

"Who turned out the lights?"

Phillips was suddenly at Vince's table. He fell over Vince and belched. "Who's that?"

"Ow!" someone shouted from down the hall.

"Get off me, Phillips," Vince said.

Doc came in from the porch. "Lang forgot to fill the generator, didn't he?"

"Yup," Phillips said.

"No," Vince said. "The generator's still on. Listen."

More swearing.

"What time is it, anyway?"

"It's…ah, forget it. My watch ain't working."

"Everybody go to bed," Doc said. "We'll whip somebody in the A.M."

Footsteps shuffled off toward bunks. "Hey," a voice said, "my watch isn't working, either."

In Vince's mind a red flag went up. Watches ran on batteries. No normal power loss would affect them. Then he remembered the nausea he'd felt. Electromagnetic pulse. Vince hurried to the kitchen, sat on the floor, pulled out his lucky cap, and put it on. His moment had come.

A yellow light flared on. Morris almost dropped his lighter when he saw Vince on the floor. "What're you doing down there? Almost wet my pants."

Vince shrugged.

Morris opened the refrigerator and took out a beer. "If the power's out, this might be the last cold one I get in a while."

Vince didn't speak. He watched Morris disappear around the corner. The orange cigarette light went with him.

He was still sitting on the kitchen floor when Delta Force

struck. Where had they come from? He never saw them, though he felt himself looked at several times. His specially dyed cap must have been working. Startled shouts—and one canine yelp—from all over the compound hinted at the strike team's location and activities.

In under three minutes a chemical torch lit the room a pale green. Two ghostly soldiers stood over him with night-vision goggles on. Strange-looking weapons pointed at Vince's chest.

"Identify yourself," one demanded.

"Vince Dreyer, FBI."

The weapons lowered.

Vince stood up. "What are those? Stun guns?"

"Affirmative, sir."

"Nice. Hey, are you guys done?"

"The target is neutralized."

"Wow."

"Nice hat, sir."

The raid on the Manning Freightways warehouse was over in thirty seconds. If the FBI special agents had been hoping for a Hollywood shoot-out, they were disappointed. The bad guys were taken completely off guard. They raised their hands very high.

"Don't shoot!"

"Hands up! Down on the floor. Now, hands behind your heads."

An agent recited their Miranda rights.

"Get away from that computer!" one of the Phoenix agents shouted to a fat man who hadn't left his keyboard.

The fat man obeyed.

Mike Gillette went to the agent. "Whatcha got?"

"He was still working on that," the Phoenix agent said, pointing at the man's computer. "Probably erasing evidence."

Gillette pulled his night-vision goggles off. The others on his team followed suit. One agent sat at a terminal and started searching the storage drives.

"Okay, everybody listen up." Gillette showed his badge around. "You all are under arrest for multiple counts of terrorism, electronic espionage, and obstructing official investigations. As of this moment, the White Company is a nonentity."

The fat man, working himself to the floor with difficulty, snorted. "The what company?"

"Shut up, you," an FBI agent said.

Gillette holstered his pistol. "Don't play dumb; we know you're part of the group blowing up old folks' homes."

"Look, FBI," the fat man said, "you got the wrong guys. We don't know anything about that."

"Yeah," a teenager on the floor said. "My Gramma got burned bad when that place in Philly went up."

Gillette scratched his scalp. Suspects almost always gave him the I-didn't-do-it speech when he arrested them, but this one had a note of sincerity. He realized there was someone at his elbow. "Sorry, Tim. What?"

"Mike, they're telling the truth."

"See?" somebody prone said.

"Stay where you are, everybody," Gillette said. He drew his pistol again. "Tim, talk to me."

"I checked their files, Mike. There's nothing in there that could be used to do the things the White Company's been doing."

Gillette swallowed. "What about Fat Albert? He probably erased everything, right?"

Tim swept his arm over the tables. "We checked all of them."

Gillette felt his ears get hot. He looked up at the snipers on the catwalk. "Then what've you guys been staking out for six weeks?" For the second time he sent his pistol back to its holster. "Let 'em go, boys."

"Fascists!" one of the guys on the floor said.

"Not so fast," Tim said.

Gillette looked at him. "What is it now?"

"I said they weren't guilty of doing what the White Company was doing. I didn't say they weren't guilty at all."

One of the teenagers on the floor leaped to his feet. He knocked the nearest FBI agent aside and bolted for the door. Weapons came up. Gillette saw the snipers swing their rifles after him.

"Hold fire!" he shouted. He spoke into his radio. "Door teams, move inside. We got us a runner."

As the teenager neared the door, two men in FBI T-shirts stepped inside and caught him. They wrestled him to the floor and applied handcuffs.

Gillette turned back to Tim. "Okay, I give up. What are they guilty of? So I know how nice I have to be."

"It's child porn, Mike. Selling the stuff over GlobeNet. Got about twenty-five terabytes of it on disc."

Gillette fought the urge to unleash on his captives his most toxic curses, the ones he reserved for the likes of…well, the likes of nobody but child abusers. Instead he established a radio connection with his counterpart on JIDIOC-P. "Max, this is Gillette. Our part of Hydra's a wash. We got the wrong group. Tell Ethan the White Company's still in business."

"Can't risk it, Mike," Max said. "Comm silence while he's in their computer."

Gillette swore. "This thing ain't exactly goin' according to plan, is it?"

"Never does."

"Right. Hey, you better tell the CIA their guy's still got a ticking bomb on his hands."

"Gotcha. We'll get the Marine bomb squad on it. Cobb out."

Gillette turned back to his team. "Okay, get this—get these individuals out of my sight."

John Hawkwood watched the FBI agents escort their captives out of the warehouse. The U.S. government, as it happened, was not the only group capable of planting hidden cameras. As they filed out, Hawkwood couldn't suppress a chuckle. It had been something of a nuisance to set up this elaborate electronic trail leading any pursuers to these porn dealers.

Hawkwood strode to the center of the battle bridge and spoke into a microphone. "Let me have your attention." Thirty sets of eyes on all four radials turned to him. "It's confirmed," he said. "We're under attack. It's a coordinated attack, striking on at least two fronts. Probably more."

He waited for the excited wave to travel the length of the room. "We've lost contact with our demolition unit in Denver, and the FBI just raided what they thought was our headquarters." He shot a patronizing look at an aide who had criticized his ruse. "I'm moving us to yellow alert. Execute Def Plan Alpha."

Hawkwood watched his men go to work. Each had been excruciatingly investigated before being allowed to join his little army. Nevertheless he awaited the day when one would betray him.

"Everybody relax," he said. "Just do your job. We're completely safe here. If you need me, I'll be keeping an eye on the henhouse. We'll see just what caliber of fox has come calling today."

The message that the bomb was still ticking did not reach the intended parties. The CIA agent inside the Denver Home for the Emotionally Fatigued didn't hear because he was grappling with the bombers, both of whom had snapped out of the DoE's mind ray. The U.S. Marine bomb squad waiting outside didn't hear because their only radio contact was with the CIA agent. The Department of Energy agents didn't hear because they were too busy trying to get their temperamental microwave gun to work again.

180...179...

CHAPTER FOUR

Ethan Hamilton eased his virtual craft to a halt just inside Bundt/Alliance Life's impressive lobby. It was a beautiful stone foyer: gray square pillars, white marble stairs leading to black double doors on either side, checkerboard gray flagstones. The whole chamber was lit indirectly by lights recessed in the cutaway ceiling. The red and white Bundt/Alliance Life seal lay on the floor like a giant's drink coaster. No one in sight.

Ethan had gotten this far before. Several times. All the simulated doors were locked, of course. Advanced encryption kept them sealed. The only thing he'd been able to do on previous trips was activate the artificial receptionist program. This was done by moving beyond the official seal.

It would be easy enough to see if the NSA's code breakers had been successful. Ethan drove his virtual craft across the seal. No receptionist appeared. One more test. He moved to the far end of the lobby and ascended the stairs. At his approach the black door raised like a portcullis into the ceiling above. He was in.

Ethan accelerated down the long corridor, coming to several cross branches. He went straight. Executives didn't take cross hallways. At length he pulled into a massive circular chamber, three stories tall. Here the decor was all wood. Rich, reddish wood, in three distinct tiers. Like an old opera house. Eight doors opened off the round room.

As Ethan neared the first door, a name hovered in the air before him. Amazing, Ethan thought, nameplates in cyberspace. Big powerful executives can't even remember which virtual office is their own. The name in the air wasn't the one Ethan was looking for, so he moved on.

The fifth door was the right one. Alexander Ironhorse Carruthers. The floating nameplate had to scroll down to get it all in. Ethan wiped his hands on his jeans. Then he pushed at the door. It opened. He was going to have to give his NSA rocket scientists due praise. Later.

Carruthers's office was appropriately ostentatious. It appeared to be a suite. Just inside the door was a receptionist's desk. Passages opened on either side behind the desk. One led to what appeared to be Carruthers's office proper, while the other passage fed into a sunken living room. And why not have a suite? Ethan thought. In virtual reality, everyone could have a corner office.

Ethan drove to the back office. It was surprisingly plain. Generic floor and ceiling textures, boring wallpaper, clipart furniture. He went to the simulated computer and turned it on.

Ethan licked his lips. Here was what it all came down to. He had to find something on this man's computer that linked him conclusively to the long-term care bombings. Financial reports, perhaps. Undeleted e-mail. Or the dreaded Internal Memo. If Ethan were caught inside this computer and his identity was somehow revealed, he and a bunch of other people would be in seriously hot water.

Ethan knew his NSA people had broken the White Company's encryption and he assumed Mike Gillette had shut them down in person. But still, this seemed too easy. Surely the White Company would've installed some kind of automatic defenses. The NSA antiencryption algorithms wouldn't have eliminated those.

He decided not to look for anything in particular on Carruthers's computer, but rather to simply download the entire contents of the storage drives. He could sort through it later.

That was when the computer disappeared.

Ethan blinked. It was gone. One second he'd been about to access this man's deepest secrets, the next he was staring stupidly into virtual space.

From behind him came a man's voice. "Looking for something?"

Who would've guessed that two disposable bomb planters would be trained in the martial arts? Certainly not CIA agent Calvin Coakley. His mission—to incapacitate the trespassers—had risen exponentially in complexity. His only advantage was the mop handle he'd broken off soon after the intruders had snapped out of the DoE's mind control gun.

The whole hall was awake now. How could anyone sleep with three men in mortal combat outside their doors? But the nurses had locked every patient's door before leaving that evening. Coakley spared a thought about what damage this would do to the psychological well-being of the permanent guests of the Denver Home for the Emotionally Fatigued. At least they were already in therapy.

And at least the bomb on the nurses' station counter had been deactivated.

He banged on the door to the custodian's closet, the room in which the DoE agents were hidden. Although *hiding* might have been more like it. "Get out here and help me!" Coakley kept the bombers at bay with his stick.

"What are we supposed to do?" a voice complained.

Coakley cursed. "Just get out here."

"We're working on the microwave gun."

That gave Coakley enough energy to launch a furious assault on his assailants. He landed a resounding blow on the younger's left collarbone but took a roundhouse kick to the stomach from the older. The younger fell to his backside. Coakley smacked the mop handle across the kid's shins. The handle broke in two and the end skittered down the concrete hallway. The kid moaned on the floor. Coakley held the remains of his mop handle at the other assailant like a switchblade.

"Sarge," the kid said. "I'm hurt, Sarge. Let's just get out."

"We can't. He's seen us." He straightened from his fighting posture and raised a finger at Coakley. "You're no janitor, darkie."

Coakley smiled dangerously.

"Sarge!" The kid was limping, holding his arm to his chest. "We've got to get out before it goes off!"

"Oh, that?" Coakley said. "I wouldn't worry about it. It's disarmed."

The older bomber went to the younger. "Okay, then you won't mind staying here until it counts down. We're leaving." He put an arm around the kid and helped him down the hall away from Coakley.

"You should stay a while," Coakley said. "I insist."

Suddenly the younger bomber was lurching forward. Coakley pushed the kid aside but fell under the older man's rapid-fire attack. Blows and kicks landed in his face, groin, stomach, knees. His mop handle flew out of his hand as if it had come to life. A spinning jump kick to the ear took Coakley to the concrete. And still the attack didn't lessen. Coakley rolled and blocked, but even his best dirty tricks failed him. He felt his consciousness slipping.

Suddenly the beating stopped. Coakley was vaguely aware of voices echoing off the walls and a flurry of movement. Maybe a scuffle. He thought it must be the inmates in their cells.

Then he was being carried down the hall. Men in green helmets with Plexiglas shields. "Who are you guys?" Coakley managed.

"Third Combat Engineer Battalion, First Marine Division. You're going to be all right, sir."

"About time."

"You were supposed to call us, sir. Denver police said you'd been incapacitated."

"Did you get them?" Coakley asked.

"Affirmative. Good work, sir."

They carried him outside. The air was cool and fresh. An ambulance had just arrived; the paramedics were opening the back doors.

"There's two other guys in there," Coakley said, although he was tempted not to mention it. "Department of Energy."

The soldiers laid him down on a gurney. "We'll take care of it, sir."

Coakley grabbed a sleeve, though his ribs protested. "The bomb, it had been disarmed, right?"

"Working on that now, sir."

Calvin Coakley passed out with a moan.

Ethan was trapped. The wood-paneled opera house was going to be his virtual tomb. The man in Carruthers's office hadn't tried to stop Ethan from leaving, obviously because he knew Ethan couldn't go very far. He ran to every door, but each was locked. Even the floating nameplates had been disabled. The passage back to the hallway had vanished.

Ethan rotated his craft to face the door to Carruthers's office. The man, dressed like someone fresh out of Starfleet Academy, strode across the carpeted floor with magnificent fluidity. Ethan sighed. "This was a trap, wasn't it?"

The man shrugged. It was a marvelous facsimile of a real gesture. In fact, the only thing that gave away that this was not live-action video was the sheer perfection of the image. It was wonderfully bright, almost luminous. The edges were crystalline. The features symmetrical.

"You could say that. A spider's web. My special additions, anyway. Bundt/Alliance Life uses it every day just like normal."

"Who are you?" Ethan asked.

"Seems to me I'm the one who ought to be asking questions, hmm?"

Ethan nodded. He realized that his gestures—inside his cockpit—wouldn't transmit to cyberspace. It took a moment for him to remember what persona he'd chosen for this mission. Ah, yes: a stealth tank. A nodding tank wouldn't make much sense anyway. "So ask me."

"Let's start with your name," the man said. "And don't bother lying because I'm reading your code right now."

"If that's true why should I tell you?"

"I like to know a man's integrity."

"They call me Brainiac."

"Yes, so I see. Did your mother hate you?"

Ethan didn't answer. He decided to look for an exit on a higher floor. In cyberspace, stealth tanks can fly. He flew up.

"I don't mind telling you my name," the man said. He was calm, as if Ethan were still standing before him. As if he knew Ethan's search was pointless. "I am John Hawkwood, humble captain of the White Company."

"I know that name," Ethan said, hovering high above the floor. "John Hawkwood, also known as Giovanni Acuto. Condottiere of the famous White Company in the fourteenth century. Under your leadership, the White Company became masters of mobility, tactics, and…and the longbow, I believe."

"Wonderful!" Hawkwood said. "A man of letters."

"Didn't you die about six hundred years ago, dude?"

"And a mathematician. You really are Brainiac."

"Just something of a medieval history buff."

"Fascinating time, wasn't it?" Hawkwood stared up at him. "If we're going to have this conversation, why don't you come down here?"

"Because I don't want to talk to you."

"Aw. Did I spoil your fun?"

"Afraid so," Ethan said. "I'll be leaving now."

Hawkwood chuckled. "So I see."

Suddenly Hawkwood was sitting on the balcony railing beside where Ethan hovered. "A prime rule of war," he said, "is to deprive your enemy of what he wants while gaining for yourself what you want."

"I see." Ethan wasn't in the mood for a lecture on strategy. Operation Hydra was going on, for good or ill, without its leader. And its leader had just failed in his objective. The prime objective. Better to get back and begin damage control. If it could be controlled.

Hawkwood was talking. "...while your true vulnerabilities remain well hidden."

Something in that sounded familiar. "What did you just say?"

"I said you make your enemy rush around after things you hold out for him, while keeping your true vulnerabilities far from him."

"That's Sun Tzu," Ethan said.

Hawkwood's eyebrows lifted. "I thought you said you just knew medieval history."

"I also know a little strategy."

"Hmm. Yes, that's Master Tzu."

Ethan thought about it. Had Hawkwood been practicing the maxim he quoted: making him rush around like a lab rat, while his true valuables remained safely out of sight? He examined the man, who seemed to be doing the same to him. Fencers prodding and testing. Where would Sun Tzu hide something in an office building? Someplace that looked unlikely. A thought came to Ethan's mind: Executives don't take cross hallways.

Ethan toggled two switches above his head, turning clipping off and map reckoning on. Without a word he dove from the ceiling straight toward the carpet. And through the floor.

His view became massively distorted. Half-rendered images flipped past one another like a rotating infinite reflection. Sound bytes—words and sound effects—caught in midexecution stuttered through his speakers like a helicopter blade. Ethan ignored the chaos on his window monitors and concentrated on the map display on the black-and-white CCF monitor. At the proper coordinates, he pulled back on his joystick.

He emerged from the floor at the end of the most remote corridor in the Bundt/Alliance Life building. He spun around. The simulated lightbulb overhead glowed faintly. Stacks of chairs clogged the hallway behind him. There were no doors on any of the three walls. Dead end.

Or was it? Ethan plunged through the farthest wall. He expected to see the between-places distortion again. Instead he popped instantly into what appeared to be a small, forgotten library. Multicolored books, all dulled with simulated age, lined the walls of the small room. At the only table sat John Hawkwood.

"I'm impressed," Hawkwood said.

Ethan's vehicle no longer responded to his moves. Hawkwood had probably inserted some kind of malicious logic that deleted his 6DOF attributes. He could likely extricate himself given time, but for now he was as stuck in place as if he'd stepped into quick-drying cement. Hawkwood got up from the table and returned the book he'd been reading to its place. Ethan kept his eye on that book.

"I'm curious," Hawkwood said. "Who are you really?"

"I told you: Brainiac. My friends call me Brainy."

"Brainy? Hmm. Are all your friends losers, then?"

"Looks to me like there's only one loser here." Ethan pressed a key.

Twenty-seven simple bots appeared in the library. Each was nothing but a shoplifter routine, configured with instructions such as, "Go in, grab something you see, then run back to base." They looked like dirty children, waifs. They ran screaming around the little room, grabbing books from the walls and disappearing.

Hawkwood swatted at them. He caught one, but it vanished in his hands. He shouted.

Ethan deferred his enjoyment. The bots would be gone fast,

and if he didn't have the necessary data by then, his one and only ruse would be gone. The problem with the shoplifters was that they couldn't be targeted. Ethan had no doubt that anything they grabbed in this room would be useful for his investigation, but the only crucial piece of evidence, if his hunch was right, was yet to be nabbed.

He launched another bot. A disembodied hand. This one had no independence. It was more like a remote control power tool. Ethan guided it through the frenzied library with the tiny joystick on the dash of his cockpit. Out of the corner of his eye he saw Hawkwood wrestling with a shoplifter bot over a particularly weighty tome.

His remote hand gripped the book Hawkwood had been reading and pulled it from the shelf. Hawkwood saw his mistake and dove for the floating hand. Too late. Ethan consumed the contents of the file, sending copies to a safe—but untraceable—GlobeNet address.

Ethan had a troubling thought, that maybe this was all another of Hawkwood's misdirections. No time to worry about that now. He'd played his gambit. He wouldn't get another chance.

The last two shoplifter bots bounded around the library, squealing. Ethan and Hawkwood stared at each other, perfectly still. In seconds the bots made off with their loot, and the room was silent again.

Hawkwood lifted a finger. "You don't want me for an enemy."

"Aw, can't we be pals?" Ethan asked forgiveness for his smart remark. God was working on him about not letting his heart rejoice when the wicked fell. The problem was he kept going up against wicked people, and sometimes it felt so good to see them go down. "You're not my enemy," he said, "the people you're protecting are."

"Were protecting," Hawkwood corrected. "I don't think they'll be interested in retaining the White Company's services now, do you? That was clever, all those little brats. I'll have to remember it. Now if you'll excuse me, I have to go break the news to my people." He turned to leave down a dark passageway. Then he said, "By the way, are you CIA or DoD?"

"Excuse me?"

"I know you're working for the U.S. government, that's obvious. Who else could coordinate simultaneous attacks against me in three different states and in cyberspace? Was it Force Recon or Delta Force that hit us in Ohio?"

Ethan didn't know whether or not to answer. This was an aspect of espionage to which he was still unaccustomed. Would it give anything away to tell him? Would it somehow put someone in danger?

"Did you know about the FBI's little fiasco?" Hawkwood said. "They raided the wrong place. It was amusing. I have it all on disc. I'll show it to you sometime."

"Okay..."

"What did you think, that I would let someone so easily track the White Company's physical whereabouts?"

Ethan hadn't thought it was easy at all. "I guess not."

"Oh, come on!" Hawkwood said. "Where's your sense of pride? No riposte prepared? Oh, well. Maybe next time." He turned to go. "Pleasure working with you, Brainiac. I'm sure we'll meet again. Tell Director Pickett I said hello."

CHAPTER FIVE

"**A**nyone who loves his father or mother more than me is not worthy of me; anyone who loves his son or daughter more than me is not worthy of me; and anyone who does not take his cross and follow me is not worthy of me. Whoever finds his life will lose it, and whoever loses his life for my sake will find it."
Matthew 10:37–39

Tamara Mack laid the Bible on her lap. Would the words ever cease to amaze her? In the two months since she'd become a Christian, it seemed every time she opened her Bible it said something else that staggered her. She highlighted every cool verse she found, which was turning into quite a sum. How could the world be the way it was with words like this there for anyone to read?

She looked at the clock on the break-room wall. Time to get back to work. She tucked her highlighter in her cloth Bible case and headed back to the lab.

When Tamara passed people in the ultramodern hallways, she saw them with new eyes. What sad, terrible lives they all lived. Why would they pass up the joy she had found? Springs of water bubbling up within her. Something like that.

In the exuberance of her first days as a Christian, she'd

taken some of her coworkers aside and told them about Jesus. She was sure they'd want what she had found. Who wouldn't? All she had to do was tell them, just like the old man in Acapulco had told her. To her astonishment, her friends had turned cool toward her. They didn't want to hear any more about Jesus. They said they'd heard enough for a whole lifetime. These days they avoided her.

Tamara was more careful now. It had become clear that there was more to it than just explaining the...the gospel—she was learning the lingo. A wise person she'd spoken with on GlobeNet had shown her another wonderful passage in the Bible. Jesus said, "No one can come to me unless the Father who sent me draws him." Whoa.

Her heart was aflame with adoration for this God. How the earth must've shaken when Jesus spoke! Why didn't the world just crumble apart when he was killed? Or explode with joy when he rose? She felt as if she were going to explode herself if she couldn't talk to somebody about her Savior, and fast.

But she still had her work to do. She'd been out of the lab long enough for a stack of new work orders to pile up. Besides, at GeneSys, religion was a taboo topic. Clipperton was too small an island to have a holy war going on, or so she'd been told. She'd have to keep her rapture bottled up until she got off work and could log on to her friends on GlobeNet.

Tamara entered the lab and put on her white coat. She pulled blond hair from the collar and fluffed it over her slim shoulders. She had sun-browned skin and a face she'd been told was pretty.

The lab was twice as long as it was wide. White counters lined both walls, packed with the tools of molecular biology: test tubes, microscopes, petri dishes, a large vat for mass-producing anaerobic bacteria, and other exotic instruments. Long white tables ran down the center of the laboratory, holding cultures from various projects. A desk at the far end of the room supported Tamara's computer. Behind the desk was a window that looked out over the crashing surf.

As expected, her In tray had ten new work orders in it. It was the one spot in the lab that never needed dusting. She grabbed them and went to her stool at the counter. She read through them, looking for something halfway interesting to kick things off.

Tamara had worked at GeneSys for two years, ever since receiving her master's in microbiology from UCLA. What a dream come true for her: fresh out of grad school she's recruited by a major biotech firm whose main campus is on an island in the Pacific ocean, and offered $150,000 U.S. a year just to fill simple work orders like these.

What had made her stand out above her classmates? She was no valedictorian. True, she did have a high proficiency with viral vectors and, she had to admit, she was a true artist with micromanipulators. But there were others just as good. Plenty of others. She didn't ask the recruiters what made them interested in her—afraid they might disappear in a puff of smoke. The fact that she had no family kept coming up.

She was perfectly happy performing her simple procedures, going home to her apartment on this exotic tropical island, spending every other weekend at GeneSys's resort in Acapulco, and collecting her obscenely high paycheck. Now that she'd become a Christian, she was thrilled to be able to donate generous gifts to churches and other worthy causes around the world. She fancied herself an eccentric rich woman living on a deserted island.

Tamara narrowed her eyes. She read over one particular work order again. She read it a third time. It couldn't say what she thought it said. Even if it did, it couldn't mean what she thought it meant. She pulled another page from the stack, just to be sure her brain was still engaged. Had all of them changed to bizarre requests, too? No, the others were plain vanilla work orders: clone these cells, split this DNA at such-and-such coordinates, build a vector to transport this gene therapy to that chromosome. She turned back to the other one. It hadn't changed.

"This can't be right."

Tamara felt her heart fluttering inside her. She left the pages on the counter and walked to the window. She stared out into the tropical sun. The ocean was never more than a mile away from you wherever you were on Clipperton, but in this wing of the GeneSys complex the water was less than a hundred yards away. She watched ten-foot-high waves crash against the coral beach, one after another.

At the extreme right of her vision Tamara could see the Rock, a towering volcanic crag, where once a murdering rapist had lived. There he had carried out his reign of terror. There the women and children he had terrorized had killed him.

Tamara felt the first twinges of what those women must've felt. Trapped on this tiny island, forced to do horrible things. She felt the presence of the work order on the counter behind her. It had life now. Power.

"It can't be right."

Dear Jesus, she prayed silently, *save me from this.*

She grabbed the offending work order off the counter, threw the door against the hydraulic stays, and marched down the hall. She pushed the door to her manager's office aside and went in, upsetting his secretary's bottled water. Tamara didn't wait to be announced. She strode up to her manager's desk, squared her shoulders, slammed the paper down. And started to cry.

Richard Thornton looked up from his printout and stared at her over half-frame glasses. "Come in, Miss Mack." Thornton's cheek twitched. He slid a box of tissues to Tamara.

Tamara took the box and sat in a chair. Her boss's face stretched and smeared in her teary vision. She willed herself to calm down. This wasn't how she'd wanted to handle this.

"Now," Thornton said, "what's wrong with you?"

"It's that," Tamara said, jutting her chin at the work order.

Thornton drew it to him and dipped his glasses to read it.

"Mmm-hmm." His eyes lingered at the paragraph describing the requested procedure. "Hmm."

"That's what I thought, too," Tamara said. "I couldn't believe it at first."

Thornton pushed it back across the desk. "What's the problem?"

She stared at him. "Didn't you read it? Somebody wants me to make a spray of botulin toxin! Botulism, Mr. Thornton. Food poisoning. It kills people." Tamara wasn't getting through to him. "This is a weapon, Mr. Thornton! It's a mistake, right? Tell me it's a mistake. They want a biopolymer or a bolete, right, not botulism? There's no way I'm making botulin airborne."

Thornton tilted his head back thoughtfully. "I see."

Tamara's heart still fluttered, but at least she'd unshouldered her burden. She put the tissue box on Thornton's desk and wadded the wet ones in her hand. "Thanks for understanding, Mr. Thornton. It means a lot to me."

The half-frames dipped. "Miss Mack, when do you think you could have this work order filled?"

Tamara couldn't move. She couldn't speak. She stared at him numbly, catatonic. Thoughts that might've become words rose then quickly dissolved.

"You look confused, Miss Mack."

She still couldn't speak, but now at least her eyebrows moved. They drew together.

Thornton rocked back in his ergonomic chair. "This client, Miss Mack, has been waiting for his product for months. The project's been plagued with problems. Now it's been handed to me. Dr. Redding says a grad student could do it, but he wants a good grad student." His fingers unfurled toward her. "That's you. Take my word for it, Miss Mack, this client is not one we want to anger. It would behoove us all to get him what he wants so he can go along his merry way."

Tamara regained the use of her voice. With firmness mixed

with all the humility God would grant her, she said, "I won't do this, sir."

"Yes, you will, Miss Mack."

"No, sir. I'm very sorry, but I can't. Airborne botulism? Mr. Thornton, I make things that help people. I don't make...I don't make things like this."

Her manager didn't move, but she could sense a gathering storm.

"Mr. Thornton," she said, her humility waning, "GeneSys shouldn't do this. It's bad business to wipe out potential customers, wouldn't you think? Bad press. Two, we shouldn't do it on moral grounds. There is no purpose for this project other than to be used against living animals—which includes us. People might die and I would be responsible. No, thank you, sir. I won't do it."

Thornton carefully took his glasses off, folded them, and placed them on his desk. "Are you finished?"

She nodded.

"Miss Mack, you will fill this work order. And—"

"No, I will not."

"—if you do not, I will find someone who will. You're not exactly irreplaceable, Miss Mack. Perhaps we should give your lab to someone who's more of a team player, hmm? I believe Mr. Donizetti is still available."

The ineptitude of former GeneSys employee Steven Donizetti was legendary.

"If you choose not to fill this work order," Thornton continued, "you will be in breach of contract. Maybe you haven't heard, but Mortimer McCall takes that kind of thing quite seriously. At the very least you will lose your job at GeneSys, your credentials as a microbiologist, your home on this tropical paradise, and— need I mention it?—your lucrative income."

Tamara held her bold expression, though she felt like a deflating balloon.

"I suggest," Thornton said, "that you return to your little stool and get to work."

Tamara turned to leave, her only thought to get away from here and go somewhere to think.

Thornton called her name. "Forgetting something?" He pushed the work order across the desk.

She took it and walked numbly out the door.

Richard Thornton put his glasses on again. He drummed his fingers on the desk impatiently. He'd gone out on a limb with Redding, GeneSys's chief geneticist, bragging about how well his department would perform this task. Thornton intended to parley this into a raise. But now this Betty Boop wanted to blow it for him. Ever since she'd found religion she'd been acting flaky. It was time to cover his rear.

He pulled a keyboard toward him and called up the internal e-memo program on his computer.

> To: Personnel Department
> From: Richard Thornton
>   Manager, Microbiology
> Re: Tamara Mack

> This is to alert the Personnel Department that Tamara Mack should be considered for possible relocation. She has shown resistance to normal work assignments, even threatening not to perform company tasks that fall well within her job description. Possible cause: religious sentiments. Recommend performance review and/or termination at earliest opportunity.

Tamara found herself at the lab window again, overlooking the Rock and the crashing surf. She couldn't exactly walk out on this job.

"Jesus, what should I do?"

She pressed her forehead against the glass, letting it cool her overheating cerebrum. A Bible verse came to her mind. Stealthily, as if emerging from murky water. "He withdrew to a solitary place."

Immediately she knew what she could do. She checked her watch. 4:20. It was almost quitting time—on Friday! And it was her weekend to go to Acapulco.

She was excited now. She went to the counter and pulled out the other work orders. Even if she'd wanted to she couldn't get that one done today. Not in forty minutes. She put it on the bottom of the stack and got to work on the others. She felt light, happy to be out from under that burden.

Her mind strayed to what she might do on the mainland this weekend. She needed to go to the church where she'd been saved. Maybe the old man would be there. Maybe she'd even stay in a local hotel this time. The GeneSys resort was first class, but this weekend Tamara wanted as much distance from the company as she could get.

Maybe (would you mind, Lord Jesus?) a hurricane would come and blow GeneSys away while she was gone. At least blow a certain piece of paper away. Maybe the place would burn to the ground. If not, at least she would have the whole weekend to pray about it. Surely she would know what to do by Monday morning.

John Hawkwood didn't like to make swift changes. He preferred to mull over decisions at length, compiling mountains of research, before acting. The better to control the situation.

This Brainiac had forced him into making a leap before he'd had time to think about it, much less do any research. Suddenly Hawkwood needed to be out of the country, and quick. If Brainiac's minions didn't get to him, the Bundt/Alliance people would. Fortunately, the White Company had a long waiting list of potential clients. One of those just happened to be outside the U.S., far from public scrutiny. Maybe it was a good decision, maybe it wasn't, but he had to leap.

He selected fifteen of his best and brightest and got them and their equipment on an airplane headed southwest. They left the country on Friday and were in business again by Saturday afternoon.

than Hamilton sat with his back against a giant pine tree, overlooking their small private lake. The Hamilton home sat right on the waterfront, directly across the lake from Ethan's position. The Texas sun reflected off the waves, almost managing to disguise the brown tinge of the water. It was a hot June morning. An inconstant breeze set the pine trees to hissing.

Special Agent Mike Gillette sat against a tree nearby, his long legs stretched out before him, crossed at the boots. His Stetson lay on the rust-colored pine needles on the ground. His eyes were closed.

"I tell you what," Gillette said serenely, "you folks shore got it right out here."

"Thanks, Mike. We like it." Ethan inhaled the pollen-rich air. "You and Liz ought to build out here. The lot right behind us is for sale."

"No kiddin'?"

Ethan nodded. "You could get the same developer we used. He'll build you your own lake."

Gillette looked out over the water, a melancholy look in his eyes. Then he snorted. "Liz'd never go for it."

"Why not?"

"She just wouldn't. Her family's all in Fort Worth. She's

already asking me when we can start having kids. She'll want them close to her folks. Maybe someday."

"I'm proud of you, Mike," Ethan said. "Putting your wife first. That's a good habit for you."

He didn't answer.

A turtle's snout broke the surface of the lake. Ethan could faintly see the outline of its shell and an occasional flash of a paddling leg.

It was Saturday morning, the day after Operation Hydra's mixed bag of results. They'd had an online briefing immediately after he'd returned from speaking with Hawkwood, tallying up their effectiveness.

A bombing had been stopped. The militia group responsible had been put out of commission. Ethan had obtained evidence that would likely lead to the downfall of the insurance executive who was the silent financial backer of the long-term care bombings. It was a major coup for Ethan's team. The only black eyes were the clean getaway of the White Company and the FBI's wounded pride. His team had scored a touchdown after all, but it was as if the quarterback had been knocked out on the play.

Ethan was proud of what they had achieved. He would've liked complete success, but if any one objective had to be sacrificed, he felt the right one got picked. The goal had been to stop the long-term care bombings, and that was what they had accomplished. The only casualties had come at the CPM compound, where two militia members had been killed. Still, none of the good guys had been lost.

Mike and Liz Gillette had driven up from Fort Worth for the weekend. Sunday evening Ethan and Gillette would be off to Virginia for a rare in-person assembly of his team. They needed to debrief fully from Operation Hydra, touch base on other projects, and—if reports he'd received could be trusted—vent some interagency frustrations. So what else was new?

Across the lake Ethan could make out two tiny shapes moving around. His children, Jordan and Katie, out playing. On the upper deck of the house, Ethan could faintly see where Kaye and Liz were sitting.

"Hey," Gillette said, "can I ask you something?"

"Shoot."

"Do you love your wife?"

Ethan looked at his friend. "Mike? You know I do."

"I know, but I mean, do you really love her, or do you just, you know, go through the motions sometimes?"

"Do you mean, do I always feel all lovey-dovey for Kaye?"

"Right."

"Of course not, Mike. That wouldn't be natural."

Gillette sat up taller against the tree. "That's what I was afraid of."

"Mike, love isn't a feeling, it's a decision. You can't expect any emotion, no matter how strong, to last forever."

"So what do you do when the sizzle goes out of your steak?"

"It's not like that," Ethan said. "Emotions are like toddlers: they're wonderful, but they shouldn't get to make the rules. Your feelings will rise and fall. They're finicky. Trying to build a marriage on them is like this story I know about a house built on sinking sand."

Gillette didn't meet Ethan's eye. "Hmm."

"I'm guessing this is about you and Liz?" Ethan said. "Your feelings for her maybe aren't what they were, so you're afraid you don't love her anymore, am I right? Maybe you're worried about the D-word."

Gillette scratched his neck. "Stupid, huh?"

"I don't think so."

"It's not only that," Gillette said. "I…" He sighed. "I keep looking at, you know, at good-looking women. Too much, I guess. I've never stepped out on Liz, but…I keep thinking about it. I'm afraid maybe one day I will, especially since it seems I've lost feelings for Liz. How did you and Kaye do it?"

"Do what?" Ethan said.

"How did you patch things up after she walked out on you and went up to her parents'?"

That whole episode was one Ethan would have preferred to forget. He'd been addicted to his computers back then, to the point that they had become like a mistress to him.

"I got my priorities straight, for one thing," Ethan said. "I put God first in my heart again. Then Kaye naturally came second and everything else fell into place."

"But wasn't she sore?"

"Sure she was."

"Didn't she lose some of her feelings for you? Didn't you lose some for her? How did you get it back?"

"Mike, you've got it all wrong. Kaye and I stayed together because we're both committed to this marriage. She didn't leave because she'd lost her love for me, but really, I think, to get my attention, to show me how out of balance I'd become. In a strange way, she left so that we could get back together."

"I'm committed to Liz," Gillette protested.

"I know you are. But that's not enough by itself. Mike, in this day and age, the only chance a marriage has is the power of Jesus Christ."

Gillette looked at him earnestly. "Is that a fact?"

"That's what I believe."

"You know," he said after a pause, "it's funny that you should bring that up."

"It is?"

"Yeah, I...I've kinda been thinking about it lately. I guess I figured to ask you about it, sooner or later."

"Oh, really? Tell me more."

"Well, it's this thing with Liz, I guess. I want it to work so bad, you know. I want us to have what you and Kaye have. I look around me and I see so many of my friends who're divorced or headed that way. Some of the stories I could tell you... I just don't want that for me and Liz.

"And there's what I said about me lustin' after other women. I know I shouldn't do it, but when I see one, I just can't help myself. Then there's this hot head of mine, and the mouth it's connected to. Liz has a whole shopping list of improvements I'm supposed to make. And on top of the whole thing I think I'm burning out in my job."

They sat together quietly for a while. The forest emanated a healing power, half heard, half felt.

"Mike," Ethan said abruptly, "you need to become a Christian."

Gillette looked stunned, as if he'd just popped a tiny green jalapeño pepper in his mouth. "Huh?"

"You need Jesus, my friend," Ethan said. "Excuse me for being so blunt about this, but I'm concerned about you. Have been as long as I've known you. You're a good person, Mike Gillette, and a good friend. But you're going to hell without Jesus in your heart."

Gillette chuckled nervously. "You don't beat around it, do you, Tex?"

"You've known me how long, Mike?" Ethan asked. "Two, three years?"

Gillette nodded. He seemed a bit shaky.

"You've known from the beginning that I was a Christian, yes?"

Nod.

"And you're not a Christian, are you, Mike?"

Gillette simply shook his head and looked at the ground. "Nope."

Ethan prayed for God to give him the words. "Mike, do you know what it means to be a Christian?"

Gillette shrugged. "You go to church, you read the Bible. Don't you obey the Ten Commandments? Oh, and you try to live right."

"Okay," Ethan allowed.

"And you get to go to heaven."

"True. Those are all true. But what most people on the outside don't see is the relationship part of Christianity."

"Right, you try to help people out."

"True," Ethan said, "but that's a horizontal view, if you take my meaning. I'm talking about something vertical—a relationship between you and Jesus. He's a real person, Mike. He's got a real personality. The greatest part of being a Christian is getting to know who he is. Learning to know him and love him. Tell me, Mike, are you a good person?"

Gillette looked at him askance. "That's a trick question, ain't it? Like no matter what I answer you'll get me, right?"

"Just: do you consider yourself a good person?"

"Not as good as some, I s'pose. Better than others."

"Better than most?"

Gillette shrugged. "Maybe."

"Don't get me wrong, Mike, I think you're a very good person."

"But it's not enough," Gillette said. "That's what you're going to say. It's not enough because I don't do the rest of it. Church and all."

"Well, sort of. You're right, just being good isn't enough. But adding a few activities onto your life isn't going to make a difference. I was going to ask you a question," Ethan said, "since you consider yourself a good person, yet you admit you're not a Christian."

"Uh, oh," Gillette said with one eyebrow cocked. "I'm trapped, huh?"

"I just wanted to ask you why. Why are you a good person, Mike? Why do you obey the law and pay your taxes and hold the door open for old ladies? And why don't you do other things? Why don't you run around on Liz? You see what I'm asking?"

"Not really."

"You're not a Christian, Mike, so you really have no reason to behave morally. You do good things and you don't do bad things, but why? See, I've come to the conclusion that non-Christians cheat themselves out of a lot of so-called fun. They ought to live it up, suck every ounce of self-indulgent fun out of this world, then I think they should kill themselves."

"Whoa, podner. I think that's overdoing it. "

"No, think about it. For the non-Christian, what meaning does this life have? None. You're a random life-form accidentally given momentary life. After a miserable few years, in which you try and fail to make yourself happy, you'll simply blip out of existence. So why not kill yourself?"

Ethan checked his friend quickly. Gillette was staring at the water's edge.

"Maybe I see what you mean," he said.

"But it's not that way for the Christian," Ethan said. "Oh, Mike. My life has meaning. There's purpose to this existence, and I have a part to play." He paused a moment. The wind blew gently. A squirrel skittered up a tree in the grove behind them.

"You can be part of it, too, Mike," Ethan continued. "There is meaning for you. The Creator of the universe wants to give you a power supply for you to love Liz with God's love. That's the only chance your marriage—or anybody's marriage—has. And Jesus wants to give you the power to overcome your anger, your lust, your burnout and all the rest. Jesus will give you hope."

They sat together without speaking. They would have to head back soon for lunch. But not before someone's eternity was decided.

"So what do you think, Mike? Does it sound good? Does it sound like something you want?"

Gillette's voice was wobbly. "Yes, sir, it does."

Kaye Hamilton and Liz Gillette sat on the second-story deck sipping lemonade and watching the children play below. Liz the beautiful trophy wife and Kaye the winsome woman of God.

These two got along well and enjoyed each other's company. Mostly they talked about married life, their husbands, and Liz's growing desire for children. At the moment they'd exhausted those topics and were wishing their husbands would return.

"Mommy," three-year-old Katie called.

"Yes, honey."

"Jordan won't let Katie pay with that." She pointed in Jordan's general direction.

Kaye couldn't see what Jordan was so jealously hoarding, but decided it wasn't worth the effort. "Why don't you go swing, Katie."

"Okay." The blond girl ran to the tree swing.

Kaye and Liz exchanged smiles. "You pick your fights," Kaye said.

"Good plan."

They heard ten-year-old Jordan call to someone. He was down by the boat pier. Ethan and Gillette walked into view.

"Finally," Liz said, standing up.

Ethan approached the house and looked up at them. He seemed happy. "Hello, my love."

"How was your nature walk?" Kaye asked.

"Wonderful. Tell you all about it later. Right now, Mr. Gillette and I were wondering what we could do to help get lunch ready."

"Um-hmm," Liz said, a hand on her hip. "That's not the Mr. Gillette I know."

Ethan put a hand on Gillette's shoulder. "You never know, Liz. He might just surprise you."

"Hmph."

To Kaye, Gillette looked a little forlorn. "Are you feeling all right, Mike?"

"Just fine, ma'am," he said, tipping his cowboy hat.

"You're taking us out to lunch," Liz said.

"We are?"

"No," Kaye said, "Ethan and I are taking all of us out. If that's all right, Ethan?"

"Always." Ethan turned to his children. "Come on, kids. Get in the car. Let's go eat."

"Yay!" Jordan shouted.

Katie scuttled after him, chanting, "Buhguh King, Buhguh King."

CHAPTER SEVEN

It wasn't the largest conference room at Langley Air Force Base, nor was it the plushest, but it would do. Ethan wondered if the conference room secured for their meetings was an indication of score. Had Operation Hydra been a maximum success, would they have the Presidential Conference Room? However, it was the CIA headquarters. It was just possible that the president was in that room today. The nerve.

The twenty-six members of Ethan's Joint Intelligence Detail, Information Operations and Counter-Cyberterrorism, Provisional team stood or sat around the polished wood table, talking. Ethan watched them from a large monitor in an adjoining room. He liked having a little reconnaissance before entering what might become a field of battle.

He noticed the representatives of the Department of Energy keeping to themselves, as far from the CIA men as possible. Probably best for now, Ethan thought. Mike Gillette was whooping it up with buddies from several agencies. He was a valuable asset, Ethan knew. If they were ever going to gel as a team, they all needed a dose of Mike's amiable nature.

It was strange to think of his twangy, door-busting, flirtatious friend as a Christian brother. Truly God still worked miracles. After his pensive mood immediately after his conversion, Gillette had rebounded to his old self. The whole flight up to Virginia, he had plugged Ethan with questions. What to do about lust, what to do about anger, what to do about undercover assignments. Good questions, Ethan thought. Coupled with an excitement that was an excellent indication that true conversion had occurred.

By now all the faces in the conference room were familiar to Ethan. In the beginning he had known only two of them besides Gillette: Captain Kelly Barnes and Major Elizabeth Lee. Both were computer encryption experts from the Army. Both were heroes of last year's near catastrophe caused by some wayward bots. Both officers had been promoted for their efforts. Major Lee was the only woman on Ethan's team.

Ethan had made it a point to get to know each team member singly. Know your enemy, know yourself, Sun Tzu had taught. Now they all knew Ethan, but they didn't yet know each other, much less trust each other. Ethan wanted to take them all on some kind of survival camp-out, something that would create the kind of bond they would need if JIDIOC-P was ever going to lose the P.

He turned to the young woman operating the conference room cameras. "Thanks, Louise. Hope you enjoy the show."

"What's not to like?"

"Right," Ethan said. "Stay awake, now."

"Always, sir."

Ethan stopped just outside the door to the conference room and offered up a quick prayer. Then he strode into the room with an easy confidence—a confidence that always amazed him, considering his inborn self-consciousness. Some greeted him warmly as he walked the length of the table; others didn't even look up. The noise level in the room receded, though, and everyone took a seat. Ethan called the meeting to order.

"Well," Ethan said, "it's good to see you all in reality for a change." He looked around the table. Most of the men and the only woman wore military uniforms. The others wore suits. "Mr. Barnes, teleconferencing does no justice to that hair of yours."

Polite laughter. Captain Barnes stroked his red hair proudly, though his face flushed.

"Let me extend congratulations to you for a job well done. As you'll hear in these briefings, Operation Hydra was, for the most part, a whopping success. As for the rest..." He shrugged. "I hope we'll always be striving to get better. Major Lee, would you start us off, please?"

Elizabeth Lee read from a sheet of paper on the table before her. "Lieutenant Bartlett reports zero casualties in his Delta Force unit, although one man was bitten by a sentry dog. He received a rabies shot and is doing fine. Enemy casualties: our nonlethal weapons have once more proven lethal. In total, two men and three dogs were killed and six others seriously injured as a result of the effects of the weapons. One man who was stunned died because he couldn't brace himself from a simple fall out of the back of a truck. Massive head injury."

"I'm curious, Miss Lee," Ethan said. "Would you have preferred it if all the CPM men had been killed?"

That got a reaction from the JIDIOC-P team members. The military folks were generally against using nonlethal weapons, as were the CIA. Messy and unreliable. Those who worked further from the business of killing and closer to public scrutiny thought them a necessary evil. Useful for PR.

"No, sir," Lee said.

"I think what the major's trying to say," said Marine Lieutenant Adam Brosnan, "is that we'd like to fight without our hands tied, sir."

Several officers in the room agreed.

"These ray guns and stun sticks make us sick, sir," Brosnan said. "Prisoners take manpower, food, and medicine from my men. No, thank you."

"The problem isn't with the ray guns, " a DoE agent said.

"No," Calvin Coakley said. "It's with the people who invent them."

"Don't start, Calvin," Ethan said. "You all know it isn't up to me about using nonlethals."

Coakley rolled his eyes.

Ethan blew out a sigh. "I am so tired of trying to hold you people together. I was hoping that Hydra would bring us together. It should've, for crying out loud. Look what we accomplished together. But I can see now that it's going to take more than that to make you give up the old feuds. More than I can give. Tell you what: why don't we just disband JIDIOC right now? You all just go on back to your old assignments. I'll tell the president."

There is something odd about a room full of silent people. An invisible influence held twenty-seven mouths shut for almost a whole minute.

"You know what I wish?" Jeffrey Larson of the State Department finally asked. "I just wish we could read about it in the morning paper when we do something good."

Voices agreed gently.

"Yeah," Captain Barnes said, "or hear our names on TV. 'Here they are, folks, the people who blew the lid off Bundt/Alliance.' But no, all we hear is that the company suddenly declared bankruptcy. They don't even connect it with the bombings."

"They don't even know they've stopped," Coakley said, a bruise dark on his brown face. "They're still waiting for the next one to go off."

"Another day, another war won," Lieutenant Brosnan said.

"Shadow wars," Max Cobb from the FBI said.

"Cheer up," Dean Berry, the other CIA agent said. "If they ever did run it in the paper, they'd probably put Gillette's ugly mug in there and we'd all die from shame."

"Har har," Gillette said.

"Talk about your nonlethal weapons."

What was this, friendly laughter? Ethan looked up. They were all still there. He'd expected to see a few empty seats at least.

"The thing of it is, sir," Major Lee said to Ethan, "it's a new way of doing things. None of us like working together because it isn't how we were trained. Remember, Captain Barnes and I wanted this duty, but the rest were simply assigned to it."

Ethan nodded.

"We all think we've got this territory we have to defend," Gillette said. "It's not just us in this room, either. It's a proud tradition in all our agencies and branches. You're supposed to think you're better than the other guy. It's part of being proud of what you do. We'll come around, boss. Just give us some time."

Ethan looked around the room slowly, trying to read faces. He left the door open for anyone else to comment, but no one did. Perhaps he'd misread them all. Maybe there was hope for this team after all.

"All right," Ethan said. "Okay. Look, I know Operation Hydra had its mishaps as well as its victories, and I know relations are strained between Energy and the CIA, but maybe it's time to put those behind us. What do you say? We can work it out this afternoon on the football field. We do have the stadium reserved, don't we, Danny?"

The Air Force officer gave a thumbs-up. "Secured, sir."

"Good. Because we're all on the same team here, aren't we? Us against the black hats, right?" Ethan smiled. God willing, they were on the way to becoming united into a cord of many strands.

After all the reports on Operation Hydra had been delivered, Ethan turned their attention to other cases.

Captain Kelly Barnes moved to the side wall of the conference room, his red hair dark brown in the dimmed light. Aerial video footage of an ocean island played on the large screen behind him. The island was small, flat, and appeared to have no vegetation whatsoever. Sun glinted on the water, showing a large interior lagoon.

"Clipperton Island," Barnes said. "Arguably the most remote spot on earth. Though officially part of French Polynesia, it is twenty-six hundred miles from the nearest French Polynesian island. Seven hundred miles north of the equator and almost as far from the nearest mainland, which is Mexico. Acapulco is six hundred seventy miles to the northeast.

"As you can see, the island itself isn't much to speak of. Only two and a half miles across at its longest point. In this shot you can also see the freshwater lagoon. Clipperton is like a big rubber band floating on the Pacific Ocean. Water on the inside, water all around. The beach is never more than five hundred yards wide, and most of it is more like fifty. The rest is lagoon.

"Clipperton Island is nature's way of saying, Keep Out. There is no ocean approach to Clipperton. No anchorage. Jagged coral reefs surround the island, which is constantly battered with ten-foot-high waves. Jacques Cousteau made a documentary about Clipperton, called 'The Island That Time Forgot,' and in it ol' Jacques had to walk his little pontoon boat about twenty yards from shore to keep from getting ripped up on the reefs.

"Man-eating sharks thrive in the waters around the island: hammerhead, blue, mako, nurse, thresher, tiger, and great white. Moray eels are there, too, sometimes even coming ashore to attack people snoozing on the beach.

"There have been several attempts to inhabit the island. All but the latest have ultimately failed. In total, ten ships have been wrecked or grounded on Clipperton. In World War II, the U.S. Navy tried to build a listening station on the island but gave up the effort when the ship with all the heavy equipment ran aground. Then two of the ships that came to rescue it ran aground. They eventually abandoned the landing ship, along with all its equipment and vehicles."

Ethan saw the Navy representatives bristle at the story, but neither interrupted Barnes.

"The most interesting story about the island," Barnes said, "concerns a Mexican garrison stationed there in the days before World War I. There was this small garrison there: the soldiers and their families. They'd been getting a regular shipment of supplies every four months or so, but then—unbeknownst to them—there was a revolution back in Mexico. The government was overthrown. All the garrison knew was that the supply ship stopped coming.

"One man, a black Mexican named Álvarez, lived right here." He pointed at a dark mark on the video image of the island. "It's called the Rock. It's the only piece of Clipperton that rises more than nine feet above sea level. The Rock is seventy feet high. They used it as a lighthouse. Álvarez lived in a shack at the base of it.

"Anyway, when the supplies stopped coming, things got bad. There are about six coconut trees on the whole island. These produced enough coconuts to keep scurvy away from the women and children, but the men, who went without, quickly succumbed. Months and months passed, until only five men remained alive: the commander, three of his soldiers, and Álvarez. Eight women and children still lived, all in various states of starvation, disease, and malnutrition. They didn't know it, but World War I had started by this time and was in full swing.

"One day the commander sighted a ship. At least that's what he claimed. No one else saw it. One account says that the island had driven him crazy. Anyway, he ordered his men to launch their small boat to try to reach the ship. When they refused, he ordered them at gunpoint. They got out in the high surf, but then something happened. One account has it that the oars broke and they lost control. Another says that the men tried to take the gun away from him. Either way, the boat went down and all four men were lost.

"Now," Barnes said, "this is when the good part starts. See, Álvarez is watching all this, too. One minute he's the bottom of the social order, the next minute he's the only man on an island of women. So he thinks he's fallen into a gold mine, right? He rounds up all the guns and proclaims himself king of Clipperton Island. It wasn't long before he started demanding the, uh, services of the women. Those who resisted, he shot.

"At first he stayed away from the commander's wife—all accounts describe her as a very strong-willed woman—but eventually he came to her and demanded that she come to his shack. The story is that she looked at the women and children around her and said, 'It's time.'"

"Kelly," Ethan interrupted.

"So— Uh, yes sir?"

"We do have other projects to discuss. Why don't you cut to the chase?"

"Yes, sir." He thought for a moment. "Anyway, they all went out to Álvarez's shack and attacked him. One of the girls bashed his head in with a hammer. One of the kids went running around the shack to get a rifle and saw, get this, a U.S. Navy ship. Right there, just offshore, sending a landing craft in.

"Imagine the crew's surprise when they landed on this supposedly deserted island looking for Germans and instead found a bunch of hysterical women who had just killed the lighthouse keeper. The sailors took everybody aboard—everybody except Álvarez, who was already getting chewed up by the crabs. Have I mentioned the land crabs yet? They infest the island like an Old Testament plague. The place stinks, too—have I mentioned that? Ammonia from the bird droppings. Have I mentioned the birds that nest there? Tens of thousands of them on that tiny little—"

"Kelly," Ethan warned.

"Sorry. Okay, let's cut to now."

Barnes pressed a button on the remote, skipping the video disc to footage of an elegant, ultramodern complex with blue ocean in the background. The buildings stood in a shallow lagoon atop massive sea legs reminiscent of offshore drilling rigs. A vertical wind turbine rotated atop one of the buildings.

"Before I go on," Barnes said, "I'd like to thank Dr. Hanover of the National Reconnaissance Office and Larry Templeton at the National Imagery & Mapping Agency for providing these graphics."

The two men mentioned nodded.

"Today, Clipperton Island is home to GeneSys Industries, a cutting-edge biotech company specializing in, shall we say, custom-made genetic products. Anything you want, they'll do it for you: clones, hybrids, self-fertilizing crops, transgenic animals, made-to-order babies, whatever. If you pay what they charge, they'll do it, no questions asked.

"That's the reason they've chosen Clipperton—a natural fortress, far from meddling superpowers, and, thanks to generous policies with France, no extradition treaty. GeneSys is essentially a nation unto itself."

Ethan heard someone mutter, "Island of Dr. Moreau."

"GeneSys has a client list that reads like a who's who of the world's rich and famous," Barnes said. "Industrialist Broderick Smythe had his dead wife cloned there. Rock star Sagamore Black had himself cloned. No surprise there. Prime Minister Tehuapec's new heart? Grown in a pig at GeneSys. Remember Eddie Jolly, the baseball player who was dying of that rare brain disease? He had himself cloned, then harvested the embryo's brain tissue to have it implanted in himself. I hear he's batting .375 this year.

"Companies use GeneSys, too. It was no coincidence that Weatherport Aeronautics announced its new ultralight aircraft design shortly after GeneSys created a bat/hawk hybrid for them. The new generation of organic computing you may've heard about—cyborganics—is being developed partly here at Clipperton Island, far from those who object to outright exploitation of animals.

"GeneSys doesn't care what you want them to do, so long as

you pay their price tag. This is what has brought them to our attention. Projects currently under development include a race-specific form of anthrax for a neo-Nazi client, rice that turns toxic when mixed with soy sauce, an enzyme that searches for a host with the so-called 'fat gene' and then attacks the hypothalamus, and—get this—an airborne version of botulism."

There were several angry outbursts and expressions of disbelief from the JIDIOC-P team. The Air Force officers were making sounds like they might go bomb the place right then and there.

"Easy, people. Dave Weinhart's working on this personally," Ethan said, naming the National Security Advisor. "He's putting pressure on France to take action, especially since at least one of these weapons will likely be used on French soil. So far they've been dragging their heels."

"Cha-ching," someone said.

"At the very least, Dave's trying to get approval for us to send about a company's worth of U.S. Marine 'advisers' to check things out."

The team members fell into raucous conversation. The bits Ethan picked out were mostly bluster.

"In the meantime," Ethan said, "I've had Captain Barnes here throwing the proverbial wrench in their gears. I realize this kind of thing is really the CIA's cup of tea, but Weinhart's asked us to see what we can do from here. Kelly's been able to do some incredible things. Tell them, Mr. Barnes."

"These scientists," Barnes said, "they may be great genetic engineers, but they're total GlobeNet boneheads. Absolutely no safeguards on their network. I've been going in at will and erasing files, scrambling data, whatever I want to do. Every one of their questionable projects has been frustrated or set back since I've been going after them. One project, the soy sauce one, was even canceled."

Barnes returned to his seat, though it was clear he wasn't finished. He sat down quietly and stared at his hands folded on the table. "About two weeks ago I got a little cocky." He pulled a legal pad closer and played with it nervously. "I thought it would be fun to swap the contents of their head geneticist's storage disks with that of their chief cook. I thought one might start engineering pot roasts and the other cooking cloneburgers." Barnes's fair face reddened deeply, almost the color of his freckles.

"The procedure took too long," he said. "I never should've done it. It was actually the cook who caught me—the scientist never had a clue. Who'd have known the cook would be Junior Whiz Boy? He stopped the file transfer and, before I saw what was going on, he'd traced the command pathway all the way out to my first alias. Of course he never found out who was doing it, but it would've been clear to him my attack was coming from the outside.

"I read their internal mail and saw that the cook had reported it, but for two weeks nothing happened. I thought maybe they'd just forget it. I went on with my job, keeping my nose extremely clean." He pulled the legal pad closer. "This weekend it was like somebody put up a Jurassic Park electric fence around the GeneSys computers. I…I can't get in."

No one said anything for several seconds. Finally Sai Cho from NSA spoke. "Somebody wised up."

"What's the status with France?" asked Max Cobb.

"No good," Ethan said. "As I said, they're dragging their heels."

Calvin Coakley said, "We need to put a warm body in there."

"Ah, Mr. Coakley," Ethan said. "That's just what I was hoping you'd say. When can you do it?"

"I'll have to ask Director Pickett," Coakley said. "But maybe somebody could leave today or tomorrow."

"What would they do," Ethan asked, "go in as a tourist or something?"

"Maybe. Maybe a potential customer." Coakley looked at Barnes. "Are they looking to hire in any position?"

"I'll find out," Barnes said, writing it on the pad.

"Okay," Ethan said. "That's good. Hopefully Weinhart can get France to cooperate. But the CIA will have to do in the meantime. Now, can we move on to other files? Mike, what's up about—"

"Excuse me, Ethan," Barnes said. "I mean, Director Hamilton."

"Go ahead, Kelly."

"There's one more thing that might be helpful. This past Friday, just hours before the new defenses went up on GeneSys's computers, I read an internal message." Barnes pulled out a sheet of paper. "There's a woman in one of the microbiology labs that's apparently starting to ask some discomforting questions of her boss. Tamara Mack's her name. Her boss wrote her up for resisting assignments. I checked up on her and found that she'd just been handed the task of making botulism airborne—and for the Algerian Chehili terrorists, no less.

"Here's the clincher: her boss thinks she may be refusing because of her religious sentiments. I checked her e-mail. Seems she's one o' them born-again Christians. I knew you'd be interested in that, boss."

"Right, Kelly. Thanks." Ethan looked at the CIA agents. "This Tamara Mack might be a good contact when your agent gets there."

The door to the conference room swung open. DCI Roy Pickett strode in, a smug grin on his face. He was flanked by two aides.

"Actually," Pickett said, coming to stand at the table, "nobody's going to this island." He looked at Ethan. "Say, buddy, could we have a word, you and me, hmm?"

"Sure."

Ethan followed the director of Central Intelligence out into the hallway.

CHAPTER EIGHT

H e's history."

Mike Gillette looked at the DoE agent who had made the comment, then at the closed door through which Ethan and Pickett had just walked. Out there stood a man who had, two years before, called the Fort Worth FBI office with a wild theory about someone electrocuting people on GlobeNet. Oh, the places they'd been together since then.

Ethan was the only true friend Gillette had. While no one was a stranger to Mike Gillette, still no one was a confidant, either. And Ethan was the one who had introduced him to Jesus. In a way, no one had ever done more for him than Ethan Hamilton.

The door swung open. Pickett sauntered in, alone. He walked to the head of the table and sat down in Ethan's chair, smiling like a cat with feathers in its mouth.

"Please," he said, "proceed with the briefing."

"Where's Ethan?" Captain Barnes asked.

Pickett didn't answer right away. To Gillette it almost seemed he was prolonging the moment deliberately. Maybe he was. Maybe he wanted to wallow in it like a hog in mud.

"Mr. Hamilton," he said slowly, "is on indefinite leave."

"What?" more than one person said.

"Who's going to lead the team?"

"Fired, you mean."

"Why?"

Gillette watched Pickett listening to the babble. "It would help things, Roy," he said, "if you didn't seem to be enjoying this so much."

Pickett's who-me look was a beautiful forgery.

"With all due respect," Gillette said, standing, "you make me sick. He was only doing what President Connor enlisted him to do. But you couldn't stand it that Ethan and Rand are close, could you? You've been looking for a chance to bring him down this whole time, haven't you?"

Pickett might've been hearing a mildly favorable stock report to judge by his expression. Then, as if Gillette had never spoken, he went on. "I told Ethan I'd hold down the fort while he was gone. He's going to take some well-deserved vacation time while we reevaluate his status."

Gillette fell into his chair. He ought to strike some blow in Ethan's honor. All of them ought to. He looked around the room. A few of the others appeared upset. Barnes looked like someone had punched him in the gut. Most wore neutral expressions. A few nodded eagerly with Pickett's every word.

The DCI was speaking. "...idea is a good one. So none of you worry. You still have your jobs. For now there will be no reassignments as far as you're concerned. We'll simply be looking for a new director. I just happen to have a man in mind." The lips-only smile stretched wider. "Okay, who's next with a briefing?"

Tamara Mack had had no revelation from God. The whole weekend in Acapulco she'd prayed and fretted and searched the Bible. Sure, she'd had ideas. Oh, maybe she should handle it this way. No, Jesus would do it this other way. But maybe this verse could be interpreted as saying she should do it yet another way. If people thought becoming a Christian would make all their problems go away, they were wrong.

She stood on an observation bridge between the dormitory and the lab building. The wind blew steadily, carrying a faint ammonia odor. The birds and the surf shouted at her. Atop the tech building the corkscrew wind turbine rotated gracefully.

Though GeneSys had seemingly mastered the art of alternative energy, they still regulated power use frugally. Tamara had found a stern warning on her apartment door when she'd returned from her weekend. Apparently she'd left a lamp on. This isn't the mainland, the letter said; she couldn't just leave things on when she left. She was sentenced to a fifty-dollar fine and five hours on the battery-charging treadmill.

The weight of The Work Order pressed her down. Though she'd received no clear word from God this weekend, she knew more than ever that she could not fulfill that order. It was no longer difficult to imagine herself defying her employer in the name of right. And now that she looked around herself, she began to see things she hadn't before.

Bits of overheard conversation resurfaced in her mind. Labs with enigmatic and sometimes euphemistic titles on the door suddenly seemed sinister. A picture of the real GeneSys was slowly forming in her mind. GeneSys was up to no good. How had she not seen it before? Was she that naive? Maybe she had gotten her word from above after all.

But what could she do about it? She was a gnat and Mortimer McCall was an elephant. The problem was still on her mind when she sat back down at her microscope.

Lake Hamilton wasn't much larger than a football field, but to hear Jordan describe it, it was Lake Superior. The Hamiltons had a near-flotilla on their glorified pond: a canoe, a sailboat, a paddleboat, inner tubes, a fishing boat, and the occasional experimental raft. Pine trees ringed the green-brown water; the banks were orange East Texas dirt. When the moonlight shone on the water, it was pure silver.

The two-story Hamilton home looked out over the lake from across a grassy hillside sprinkled with pine needles. They were less than a twenty-minute drive from Tyler, Texas, but they might as well be in the middle of the wilderness. It was close enough to shopping malls for Kaye and far enough away from concrete for Ethan.

Ethan lay in the cockpit of his little Sunfish sailboat, rocking rhythmically out in the middle of Lake Hamilton. A small anchor held the boat more or less in place. The light breeze jangled the rigging occasionally. The sun was hot on his arms and legs. It was Tuesday afternoon, June 26.

The first splash sounded like a fish jumping. Ethan hardly turned his head. By the fourth splash he knew he was under attack.

Jordan stood in a canoe fifty feet away, heaving yellow tennis balls into the air like grenades. Beside Jordan a small paddleboat chugged across the water, carrying Ethan's wife and daughter. Ethan was being waylaid on the open seas. Nothing to do but heave to and wait to be boarded.

"Daddy!" his daughter Katie said when the paddleboat was near the Sunfish. "I came to see you."

"Hello, ladies. Thank you for coming to see me, Katie."

"We thought you'd like some company," Kaye said.

Ethan, a wet tennis ball sequestered in his hand, watched Jordan out of the corner of his eye. "Wonderful."

Kaye pulled up next to Ethan's sailboat and passed him a cold drink. Ethan went to reach for it, but crouched and threw the ball instead. Jordan squawked and almost tipped the canoe. He paddled furiously toward ammunition floating nearby. Ethan finally took the drink.

"Thank you, honey." He saw Jordan rise in the canoe. "Ah-ah, Jordan, don't." He gestured to the paddleboat. "Truce while the civilians are on the battlefield."

"Dad!" Jordan complained. "This is war. Civilians don't belong." His complaint lodged, he wisely refrained from throwing any more tennis balls. He turned instead to a thorough collection campaign, paddling around picking up yellow projectiles.

"Please, I get on the boat with you, Daddy?" the little girl said, struggling at the paddleboat's harness.

"No, honey," Ethan said. "Stay with Mommy this time."

She whined but settled down. "Jaggonfly, Mommy!" she yelled, pointing over the water.

Kaye Hamilton studied her husband. "Were you thinking of staying out here all day?"

Ethan smiled. "The thought had occurred to me."

He knew what she was saying, why the flotilla had sailed. She was saying, Snap out of it. He'd been moping around like a hound dog ever since he'd returned from Virginia yesterday afternoon. Now she was ready to have her husband back. She was right. It was time to quit feeling sorry for himself. The righteous martyr bit only took you so far, especially when you're not completely innocent in the matter.

He felt as if he'd had the wind knocked out of him. How could he be "reassigned," as Pickett so delicately put it, when all he'd done was what he'd been asked to do? The president of the United States had given him an offer he couldn't refuse, personally selecting him to head up this experimental task force. And it had worked, for goodness' sake. Operation Hydra was a huge success, a major feather in President Connor's cap.

Yet all along Ethan had felt the resistance new paradigms always generated. Connor got to whip together the team, select its leader, then go off to reap the glory. It had fallen to Ethan to try to make the thing work. In his task he had faced, both from within his team and from without, fierce territorialism, old scores left unsettled, ridiculous posturing, internecine rivalries, a habit of mistrust, and a veritable slag pile of apathy. "No one," Jesus once said, "after drinking old wine wants the new, for he says, 'The old is better.'"

There were a few people on his team, not to mention in the Oval Office, who believed in the new multiagency system. They knew that the traditional division of labor wasn't cutting it anymore. The bandits were outdistancing the posse. For these few, and because Ethan himself believed in what he'd been doing, he wanted to be back at the helm of JIDIOC-P. The Roy Picketts of the world would come around when success piled atop success.

Roy, Roy, Roy. Ethan had slandered him repeatedly, if not aloud then certainly in his heart. Even now he felt the anger rising. He just wanted that team for himself, a sly voice told him. All the things that Pickett had reportedly done against Ethan came back to his mind.

At the beginning Ethan had felt like a Christian Mr. Smith going to Washington, eager to bring not only decency but also a Savior to the nation's capital. Now what was he? Just another reject from Capitol Hill. Kicked out in a political power play. Nothing special, nothing distinctively Christian about him or the whole situation.

Snap out of it, Curly, he said, calling himself by his self-deprecating nickname. *Wallowing in it doesn't help.* He looked up at his wife and found her watching him.

"You know what I think?" she asked.

"Tell me."

"I think people have to see the need to change before they will."

He smiled wanly, feeling that sad part of himself begin to cave in. "How do you do that?"

"Do what?" Kaye asked.

"Always know the right thing to say." He leaned across the boats carefully and kissed her. "What would you say to a vacation?"

"A vacation? Where?"

"Oh, I don't know," Ethan said. "We've talked about somewhere in the Caribbean." He decided to plant an idea he'd been toying with all day. "Maybe even Acapulco. What do you think?"

"You mean now?"

"Sure. This week. Tomorrow, if we want to."

Kaye's eyes widened. "Tomorrow?" Little Katie whined in the seat, wanting to get moving. "We'll talk about it," Kaye said to Ethan.

"I'm ready to go in," he said.

She pointed with her chin. "I think you'd better deal with Blackbeard over there first."

Ethan saw Jordan, sitting in his canoe with the sun behind him, waiting like a buzzard for his opportunity. A sea hawk. "Right. You'd better get to cover," he said to Kaye. "I think it's going to get ugly."

"Come on, Katie," she said. "Let's go fix supper."

"Avar and avast," Ethan called to his son when the paddle-boat was away. "Ye scurvy, landlubbin' scalawag. Be off with ye before I split ye keel to yardarm."

Jordan was unimpressed. "Dad, you are so unbelievably toast. Do you know I have twenty-one tennis balls and you have none? They're all nice and heavy. And they stink from lake muck. Mom's gonna be mad when she smells you."

"Here," Ethan said, "I'll raise my sail so you have a bigger target. I know what a terrible shot you are."

Ethan was right: it got ugly.

Wonder of wonders, miracle of miracles. Tamara Mack wasn't especially fond of Broadway musicals, but this song kept running through her head today. She'd found a temporary fix, a way for her to ethically keep her job a little longer and yet delay working on the work order that haunted her.

GeneSys work orders were sent out in triplicate. One copy went to the lab assigned to fill the order, another went to billing, and a third copy went to the materials stockroom. Botulinum cultures were normally kept on hand. But the woman in charge of keeping the laboratories well stocked had been sent to the States because of a problem pregnancy. The young man filling in for her had not ordered new bacterial cultures far enough in advance. As soon as the work order arrived, he placed the order for more cultures, but they wouldn't be available for some time. Consequently, Tamara couldn't do any work on it until the next supply ship arrived, even if she'd wanted to.

"And people say there is no God."

She almost enjoyed doing the other mundane work orders now. For six glorious days, until next Monday's supply ship, she didn't have to worry about what she should do.

"No, Ethan. No."

Ethan looked at his wife. "No?"

"No," Kaye said.

He nodded. "It was just a thought."

"Ethan, you don't work for the CIA. You're not a spy, you're a manager."

"I know."

They were sitting on the couch in their living room. It was a huge, cavernous room, with a wall of windows overlooking their moonlit lake, a metal spiral staircase leading up to the bedroom level, and a stone fireplace reaching up to the vaulted ceiling.

"If you went to that island…It's just crazy," Kaye said. "I don't even want to talk about it."

They sat together silently for a while. Ethan sighed. "It's just that I feel responsible. I'm—"

"You're not responsible for this. Honey, you got fired. Somebody higher up than you fired you. It's his problem now."

"You're probably right. The only thing is, I'm not sure he's going to do anything about it."

"That's not your problem."

"But Kaye," Ethan said, sitting up straight, "if I don't do anything, knowing what I know, won't I be held accountable? Don't I have some responsibility because of what I know?"

"Fine, write your congressman. Call the president yourself; I'm sure he'd put somebody on it."

"You're right, Kaye. You're probably right. But let's both still pray about it, okay?" Ethan said. "Let's not just shut the door without asking God."

"Does this mean you don't want to go on vacation?"

"Nope. I still say we should go. We haven't been away together in a while."

"Great. Where, then? Jamaica? Bermuda? Virgin Islands?"

"Wherever," Ethan said. "Honey, you are still keeping your mind open in case God wants us to go to Acapulco, right?"

"Oh, right."

CHAPTER NINE

In 2007, terrorism was a business. Rising costs, employee benefits, even industry guidelines of a sort beset the modern terrorist as they did the rest of the world. Gone were the days of ski masks and VW vans. If you wanted to survive in this climate, you had to evolve.

Ali al-Fashir wanted to survive. Before he'd even officially formed his group he'd done research on how to do terrorism in the twenty-first century. Thus at its first meeting, the Algerian Sirocco Front was already equipped with encrypted computers, an extensive freelancer list, and anonymous donors. The ASF—nicknamed Chehili for the hot, dry wind that every summer blew into Algeria from the Sahara—was a group whose only purpose was revenge.

In 1992 a popular election was held in Algeria. As votes were tallied, it became evident that the militant Islamic party's candidate was going to carry the election. The secular government stepped in and cancelled the election, thus retaining the presidency. In response, Muslim rebels attacked remote villages, massacring everyone who didn't run fast enough.

The violence continued over the years. What began as a politico-religious protest settled into a seasonal tradition of massacre. The rebels, who later called themselves the Islamic Liberation Army (ILA), were organized and well equipped.

Every year, especially during the Islamic holy month of Ramadan, armed rebels slaughtered civilians like sheep. Muslims killing Muslims—men, women, children; newborns and the aged—in the holiest of months.

Always the government security forces arrived at the village too late. Some wondered at the coincidence, even suggesting that the "rebels" might actually be government troops. If the people were distracted by the massacres, the reasoning went, they wouldn't stop to think about other more mundane problems, such as poor sanitation, food distribution, and medical care.

One day in 1997, the rebels chose Ali's village.

Everyone said he'd been so lucky that day. Out of town with friends. He'd come back to find his village in flames. The houses not aflame were awash with the blood of his neighbors, their decapitated heads sitting on thresholds or in windows.

He'd arrived at his family's home just as the photographers were leaving. How honored he should have been that they'd chosen to use that photo for their newspapers. It was the photo they'd run on CNN. A shot of their little kitchen, perfectly clean as his mother always kept it, except for her blood on the floor. Splashed up on the cabinets.

Ali's mother had been pregnant. After all these years Ali was finally going to be a big brother. The ILA butchers had evidently deemed themselves skilled surgeons.

That single image, of his sister's tiny body in the hands of an ILA soldier, was Ali's constant power supply. It was refined now, compressed, but it had lost none of its power. He glanced at it in his mind whenever he needed to get angry about something, which was often.

As the attacks continued across the Algerian countryside, the ranks of Ali's group swelled. For there were only two responses possible to such atrocities: fear or rage. As the government sputtered and whined—and blocked human rights investigations—men such as Ali al-Fashir swore to avenge their dead.

The image of his sister—or perhaps her spirit—had guided him to the idea of a biological weapon. Something that would make the guilty rot on their feet. Something that would make them suffer tremendously before finishing them off forever. He didn't know details of delivery or detonation, but he knew it was the solution he'd been looking for. Chehili might make only one strike and be snuffed out forever, but it would be a mortal strike, like the plunge of a dagger.

Very few private companies made biological weapons, and those that did were usually under government contract and would not sell them. Ali, once he set his course, could not be swayed. He'd found a company on a deserted island in the Pacific who would do it. Though their price was criminal, to whom could he complain?

He'd paid the money gladly. Their sorcerers had listened to his requirements and gone to work. Two months, they'd said. Ali checked the calendar on his wall. That had been sixteen weeks ago. Troubles, setbacks, accidents, so they said. If Ali ran Chehili like GeneSys ran their labs....Finally they'd told him they were finished. He'd gone for a demonstration. But they had not heeded his desires. The weapon they'd created was too gentle to its victims. He convinced them to begin again.

Botulism. That's what they were working on now. Food poisoning. Ali had done some research and decided that botulism would meet his requirements nicely. A simple process, he'd been told. A week to ten days, at most. That was two weeks ago.

Ali brought the image of his unborn sister to his mind. She always told him what to do. This time was no different.

"I take it you guys didn't play football?"

Mike Gillette's face puckered. "'Fraid not, cowboy. Roy sent us home before lunch."

Ethan nodded. He sat on a swiveling stool, addressing his friend on the giant flat-screen wall monitor in his underground game room. "So he told the president I couldn't take the stress, did he?"

"He had to come up with something like that," Gillette said. "It had to appear to be coming from you."

"I guess." Ethan sighed. "Well, how's Fort Worth? Was Liz glad to see you?"

Gillette blushed suddenly.

Ethan laughed. "I guess she was."

"You call for any other reason, Tex, or was that pretty much it?"

"Sorry, Mike. Didn't mean to hit so close to the mark. Hey, did Roy say anything about a replacement for me?"

"He didn't name names. Though to hear the rascal talk, sounds to me like he intends to do the deed himself."

Hateful words jumped into Ethan's mind. He veered away from them with difficulty. "What was the reaction in the team?"

"'Bout what you'd expect. Commander Dunbar looked like he'd just won the lotto. I thought Kelly Barnes was gonna break down and cry right there at CIA headquarters." He shrugged. "Most of 'em didn't show much at all. You're in the business long as we are, you learn how to roll with the punches."

"So you think Roy's going to disband the team?"

"Can't," Gillette said. "Take an act of Congress. What he'll probably do is keep the JIDIOC name alive but use it as a front for CIA activity. Like he needs another front. That's one thing we could count on with you, podner: you didn't play favorites. Whichever group had the best tools for the job, that's who you used."

It looked to Ethan as if his friend wanted to say something more. "Mike?"

"Ethan, you...you know how I feel about you, right? I just...I'm just sorry, that's all. Sorry you got chewed up and spit out like this. You deserve better." Gillette took a deep breath. "If I ever meet Roy Pickett in a dark alley somewhere..."

"Thanks, Mike. I appreciate what you're saying. It probably

wouldn't be a good idea to beat up the director of Central Intelligence, though."

"Who said anything about beatin' him up? I just want to resurface his cranium."

Ethan smiled in spite of himself. "Thanks, Mike. You're a good friend. Don't worry, though, God's got something planned for me. This was all part of it, part of preparing me for something bigger, maybe."

"That's one way to look at it, I suppose."

"So how's your spiritual life going, Mike?"

"Good. Fine, I guess. I...I thought..." He lapsed into uncomfortable silence. "Shoot, Hamilton, I just thought I'd feel different, you know? But I just feel the same. I just feel dead inside. Numb-like. Especially since..." He nodded at Ethan. "That with Roy."

Ethan smiled wearily. "I should have told you things would get bad as soon as you became a Christian. The devil and his tricks. But I just thought it would get bad for you, not for me!"

"It's confusing, is what I'm trying to say." Gillette paused again. "You know, before I would've gone up to Pickett and told him what I thought. If I'd gotten worked up enough, I might've *shown* him what I thought, DCI or not. But now..." He spread his hands helplessly. "Now I don't know how to act."

Ethan felt like saying, Join the club. "You didn't know how to act, Mike, because you're not that old person anymore. That old guy had all his ways of dealing with life, some good, some not so good. But now you're a new creation and you want to act a different way. But you don't know many new ways yet."

"I suppose."

"Don't sweat it, Mike. You're going to feel this way for a while. When you get to know God and your Bible better you'll begin to see how to behave and what to do. Most of the time, anyway."

"It makes sense, Reverend."

"Mike, did you get any feel about whether Roy was going to

do anything about GeneSys? I mean, was he serious when he said no one was going to Clipperton?"

"Hard to tell."

"Did Kelly finish his briefing?"

"Yup. Pickett sat there with that fat-cat grin of his, acting real chummy with everyone. He may be many things," Gillette said, "but he's no fool. He knows better than to ignore biological weapons getting into the hands of terrorists or next time it'll be his can booted like he booted yours. I imagine he'll do something. But he'll do it CIA all the way, o' course."

Ethan chose his next words carefully. "Mike, what would you say if I told you that I knew of…a person…who just happened to be going on a vacation to Acapulco this week?" That wasn't set yet, Ethan knew. In fact, Kaye was currently reading a travel book about Grand Cayman. She had no intention of going to Acapulco.

"Does this person plan to just see the sights," Gillette asked, "or does he intend to attempt something he's not even remotely qualified for?"

"I would have to guess that this person would say, 'It depends on what Roy does.' If Roy sends someone in to make contact with that girl, then the person in question would be going just for the sights. He might not even go to Mexico at all, in that case."

"Tell you what," Gillette said. "I'll find out for you—for this person, I mean."

The war ravaged on, unchecked by casualties, peace talks, or environmental groups. The forces were evenly matched, equally determined to win the campaign that was even now in its sixth year. The entire planet was the battleground. Gains on one front were countered by losses on another. Weapons were developed that gave one side an advantage but were quickly countered by enemy scientists. Strategies that once carried the day were now crushed by battle-seasoned commanders.

The two superpowers had fought to a stalemate. In truth, they had been at stalemate the whole time. Nevertheless the battle was joined daily with vigor by combatants on both sides, each determined that this time the decisive edge would be theirs.

This was Argon 3, the most massively multiplayer-persistent game world on GlobeNet. Most such multiplayer games were fantasy realms where players could merely socialize online and ride out to fell the occasional dragon. But Argon 3 was unique in that its only purpose was to wage war.

The designers had gone to great lengths to ensure that the two forces, SyCant and DotMil, were perfectly balanced. If they had done their job right, neither side would ever win this war.

Every ship captain, tank gunner, infantryman, AWACS operator, and admiral—on both sides—was played by a human jacked in from somewhere on GlobeNet. When there weren't enough human players to go around, the computer supplied artificial intelligence characters—bots—to fill the gaps. Rain or shine, day or night, human or cybernetic, the war on Argon 3 rolled on.

Jordan Hamilton would've spent his every waking moment on Argon 3 had his mother allowed it. She had the annoying habit of reminding him of drudgeries like eating and going to school. Jordan found self-expression in this war-torn world: now playing as a grunt on the battlefield, now as a strike fighter pilot, now as a spy infiltrating enemy headquarters. He even took the odd turn at officer when the mood hit him, though command was more the realm of his dad. The fact that his father loved the game almost as much as he did was Jordan's shield against his mother's scoldings.

Now Jordan hovered in his attack helicopter just behind a sand dune, with only his radar mast protruding above the crest, waiting for the enemy to appear.

His wingman spoke. "This is another scrub, ain't it?"

"Looks like it," Jordan's copilot said.

"Who died and made this loser our general?" the wingman said.

"Knock it off, you guys," Jordan said.

"It's a total wash, Stark, baby," the other pilot said, using Jordan's game name.

"Stark naked," someone teased.

"Okay, okay," Jordan said. "If you guys think it's a wash, why don't you head back to base? But don't blame me when I come back with ten kills and you get zip."

"I can't leave," Jordan's copilot said. "You're driving."

"Then jack out," Jordan said. "I'll take a bot over you any day. At least they don't whine about it."

"Take it easy, Stark attack," the wingman said. "Why're you defending this general, anyway? He your girlfriend?"

"Why?" Jordan said. "You jealous?"

"Hey!" the wingman's copilot shouted. "I got blips!"

"Where?"

"I got 'em, too."

"Two, no...six bogeys at two-zero-fifty," Jordan's copilot said, excited. "Tons more behind. Looks like the big guy got it right after all."

The wingman whistled in astonishment. "I take back everything I said about your girlfriend, Stark. He done good."

"Okay, Deadeye Squadron," Jordan said, "hold position. You know the op: seal 'em in, front to back."

"Then it's barrel-shoot time!"

Despite his preference for independence, Jordan seemed always to gravitate to leadership positions. Officially the wingman in this flight outranked Jordan, but everyone deferred to the ten-year-old's orders. No one knew he was ten, of course.

"We wait for the Navy flyboys to seal the pass," Jordan said. "That's our signal."

Jordan was regularly impressed with his father's strategies. This one—a multiplatform coordinated assault—involved so much advance planning and well-timed placement of so many units that it made Jordan dizzy to think about it. He knew he held a slight edge over his father in the actual executing of things in cyberspace—which was why he preferred front-line roles to command—but the elder Hamilton definitely took the prize in the strategy department. If all went as planned, this ambush would win their force a decisive victory.

All didn't go as planned.

Jordan heard his father's voice over the intercom. "All units, this is General Curly. SyCant air elements have downed the Navy jets. Our blockade's not going to happen. We're going to have to rethink."

"Great," Jordan's copilot said.

"They're in the pass already!" the wingman shouted.

"All long range artillery commence firing on hex points JP-70 and JL-62," Ethan "Curly" Hamilton continued. "Try to seal those passes that way. Now, there's no stopping the nukes; they'll impact in less than thirty. After the wave passes, everybody up and at 'em. Tank brigades, fire at will. Air units, do your stuff. Try to clog the road with wreckage. This can still be a huge victory for DotMil, so do your best."

Jordan's speakers picked up distant explosions: the big guns opening up. He itched to crest the dune and let loose with his own ordnance. But he knew better. He eased his craft lower. "Everybody stay put."

"No way!" his wingman shouted. "I'm sick of hiding. I'm in command here, anyway. Deadeye Squadron, attack!"

Jordan saw the Longbow attack helicopter on his right rise. "Wait! The shock wa—"

Twin flashes lit the sky like, well, like atom bombs. The Longbow disintegrated without a sound.

"Stupid," Jordan said.

The shock wave from the tactical nuclear missiles washed over the sand dunes like an invisible tidal wave, flattening yet further the lifeless desert. Before the war, it was said that this entire area had been lush farmland. Only seconds later did the boom-BOOM reach them. It rocked Jordan's Longbow. He only narrowly avoided crashing.

Jordan segued his course correction into an attack move, cresting the hill and letting loose with a full spread. The few enemy vehicles that hadn't perished beneath the tactical nukes soon fell to combined fire from Longbow and tank.

Once again, Hamilton and son had saved the free world.

"Come in."

Jordan Hamilton poked his head into his father's VR cockpit. "Nice going, Dad. That's three wins in a row for DotMil."

Ethan smiled. "You think the war's almost over, then?"

"Yeah, right."

"Thanks, Jordan. It was fun. I saw you lost your wingman."

"Yeah. Total bonehead. I told him not to go until after the shock wave."

"Oh, well," Ethan said. "Not everybody's as dominating—" he said it in his best monster-truck-and-tractor-pull voice—"as you are."

Ethan's game room computer hailed him.

"What is it, Penny?"

"Incoming transmission from—" a tiny pause—"Michael Eugene Gillette."

Ethan and Jordan locked eyes. "Eugene?"

"Okay, Penny," Ethan said. "I'll take it in here."

"See you later, Dad," Jordan said, shutting the cockpit door.

Ethan turned to his center monitor, upon which Gillette's face appeared. "Whatcha got, Mike?" *Eugene.*

Gillette had his poker face on as usual. "You're not going to like it, cowboy."

"You talked to Roy?"

"To Colin Bates, his assistant."

"Tell me," Ethan said. "Is he moving on GeneSys or not?"

"Yes and no. He's ordered a full workup."

For whole seconds the two men stared at each other across the miles, the only sound a faint speaker hiss.

"A full workup?" Ethan finally said. "Mike, we've already done a full workup. I thought you said he heard Kelly's briefing."

"He did."

"So why is he—"

"He's doing a full CIA workup."

Ethan puffed. "What's wrong with the one we had? CIA's is going to be better than the National Reconnaissance Office's and National Imagery & Mapping Agency's?"

"He thinks so."

"CIA contributed to that workup, Mike! I don't get it."

"He says he'd feel better doing it in-house." Gillette looked at the screen blankly, though his eyes probed. "He says he doesn't want any more agents put in danger unnecessarily."

"Like I did," Ethan finished.

"Like you did."

"Wonderful." He looked at the date readout on one of his monitors. "How long will this workup take?"

"No tellin'. If you're doing one local, usually five or six days. One out on some treasure island somewhere, who knows? Could be weeks."

"And when was that weapon supposed to be handed over to the terrorists?" Ethan already knew the answer.

"Sooner than that."

"How do I let you talk me into these things?"

Ethan patted his wife's knee. "Because you love me."

"Humph. I loved you at home. I would love you on the moon. I don't think my love is the issue here."

The 767 taxied across the well-lit runway. Jordan and Katie sat in the seats across the aisle. Katie was coloring and Jordan had already discovered that the man next to him was a computer gamer; they were looking at Jordan's laptop computer.

Ethan kissed his wife's cheek. "I think it's because you are a heroic person," he said.

"Ha. Heroic is packing for this trip in one day." Nevertheless Kaye laid her head on his shoulder. "You're the hero. Going into this horrible place when the CIA won't even go. Besides," she said brightly, "I intend to spend the time shopping."

"Don't forget," Ethan said, "there's cliff diving and historic—"

She put her hand over his lips. "You'll be careful, won't you?"

He nodded.

CHAPTER TEN

Liz Gillette cuddled up next to her husband on the couch. "Whatcha watching?"

"Zip." Mike Gillette put his arm around Liz and kissed the top of her head. It was his first Friday night back in Fort Worth. "Want to do a movie?"

"Sure."

Gillette used the remote control to select a movie-on-demand. The opening credits began.

"Sweetheart?" Liz said.

"Hmm?"

"You'll be home more now, won't you?"

"Mm-hmm."

She folded herself into him. "Good."

Gillette tore his eyes from the screen. "What'd I say?"

"Hmm?"

"I get the feeling I said something important, but I don't recall what it was."

"You said you'd be home more now," Liz said, looking up.

"Now that what?"

"Now that you're not on that Kitty Hawk team anymore."

"JIDIOC, darlin'. Since when am I off it?"

Liz sat up. "Since Ethan." She was suddenly agitated. "You don't have to do it anymore. You said yourself it was as good as disbanded. Now you'll go back to being just a case agent here in Fort Worth. And you'll come home to me every night, instead of flying off to Phoenix or wherever all the time."

"Liz—"

"That's what married people are supposed to do, you know: sleep together."

Gillette turned the TV's volume up. "What's got into you?"

Liz stood up. "Me?" She brought her finger up and opened her mouth to chew him out. Instead, she burst into tears and ran from the room.

Mike found her in their bedroom, crying into a pillow. He sat on the bed and stroked her black hair. After a moment her tears subsided.

"You've been to the doctor," he said.

The tears began again, harder this time.

"What did he say?"

Several tissues and a trip to the bathroom later, she was able to talk about it. "He says that if I want to have babies, I'd better have them now. He says I'd better have them as quick as I can—one, maybe two—then have it all taken out."

Gillette stroked his wife's hair. "What would you think if I...prayed about this?"

Liz's eyes glazed slightly. "Be my guest."

"I won't, though, if you don't want me to. I just thought...I mean..."

She watched him mercilessly.

"Darlin'," he said, "I sure do wish we had this in common." He swallowed. "All right. Here goes. God, I just...I just want to come to you and say thanks for my beautiful Liz. And God, she's sure hurting over this. You know how much she wants babies, but...Sir, we were kinda counting on a few years of just the two of us, you know? God, I know you're the real Head Honcho. Help me and Liz have a baby or two or three whenever you want us to. And," he said with a glance at Liz, "help us come to you, you know, maybe together. Amen."

Liz didn't say amen, but he wanted to believe he saw it in her eyes. At least she hadn't cut him off.

"So," he said, "if what the doctor says is true, we should get busy then, huh?"

Liz almost smiled. "It would help if you could say it without leering."

"Without what?"

"Without lifting your eyebrows like that."

"Like this?"

She did smile. "Yes, you stud, you. Like that."

They kissed.

"Girl," Gillette said, "you give a man something to stay home for."

"Good. Shut up."

"How can I help you, sir?"

It took a moment for Ethan's eyes to adjust from the Acapulco sun. At length he saw a young man in a bright yellow polo shirt looking up at him over a computer terminal.

"Oh, hi. Yes, I'm interested in getting out to Clipperton."

The man touched a button on his keyboard. "Name?"

"I'm not expected. I mean, I haven't told anyone I'm coming, so I won't be on your list or anything. Do I have to get an appointment? I didn't even…know I was going to want to really go. But…" A glance at the stack of GeneSys brochures on the counter gave Ethan an idea.

"The kind of thing I'm contemplating," he said seriously, "is not something you do lightly. To tell you the truth, I'd actually decided against going through with it. But just this minute, when I walked down this street and saw the GeneSys logo out there, I changed my mind. I've come all the way out here and now GeneSys is just a stone's throw away; it'd be a waste not to just go through with it, right?"

The man's expression hadn't changed. "Name?"

Ethan blinked. This part should've occurred to him. If Mike had been doing this, he would've gotten false passports or a fake head or something. Unable to think of a good reason not to—and unable to think of a good alias on the spot—Ethan told the man his real name. If he recognized it, he was an expert at hiding the fact.

"All right, Mr. Hamilton," the man said, sending something to the printer, "I've got you a seat on the Monday morning transport for the day after tomorrow, July 2." He pulled out a map of the city and circled a spot with his pen. "Be at the GeneSys helipad no later than 7:30. Flight time both ways and tour time will take all day. The transport usually touches down around 8 P.M. Three meals are included in the two-hundred-dollar fare, with an option to stay overnight for an additional hundred dollars, U.S."

Ethan paid the fare.

For two glorious days the Hamiltons were on vacation together. They took guided tours, sampled exotic seafood, watched the cliff divers at La Quebrada, shopped, rode bicycles, stayed up late, and laughed themselves silly. Jordan and Katie played in the surf and the hotel's beautifully sculpted pools. Ethan and Kaye played tennis. On his father's dare, Jordan took a private golf lesson.

Neither Ethan nor Kaye mentioned what Ethan was going to do Monday morning. It was as though they had all agreed to capture this time, as if in a bottle, in case another one like it never came.

The Mark-3 Condor was the largest VTOL passenger plane currently in service. It was a distant cousin of the V-22 Osprey and twin sister to the Marines' new V-31 Hopper tactical transport. It could hold sixteen troops with their gear, heavy armament, and three crewmen. This Condor carried passengers and baggage instead of soldiers, and a load of biotech supplies instead of weapons.

Ethan had never ridden in a helicopter before, much less a vertical takeoff plane. He stared out the window like a kid, eager to see the helipad fall away beneath them and to watch the propellers rotate forward.

He felt light this morning. Though he knew he had to be cautious this day, careful not to say too much or accomplish too little, still he'd almost felt like skipping out to the plane. Now, waiting for the other passengers to take their seats, Ethan felt like he was on a mission, capable of any feat of derring-do. If God is for us, who can be against us? He imagined that he would find this Tamara Mack quickly, perhaps in the cafeteria at lunch, instantly convince her to play informant, and then simply enjoy the rest of the time on the tropical island.

What could be easier?

As a rule, Ethan stayed away from so-called "in-flight entertainment." Canned audio carefully selected to offer a broad, politically correct spectrum of music or instructional material. To Ethan it merely made the air inside a pressurized cabin taste that much staler.

This time he made an exception. The Condor had one channel of music, Mexican—no Michael Card ballads on this trip—and six channels of speech. When he finally found the one for English, he discovered it was giving a history of Clipperton Island.

Clipperton, it seemed, was named for a pirate. John Clipperton was a privateer who terrorized shipping lanes in the early 1700s. While he probably never set foot on the island, much less buried any treasure there, he most certainly sighted it. Nonetheless, over the centuries the legend of pirate gold drove many of the island's hapless inhabitants to distraction.

When the narrator turned to the riveting saga of guano harvesting on the island, Ethan lost interest.

He took out the only book he'd brought with him for the trip: a copy of Andrew Murray's classic *With Christ in the School of Prayer*. Things had been going so smoothly for Ethan: first Patriot, then Yoseph, then JIDIOC-P. His life seemed finally to have found its divine groove. But then he'd been booted from JIDIOC. Maybe he hadn't heard God correctly, after all. It heightened his desire to learn how to hear God's voice. This book, or so he'd been told, would teach him how. He read for over an hour.

His attention snapped back to the narration when the tale turned to the lighthouse keeper, Álvarez, and his captive harem. The horror of the story—and the almost poetic beauty—enthralled him. How could people look at things like the "coincidental" arrival of the U.S. Navy at just the right moment and not believe in a God behind all of history?

He took the earphones off and dozed for an undetermined period. His mind, half dreaming, explored a surreal Clipperton Island. The isolation, the tropical storms, and the sharks all blended together into a montage of inescapable danger. Something about a disease troubled his hallucination, a horrible, rotting leprosy that peeled the skin from women and young girls. And a madman's face, pockmarked with hate.

He awoke, looked out the window, and saw that very face.

No. He shook his head. It wasn't a face. Yes, it was. It was a face lying on the water like a drowned man.

He heard another passenger speaking in an elusive language. The only word he caught was "Clipperton." Ethan looked around. People were peering through windows on his side of the plane, jabbering in several languages.

Ethan looked again. It was an island he'd seen before. Oblong, outlined in ashy white against the blue Pacific. It held the general shape of a man's head. A deep hole where one eye should've been. A curving scar along the cheek. Truly the head of a pirate. Or a murderer.

From this position, directly over Clipperton, the island was invisible. It was too small to show up beneath them. All Ethan could see, as the Condor descended straight down, were thousands of circling seabirds. He didn't know a tern from an albatross to tell what kinds he saw; he only knew there were jillions of them. How they avoided colliding with the airplane was anyone's guess.

He began to see cresting waves at the bottom of his window and, finally, land. Surely it was some trick of the tropical sun, but Ethan thought he caught a glimpse of orange about the barren landscape. Perhaps they'd flown out of the earth's atmosphere by mistake and were making a landing on Mars.

There was, truly, something otherworldly about the experience. He could feel the island beneath him, almost like a presence, welcoming him into its clutches like a spider welcomes the fly.

The VTOL aircraft rotated. Ethan saw the narrow white beach skinny away, quickly curving, circling the lagoon. He saw jagged coral reefs just below the lagoon's surface. He saw, as they descended, breakers that had seemed flat now rising above the highest point of the beach and hammering down. And everywhere, birds. Whipping around the plane like debris in a tornado. The ocean sky was clogged with their bodies.

At last Ethan saw the GeneSys complex. White buildings, five at least, sitting in the lagoon like ducks. Tethered together by taut walkways. Each building ultramodern in design. Solar panels gleamed atop every roof. Windmills like propellers here and there. And in the center of the campus, a spiral wind turbine. He saw small fan-driven airboats on the water, and at a wide spot of beach, what appeared to be a passenger hovercraft.

The engine roar changed pitch. The Condor jostled. It wasn't until people began unbuckling seat belts that he realized they'd landed. Some kind of elevated helipad, it seemed. Why hadn't the captain killed the engines, then?

It turned out the engines were off. When he stepped onto the passenger staircase, he realized why he'd been fooled.

Clipperton struck Ethan like an uppercut. Stench and racket belted him with a quick one-two. He gripped the railing, suddenly dizzy. He forced himself down the stairs, if only to let the other passengers disembark. Yellow-shirted GeneSys employees, smiling insipidly, stood around the helipad, guiding the line toward double glass doors. Ethan stood as if in a stupor, staring at the ribbon of white coral beach.

He felt as if he were being watched. It was the presence he'd felt before. A consciousness. Malevolent, ancient, endlessly patient. He scanned the passengers and GeneSys employees, knowing it was not any of them. He turned back to the beach and saw the watchers. Eyes. Thousands, perhaps millions. Alien eyes. Crouching in the shadows of boulders or shrubs. Watching him.

A touch on his shoulder made him jump. A yellow-shirt beckoned him toward the double doors. The rest of the passengers were already inside.

"What are those?" Ethan had to shout and point and pantomime to get his meaning across.

The yellow-shirt shouted something, but Ethan could hear only birds. The man mimed pincers and antennae and made a creepy face. He seemed to be telling Ethan that extraterrestrials had invaded the island and everyone was quite all right with the notion, so would he please come inside now?

He went inside.

The steel-reinforced doors shut behind him, leaving Ethan's ears ringing in the sudden hush. They stood in a wide, carpeted corridor. The tail end of the line of passengers was just disappearing around a corner. Ethan walked that direction.

"Land crabs."

Ethan looked at the yellow-shirt. "Excuse me?"

"*Gecarcoidea planatus,* or red-orange land crabs. That's what you saw under the rocks out there."

Ethan shivered. "Land crabs."

"About five million of them. More of an infestation than anything else. I'm Albert."

They caught up with the line. An attractive woman stood at the front, introduced herself as Sue, and welcomed them to GeneSys Industries.

Albert whispered to Ethan. "They're smart."

"Who is?"

"The crabs. They have some kind of hive communication. Dump food in one spot today and tomorrow you'll have two hundred crabs lined up for dinner at that same spot, at that same time. They eat anything organic: wood, plants, cloth, flesh, anything."

"Fascinating." By which Ethan meant to say, I'm through listening to you now.

The crowd was moving again. Ethan had heard Sue say something about a tour.

Albert kept pace with him. "But you know the worst part?"

"Tell me."

"They know."

Ethan looked at the man, allowing him the suspense he obviously relished. "Know what?"

"They just know. Secrets, human nature, everything. They know, for one thing, that Clipperton is really theirs."

"Theirs?"

"Sure. Humans have been trying to live on Clipperton for two hundred years. It never works. They always leave."

"But the crabs stay," Ethan said.

"The crabs stay."

"What about the birds? They stay, too."

"Only because the crabs let them."

Ethan stifled a smile. This guy had obviously spent way too much free time thinking about crustaceans. "Uh-huh."

"Think about it," Albert said. "What's a land crab going to eat on Clipperton Island? There aren't more than thirty plants on the whole rock. If we didn't have those protected, they'd be gone in a day. There's the occasional skink and plenty of roaches, but the crabs' staple food is bird. Mainly from boobies."

Ethan had to bridle another smile. "Mm-hmm."

He was watching Ethan's face. "You think I'm crazy."

"No! I mean, I guess I just never thought about what they'd eat."

"I'm going to tell you something amazing," he said, once more conspiratorial. Ethan got the feeling that people didn't often let this guy talk. "Boobies—gannets, you know?—lay two eggs. As soon as a booby picks a spot to nest, a crab claims her. He burrows into the sand and waits. When the eggs come, he starts creeping closer and closer. All he needs is a second when the mother's not watching, and he's an inch closer. It's a siege. And believe me, the crab is going to win. They will wait it out. That's why they'll have Clipperton back eventually.

"Anyway, this siege can go on for a week, nonstop. The crab doesn't sleep, so the mother can't either. Exhaustion sets in. Sometimes he gets in there and grabs one of the eggs and rolls it off. Other times—now here's the amazing part—other times, if the crab hasn't won, the booby will give up one of the eggs herself! She'll pick one and roll it out for the crab."

Ethan was intrigued, despite his best efforts to the contrary. "Unh-huh."

"Yes, sir. She'll roll it right out there. He'll make off with it with not so much as a thank-you-ma'am. If he's careful, he'll get it back to his spot where he'll wait for it to hatch. Then he'll eat the chick. Yum yum. If he's not so careful and the egg breaks, he'll eat the yolk as fast as he can, because seven hundred of his best buddies will converge on his feast in about fifteen seconds flat."

Ethan looked at the man. "You sure know a lot about this."

"What else is there to do here?"

"Don't you have a job?"

"Sure, what do you think I'm doing now?"

"Oh, right."

Ethan felt sure he was missing valuable information in the lecture up ahead, but he found himself unable to terminate this discussion. He took note of the modern open spaces and clinical lab wings around him. GeneSys felt like a high-tech corporation. No surprise. There didn't seem to be anything unusual about this place, except for their product portfolio, the client list, and exotic location, of course.

Albert continued. "You want to hear the kicker?"

"Give it to me."

"They never take both eggs. They could, you know. Why not? Boobies are brain dead, the bird brains of the bird kingdom. But it's like a tax. An egg tax. When a nest has been raided, somehow the entire crab population—five million, remember—gets the message to leave that nest alone from then on.

"It's a hive, I'm telling you. A collective brain. Each little crab like a neuron and the whole island like one huge brain. All exoskeleton, eyestalk, pull-your-pincer-off-and-grow-a-new-one, voodoo-usin' neurons." This time it was his turn to shudder. He looked at Ethan severely, as if just thinking of something critical. "They're prehistoric, you know."

"Prehistoric?"

"They'll outlive us. You watch. GeneSys won't stay more than a few years. They could drive us out today if they wanted to. They know how to climb ladders and ropes, you know. Sneak into our beds and pluck our eyes out. But they're too smart for that. They'll just wait. They know the shriek and the stink and their ESP will drive us out in the end."

CHAPTER ELEVEN

The morning tour, the fourteen visitors were told, was designed to impress. And so it did. They rode an electric tram down hushed hallways, through elegant arboretums, past stately conference rooms. They saw all seven buildings of the GeneSys campus, everything from the corporate building to the warehouse to the fitness facility. They heard brief statements from various executives and even watched a short movie about GeneSys's history. The multibillionaire Mortimer McCall made a cameo appearance in the movie.

The GeneSys staff was most self-congratulatory over the company's use of alternative energy. Certainly the towering wind turbine was a marvel, and the wave towers, with their curious use of compressed air, were worthy of note. Banks of solar panels and battery-charging exercise cycles were common fare. But the high point, from their perspective, was their ability to claim energy from their sewage. Special bacterial microbes, engineered by GeneSys geneticists of course, broke down the septic fluids in such a way as to enhance the reclamation of methane gas. Any entity that could reclaim energy from its own waste, so the rhetoric went, was truly evolved.

Ethan couldn't decide if he was in Jurassic Park or a James Bond film. Definitely not in reality, that was certain.

For the duration of the tour, and now in the cafeteria where they awaited lunch, Ethan had kept an eye out for Tamara Mack. Not that he knew what she looked like. Maybe she would wear a big sign on her back or something. No one but their tour guide, Sue, wore a name tag.

He scanned the hundreds of GeneSys employees in the cafeteria. He knew Tamara was a technician, so he could ignore the legions of yellow-shirts right off the bat. That left about a hundred others, some wearing white lab coats, others in surgical gowns, still others in work clothes. He even saw a team of scuba divers, still in their wetsuits. It was hopeless to find her this way.

He took his tray of gourmet something to a relatively unoccupied round table. He had just spread his napkin in his lap when a yellow-shirt, a woman this time, pulled up a chair next to him.

"Hello," she said, extending her hand. "Evelyn LaBrea."

He shook her hand. "LaBrea?"

"Like the tar pits."

"Oh."

She produced a clipboard. "You're enjoying your visit, I trust?"

"Yes, sure. Very nice. You want my name?"

"Oh, good," she said, pulling out a pen, "you guessed."

"Ethan Hamilton," he said.

She scanned the list to the bottom. "Yes, here you are, Mr. Hamilton. What area of GeneSys are you most interested in? Perhaps I could get you an appointment with someone."

"I'm interested in microbiology."

"Ah, fascinating business," she said. "I'm taking a class in it this semester."

"You have classes here?"

"Sure. Continuing education. We have some of the leading people in their fields here. Why not set up a little ad hoc graduate school?"

Ethan spread his hands. "Clipperton U."

"Exactly. So, microbiology then." She wrote it down. "What

application exactly did you have in mind, Mr. Hamilton?"

Ethan swallowed. He'd come very quickly to the uttermost limit of his knowledge of genetics. He'd hoped the microbiology bit would be enough to get him on a tour down Tamara Mack's hall. He didn't have anything to back up his story.

"You hesitate," Evelyn said.

He smiled uncertainly.

"It's an incurable disease, isn't it?" she said.

"Hmm?"

"It's all right, Mr. Hamilton," she said, patting his shoulder, "you don't have to tell me. I just know people don't usually come to Clipperton asking about microbiology unless they or someone they love has got some incurable disease. Something regular treatments can't reach. They come to us out of desperation, looking for some miraculous, experimental new technology that will save them."

It hadn't occurred to Ethan that people might come to GeneSys for altruistic reasons. Terrorists, he realized, weren't the only people who felt forced to go outside traditional ways and means.

He found her watching him, not unsympathetically. "It's…It's hard to talk about," he said.

"Quite all right," Evelyn said, pushing back her chair. "I understand totally. Let me do some checking. I'll see who's available in microbiology this afternoon. Maybe I can get you in with the woman who teaches my class."

Ethan tried to appear only mildly interested. "Great, great. What's her name?" Oh please, oh please.

"Beverly Jau." She stood up. "I'll see if she's available. If I haven't gotten back to you before the one o'clock tour, go ahead and go on it. I'll catch up to you if I can line something up."

Only five of Ethan's fellow visitors joined him on the one o'clock tour. The others had prearranged appointments with various specialists. In fact, Ethan was the only one in the group who didn't have an appointment at all—the other five were staying the night for morning meetings.

While the earlier tour had focused on the GeneSys facilities, this one featured their various projects. Ethan saw, from the electric tram's padded seats, more "enhanced biology" than he ever hoped to see again.

He saw geeps (a cross between a goat and a sheep) and zebroids (half zebra, half horse). He saw a pineapple tree tricked into growing in arctic temperatures. He saw cows whose milk contained human insulin. He saw self-fertilizing, self-insecticiding grain crops. He saw pigs whose organs were so similar to humans' that they could be transplanted with a negligible rejection rate. He saw a lab in which engineers were splicing DNA to create wholly new creatures—literally tinkering with the building blocks of life. And these were just the more presentable projects.

Ethan learned to detect when they were passing potentially objectionable areas. Whenever Sue, still their tour guide, engaged in small talk or launched into a history of this or that, Ethan paid close attention to what he could see.

"I want to see the cloning," he said at one such moment.

"We've already seen that, sir," Sue said in a my-aren't-you-slow voice.

"Not cows, ma'am," Ethan persisted. "People. I want to see the human clones." He didn't, especially. He just wanted to penetrate the earth-friendly veneer the whole company exuded.

The tram pulled to a stop beside a row of windows overlooking the lagoon. "You'll have to make an appointment, sir," she said. "This tour doesn't—"

"And what about the biological weapons labs? Don't tell me, those aren't on the tour either, are they?"

"I don't know what you're talking about, Mr—" Sue checked her clipboard— "Hamilton." Then, as if calling him by name had effected some kind of victory, she switched back to her mouth-on/brain-off verbiage about the virtues of GeneSys Industries.

Ethan interrupted her. "I want to see the headless babies."

"Mr. Hamilton! I am trying to conduct a tour here, and I don't appreciate your heckling."

"I'm not h—"

"If you have a complaint about how I lead tours, then I will take you to my supervisor's office. After the tour."

"I don't have—"

"For now, just sit down and, if you can't enjoy the ride, at least have the courtesy to let the others enjoy it."

Evelyn LaBrea rounded the corner. "What's the problem here?"

Sue faced forward in the tram. "Nothing."

"I thought I heard voices raised."

"We were having a spirited discussion," Sue said.

"I see," Evelyn said, scanning the passengers' faces. Her eyes locked on Ethan's.

"I said I wanted to see the headless babies."

Evelyn blanched. Sue snarled. Ethan grinned devilishly.

"I know you grow them here," Ethan said merrily. "I just wanted to see them."

Evelyn took swift action. "Very well, Mr. Hamilton, I'll take you. Sue, you take the others on."

The tram almost sprinted away.

"That was a very naughty thing you did," Evelyn said to Ethan.

"I know. I'm sorry."

"Come on," she said, heading down a crossing hallway. "I've got you lined up with Dr. Jau."

"You mean you're not taking me to the headless babies?"

"Not in a million years."

Ethan tried to keep his bearings as they went, but stairwells, raucous open-air crossings, and double-back hallways quickly did in his feeble sense of direction.

"You do grow them, don't you?" he said as they passed through a large library. "Tell me the truth."

She sighed. "Mr. Hamilton, there is a tremendous demand for organ transplants in our world. I'm sure you are aware of this. The demand far exceeds the supply. You are also aware, no doubt, of the black market for human organs. People in third-world nations are being executed for their hearts, livers, and kidneys. You strike me as an ethical man, Mr. Hamilton. What do you say to that?"

"I say that's terrible. But that doesn't justify—"

"So what if I told you I could come up with an endless supply of human organs in a way so that no one would have to be killed?"

"What about your superpigs?"

"Natural human organs are always going to have a lower rejection rate even than organs harvested from engineered pigs or monkeys."

"You say you could provide these organs without killing anyone," Ethan said, "but that's not true. If you take the heart out of any baby, even a headless one, you kill it."

She stopped abruptly. "Mr. Hamilton, I will not get into a debate with you over the definition of life. Or the value of a normal person's life over that of a body with no soul."

"No s—"

"So I suggest we—"

"To purposely bring a baby into the world for the purpose of harvesting—"

"Mr. Hamil—"

"—their organs is completely unethical!" Ethan knew he was behaving badly, badgering this poor girl who was not responsible for the practices in question, but he found himself unable or unwilling to restrain himself. "And breeding them with no heads! What kind of monsters are you people?"

She turned and strode away. Ethan noticed, belatedly, people at lab and office doorways, brought out by the shouting match in the hall. This was not, he decided, the place to be left alone just now. It was something akin to insulting a group of gang members then running into a dark alley.

Evelyn came stalking back. "Look, I don't know why you've come all the way out here, since you're obviously opposed to what we do. Maybe you have an incurable disease and maybe you don't. If you still want to talk to Dr. Jau, then come on." She walked down the hall, Ethan in tow. He heard her muttering, "Pigheadedness, now there's an incurable disease."

They rounded a corner and stepped into a wide corridor. A no-nonsense sign read: Microbiology—Laboratories and Offices. Heavy doors punctuated both walls at spacious intervals. Ethan saw plastic nameplates on the doors. Apparently each lab was the territory of an individual specialist. Perhaps they were the lead engineers in each lab and various nameless underlings belonged there, too. If Tamara Mack were one such nameless one, Ethan might be out of luck.

Jau's lab was apparently far down the hall, for Evelyn showed no sign of turning aside. Then, two before the end, Ethan saw a blue plastic plaque—MB Lab #4: Tamara Mack. He stopped in front of the door, his pulse thumping in his throat. "Uh, Evelyn?"

She wheeled on him, a vicious What? on her face.

"Is this...I mean, I think I..." He swallowed. "I saw this name and...I think I know this person."

She looked at him warily. "You know Tamara Mack?"

"I know of her, anyway. I've...I mean, in my research about my, you know, problem, I think I may've come across her name. In fact, I'm sure of it. She's made rather a name for herself in the aspect of microbiology that I'm interested in."

She stared at him ruthlessly, like a horde of land crabs waiting for him to make a mistake. Ethan felt a trickle of sweat streak his rib cage. He heard an electric tram drive by behind him.

"Fine," she said, suddenly walking. "Dr. Jau's lab is right there. She's expecting you. She can direct you to the cafeteria when you're through. Dinner is at five; the transport leaves at six."

Tamara didn't look up from the micromanipulator when the door opened. If she stayed focused, she could have her entire stack of work orders filled before quitting time. It was a rare and fine thing to begin a new day without having work left over from the old one. She was eager to get back to her room to get online with her Christian friends.

"Hello," a man's voice said. "Excuse me."

Tamara turned from the eyepiece. She didn't recognize the man standing in her laboratory. He was in his midthirties, she guessed; fit but no athlete; thinning brown hair. He looked like a nice person.

"Hello," she said. "Are you looking for someone?"

"Are you Tamara Mack?"

"That's right."

"Then I'm looking for you."

"For me?" She pulled her lab coat shut self-consciously. "Why are you looking for me?"

The man looked around the room, up in the corners mostly. "Are there any cameras or microphones in here?"

Tamara nodded toward the computer at the far end of the lab. "Just there."

"No, I mean surveillance cameras."

"Oh." She looked around. "I don't think I've ever taken the time to notice. But I don't think so, no."

He seemed unconvinced. "Could we go outside and talk?"

"You want to go outside? Who are you?"

"Oh, right." He crossed the lab and extended a hand. "My name's Ethan Hamilton."

"Nice to meet you, Mr. Hamilton."

"Call me Ethan."

"All right. Call me Tamara. Ethan, who are you, what are you doing here, what do you want with me, and why in the world would you ever want to go outside to have a conversation?"

"Humor me?"

Something about this man's manner was disarming. What could he do to her, she reasoned, if he was up to no good? He certainly couldn't make a quick getaway if he had something distasteful on his mind.

"Okay," she said. She put her work away properly then guided him to the nearest outdoor exit.

CHAPTER TWELVE

Ethan followed her out onto a covered walkway. Metal stairs led up to the building's roof. They went up. He expected to find a trillion bird nests when he got there, but found none.

"The birds don't roost on your roof?" he asked.

"They can't take the hypersonics."

"Excuse me?"

"Hypersound," she said. "We use special speakers to keep certain areas cleared. It's how they clear the helipad and the airspace above it. Some kind of sonic cone." She outlined an expanding and rising space with her hands. "They explained it once, but I didn't really get it."

They removed plastic covers from two deck chairs and sat down. The noise from fowl and surf, while significant, nevertheless seemed less overpowering now.

"I wanted to come out here," Ethan said, "in case anyone might be listening in your lab." He indicated the whirling mass of seabirds around and over them. "I figured they would frustrate any microphones."

"They frustrate more than microphones, I can tell you. You should see them in nesting season."

"You mean it gets worse?"

"Lots."

Ethan felt suddenly awkward. Here he was, sitting in a lounge chair on a tropical island with an attractive young woman who was not his wife. He drew a blank for a good way to begin, so he just started. "Tamara, I work for the United States government." That sounded strange, even to himself.

She inhaled.

"What?" he asked.

"Am I in trouble?"

"Not at all. Tamara, I work for...the intelligence community."

"You're a hit man for the CIA?"

"You've been watching too many movies."

"But you do work for the CIA?" she asked.

"Not exactly. Tamara, I need to talk to you about GeneSys."

"What about it?" She inhaled again. "Are they in trouble?"

"Do you know everything that's produced here?" He waved a hand over the buildings standing in the lagoon like boys looking for tadpoles.

She hesitated. "Not...not everything, I don't think. It's a big company. Twenty-seven departments, last I heard. I only know microbiology, and I'm not even sure I know everything we do."

Ethan waited for her to go on. After an awkward pause of no more than fifteen seconds, she blurted, "They're rotten to the core, aren't they?"

"Why do you say that?"

"I've seen...I mean... Things I've seen, things I've heard. Things that don't add up. Rumors. I've heard names of some of our customers in the news—and not in a good way, either. And..."

Ethan waited. For a full minute she said nothing. Ethan began to worry about being missed by some zealous yellow-shirt. On the blue horizon, he thought he saw a speck. It might be a ship.

"Do you believe in God, Mr. Hamilton?"

"Yes, I do," he said easily. "I'm a Christian. I love Jesus with all my heart."

Her face brightened. "Oh, that's wonderful! I'm a Christian, too. Oh, thank you, Lord. You have no idea how much I've needed to talk to another believer." Tears came to her eyes.

"Tamara, GeneSys is bad news. We've been watching them for over a year. Watching helplessly, for the most part, because of their special 'arrangement' with the French government. So far they've been very careful not to do anything that would demand international action. But now they've crossed the line. Have you heard of Chehili?"

She shook her head.

"It's an Algerian terrorist group, Tamara. Very bad news. Anyway, Chehili has commissioned GeneSys to build a biological weapon for them. We think—"

"I know that!" Tamara said, sounding surprised. "They gave that project to me. But terrorists? I didn't know…I mean, I…" She looked at her feet. "Maybe I did know." Tears returned quickly. "That's what I needed to talk to someone about. They want me to make the toxin that causes botulism to become airborne. But I can't do that! I mean, I could, but I won't. Oh, Mr. Hamilton—" she grabbed his arm— "what should I do?"

"That's what I've come to Clipperton to talk to you about."

"Why is everyone so interested in me? Who am I?" Tamara asked. "How did you even know my name?"

"The organization I work for uses computers to, among other things, monitor certain companies that we have reason to suspect might be up to no good."

"You're spies, then?"

"We intercepted an internal electronic message that mentioned your name."

"You did what?"

"It said that you had shown resistance to some work assignments, possibly because of 'religious sentiments,' was the wording, I believe. We did some digging and found out that you were a Christian."

"Yes, I— What do you mean, you did some digging?"

Ethan swallowed. "We found some of your old e-mail."

"You went through my messages?"

"Miss Mack, in the interest of international security we have to make the occasional trip into what some people consider gray areas of privacy." Was it just his imagination, or did this new "official voice" sound just like Mike Gillette's? "I apologize if this has upset you, but I can assure you that we only wanted to find out if you would be a suitable contact for us here."

She perked up at that. "Contact? What do you need a contact for?"

Ethan explained JIDIOC's sudden inability to access GeneSys's computers.

"Well," she said. "You've contacted me. Now what?"

"All we ask is that you keep us informed. I understand you have new security measures with your computer systems. Is this correct?"

"That's right," she said. "Everything's hush-hush now. Got to remember seventeen passwords, and they change every week! I don't know what all the fuss is about."

"Do they still let you send out e-mail?"

"Sure, but I think they run it through some kind of scrambler before it goes out."

"That's fine." Ethan handed her a card with a safe GlobeNet address written on it. "Just send us an e-mail every evening, telling us what's going on. Act like we're friends and you're just telling us what's going on around you. If they set up any more security rules, abide by them, but try to subtly let us know."

"Don't you have some kind of code for this sort of thing?" Tamara said.

"You mean like, 'The dog flies alone'?"

"Right."

"Sorry, that's too Get Smart for me."

She examined the card. "Just an e-mail every night. That's it?"

"We're especially interested in this Chehili/botulism project.

When it's ready, let us know. When they come to pick it up we'll have a nasty surprise waiting f—"

"It'll never be ready!" she said. "Because I won't do it. I'm quitting."

Ethan nodded slowly. Out in the ocean, he noticed the ship again, perhaps minutely larger. He looked at Tamara, who had folded her arms and was not looking at him.

"I understand how you feel, Tam—"

"You have no idea how I feel. You couldn't. Not until someone's told you to make something that will kill thousands of people. And not only kill them, but kill them horribly. Have you ever seen a person die from botulism, Mr. Hamilton?" Her eyes struck him. "I didn't think so. Their bodies quit working, but their minds stay sharp. They fall, they blubber, they drool. Finally their involuntary organs stop working and they suffocate in their own perfectly normal bodies. It's hardest on babies and old people."

"Miss Mack," Ethan began solemnly. "Tamara. You're right: I have not seen a person with botulism. But I have seen death. I've seen people electrocuted, their socks literally blown off, their temples blackened. My own son was nearly electrocuted. I've been there when millions of people were almost killed by nuclear and chemical weapons. I am here," he said, finding his stride, "wanting the same thing you want: to prevent these terrorists from having their weapon. But let me ask you something. If you quit, will GeneSys back out of its contract with Chehili?"

She laughed bitterly. "Not likely."

"Someone else will complete the project, won't they?"

She didn't answer.

"And we will have lost our contact on the inside," Ethan said.

She stared into space. "I suppose."

"So really your quitting will have no effect on this project. And worse, you will have greatly hindered the only people who had a chance of stopping it. You may think that quitting will save you from having deaths on your conscience, but if you quit and we can't use you as a contact, those deaths may happen anyway."

"You want me to build their botulin bomb for them?" she asked incredulously.

"Yes," Ethan said. "But slowly. Slowly enough for certain people on my end to be convinced to take action."

"How can you ask me to do such a thing, if you say you're a Christian?"

"I can't, Tamara. If you say no, I'll understand. But I'll tell you this: if you help us, we have a chance of stopping Chehili and maybe also shutting GeneSys down for good. If you don't help us…" He shrugged.

"Why don't you just send in the Marines and shut the place down now?"

"They haven't done anything illegal yet," Ethan said. "But rest assured we will not let the terrorists off this island with their bomb." How he hoped that would be true.

"I can't build it slowly," she protested. "They'll know. Or my manager will tell them. He would do that." She wiped away new tears. "At least I've got until next Monday when the supply ship gets here."

"You mean that's not the supply ship right there?" Ethan said, pointing to the growing white speck in the blue ocean.

She shaded her eyes. "I don't know who that is. Sometimes people come out here to fish for sharks. Maybe it's the tuna boat."

"So you'll help us then?" Ethan said.

She stared at the card he'd given her. "'Build it slow,' he says."

Tamara headed back to her lab, almost literally dragging her heels. She directed Mr. Hamilton to another entrance so they wouldn't be seen together.

Why couldn't everybody just leave her alone? She'd been minding her own business, dutifully filling straightforward work orders for simple retroviruses and recombinant DNA. Nothing flashy. Just what she'd gone to school for. Even this airborne botulism was nothing terribly difficult.

A horrible thought struck her. How many of the straightforward work orders she'd filled over the years could have been intended for malicious use? They came back to her in a rush, all the nonsensical jobs she'd done since she'd started at GeneSys. What kind of monster was she? How much suffering—how many deaths—had she already caused?

No! Her mind wouldn't tolerate the thought. She was incapable of such evil. Her mind would've alerted her. Her Lord would've alerted her.

She pushed through the door to her lab. There on the counter was a sticky note. She read it: "Tamara, you're in luck! Your cultures arrived on today's shuttle. Come pick them up whenever."

Oh, Father! she prayed. *Help!*

Ethan was much relieved. He'd come, he'd seen, and he'd conquered. This undercover stuff wasn't as hard as it was always made out to be. Maybe the agents kept it secret so no one would come take their jobs.

With nothing to do until dinner at five—still two hours away—Ethan decided to see the few sights Clipperton had to offer. He took another tour of the GeneSys campus, behaving this time; grabbed a snack in the cafeteria; shot a round of pool in one of the rec halls; and, despite warnings to the contrary, took a walking tour around Clipperton's narrow beach. A yellow-shirt took him from the buildings to the beach aboard an airboat.

He stood now staring at the Rock. It seemed completely out of place. Where on this flat coral zero of an island did this seven-story tower of rock come from? It was long and narrow, like a dorsal fin the length of a football field. The in-flight narration had told him the Rock appeared to sailors as a sailing ship leaning hard into the wind.

Staring at it now, with the empty Pacific behind it, with hundreds of terns nesting in stinking caverns, and with the roaring surf on three sides, it was impossible to tell when he was. Was it 2007? Surely not. 2,000,000 B.C. seemed more likely. Surely man had never set foot on this island.

Ethan searched the base of the Rock for signs of Álvarez's shack, but of course the island would not tolerate that murderer to leave his legacy behind. Nor would any man's legacy be long tolerated. He found the double column of bronze plaques affixed to one wall of the Rock—ridiculous attempts by mankind, in this case the French navy, to establish a claim on Clipperton. Four of the six plaques showed green signs of corrosion, the oldest being almost illegible beneath the patina.

If he could find no visible sign of Álvarez, nevertheless Ethan imagined he felt his presence. If time did indeed flow unusually around the Rock, perhaps the lightkeeper was alive still, watching him from some hiding place.

To what did Clipperton owe its otherworldly aura? Was it only the ceaseless howl of the waves and the surf? Was it the land crabs' alien patience? He'd seen their eyestalks tracking him from the shadows as he passed. Or was Clipperton a link to the realm of the demonic? Perhaps it was all of these things. Ethan headed back toward the lagoon, convinced that, like several who had tread here before, if he stayed long on this island, it would take his sanity.

He walked briskly, letting his footfalls provide a rhythm of their own making. It helped assure him he did exist and was not merely a speck to be swallowed up by the island's massive presence. Greater is he that is in me, Ethan reminded himself, than he that is in the world.

The GeneSys buildings took shape before him. The lagoon reflected them imperfectly, like a heat mirage. He saw men atop the helipad, readying the Condor for its return to Acapulco. The corkscrew wind turbine rotated elegantly. Now Ethan could imagine himself in the far future, not the distant past. The ship he'd spotted before now lay at anchor five hundred yards off Clipperton's northeast shore. He saw a black shape near the ship's hull, about the size and shape of the hovercraft he'd seen before. From the looks of the sky to the southeast, a storm was on its way.

One thing remained for Ethan to do on this trip, and he chastised himself for not having done it already. Defenses had arisen around GeneSys's computers as if they'd developed proton shielding. If he could inspect the personnel or equipment they had recently acquired, it might make JIDIOC's job of repenetrating the system at least possible. Not that he had anything to do with JIDIOC anymore.

The airboat that had brought him to the shore was nowhere in sight. He walked around the beach, conscious of the lengthening shadows, into which the crabs were already venturing. He didn't want to be stranded on land when night fell. In fact, when this night fell he wanted to be back in his wife's arms. He was determining the shortest distance for a swim when the airboat appeared.

Ethan followed the teenager through the door. Not so closely as to alert the kid to his presence. Not so far behind as to have to open the self-closing door a second time.

The yellow-shirt on the fanboat had known where "those computer guys" had set up shop. He dropped Ethan off at the right building, equipping him with directions to the area. Ethan had spotted this kid from behind and caught up stealthily.

He found himself in what had once been an entertainment room. Stand-alone video game cockpits, not unlike his own back home, lined the walls and stood back-to-back in the center of the dim room. One end of the long room was given to these electronic games while the other hosted more traditional recreation. Foosball tables, air hockey, billiards, dart boards, even an ancient pinball machine.

It was at this end of the room that folding tables had been set up and something on the order of twenty-five computers were in operation. A dozen or so young white men worked at the keyboards. The kid he'd followed inside began handing out snacks and drinks.

Ethan stepped between two cockpits. Thus far he'd remained unnoticed. He peeked out, his trained eyes tracing cables and peripherals, assessing the computing power arrayed before him.

Bingo, Curly.

He was about to go for the door when someone at the tables shouted.

"Sforza, you idiot, this is lite beer!" The speaker, potbellied despite his obvious youth, smacked the delivery boy on the back of the head. "When have you ever seen me drink lite beer?"

"Take it easy on him, Werner," someone else said. "Maybe he thought you needed to start."

Others in the room laughed.

Sforza? Ethan thought. *How do you know that name, Curly?*

"Who are you?"

Ethan was spun around. A short teenager, prematurely balding, held his arm.

"What are you doing in here?"

The teenager's voice alerted the others. Chairs scooted, help started coming.

"I'm sorry," Ethan blustered, edging toward the door. "I thought this was the game room. I'm just here for today and I wanted to play a—"

"Well, this ain't no game room anymore," the balding kid said.

"Sorry," Ethan said. "I'll leave." He was out the door and around two corners before anyone else could question him.

When he was certain pursuit was not coming, he headed off toward the cafeteria as quickly as he could. Now he had a piece of information that even Roy Pickett could not ignore.

Sforza was the name of a famous Italian mercenary in the fifteenth century. The White Company was here.

Ethan passed through several busy hallways and laboratory wings. He ascended a set of stairs, wondering what was for dinner. He almost skipped along, so pleased was he with his first clandestine mission. Perhaps he had missed his calling. He wondered what Kaye would say if he told her he had decided to go to spy school. He determined to eat lightly at dinner so he could take Kaye out to the nicest restaurant in Acapulco.

That was when the terrorists blew up the plane.

PART TWO

Biotech terrorism is a catastrophe waiting to happen.
Dr. John Fagan
Internationally recognized DNA researcher

CHAPTER THIRTEEN

Ann Rydel should've retired years ago. No one her age worked anymore. All her friends had given up the rat race a decade ago. How they enticed her to come live with them at the retirement community, to go see the Everglades with them every summer, to go see the lights at Christmas. "Come get crusty with them, they mean." Ann was afflicted with a rare and untreatable malady: she loved her job.

In her tour with the National Hurricane Center, she'd seen a science develop before her eyes. She was a summer intern there in 1966 when the first geosynchronous weather satellite went online. Her first category five hurricane was Agnes in 1972, the year she got married. She'd just been promoted to the command staff in 1988, the year Gilbert devastated Jamaica.

Every year seemed to bring either a huge advancement in the science—Doppler radar or drone reconnaissance planes—or another big storm. Except for the occasional emergency evacuation of their Coral Gables, Florida, offices—like when Hurricane Andrew toppled the NHC satellite dish—what was not to like?

And now, in 2007, the scientific advancements were coming more quickly than the storms. Even more exciting things—such as tropical disturbance management—lay just beyond the horizon. There had never been a good time to leave the NHC, and it wasn't a good time now.

Ann waited for her student to answer. He was a bright young boy from New Jersey, though she had determined not to hold his birthplace against him. He stared at the large computer monitors before him, watching real-time data overlaid with a thirty-six-hour enhanced satellite replay. Something was happening in the eastern Pacific. The question was what.

"Well?" Ann prompted.

"It's a tropical storm," he said. "Tropical Storm Flossie, pure and simple."

"If it's pure and simple, why did it take you so long to answer? Millions of people count on us to get it right and get the information to them fast. Now"—she looked over her glasses at him—"are you sure?"

"Yes." Then he looked at her unsteadily. "Right?"

Ann sat beside him and pointed at a monitor. "Do you see how the winds peak here? And do you see the beginnings of a parabolic path, here on the thirty-six? And the pressure levels at this point—" she pointed— "as compared to this?"

He looked at the readings. "They're dropping. I didn't see that."

"You have to see it, Michael. But the main thing is the windspeed. That's your big giveaway."

"So it's a hurricane then?"

Ann smiled. "Officially. Hurricane Flossie. Let's put out the advisory."

This would be a good storm for him to track, Ann thought. Just a mild hurricane doing its dance in the uninhabited eastern Pacific.

The terrorist takeover of Clipperton Island had gone like this.

When the ship carrying Ali and his men approached the island, Ali radioed GeneSys saying that he had a number of Arab dignitaries on board who wanted to talk about a large-scale project, so would they please send some kind of transport when they dropped anchor?

Before the anchor had even splashed down, the GeneSys hovercraft was alongside. Ali climbed down a rope ladder.

"Hello," the yellow-shirted operator said to Ali. "Welcome to Clipperton Island." He sat in the pilot's seat, working controls with both hands and pedals with both feet.

"Thank you most kindly," Ali said. They had to raise their voices over the whine of the air-cushion engines and the maneuvering fans mounted above the hovercraft's stern.

"The others with you, they will be along soon? Or am I taking you ashore alone this time?"

"Oh, they are coming," Ali said. "You know how rich men are: deliberate and—what is the word in English?—prissy."

The hovercraft operator nodded. He shifted his attention to keeping his small craft in position beside the tanker.

"This is a fine boat," Ali said.

"I love it. It's perfect for our needs. Fast, light, carries about eighteen passengers, and can take you straight from your ship to the front door. There's nothing quite like driving over water and land without so much as a bump."

Ali nodded as if entranced. "How does one pilot such a machine? You must have Allah's own wisdom."

"It's easy," the operator said, pleased. "This throttle here controls your motion forward and back. See? The rest is pretty much like an airplane. The stick controls pitch." He lifted and dipped the hovercraft's nose to demonstrate. "And these pedals do the left and right, what they call yaw."

"Fascinating. May I?" Ali indicated the driver's seat.

"You know, I'd better not. The waves are a little tricky. Maybe when we get back to the lagoon."

"Then take us away from the ship. When the rich men are ready, we will move in again."

"I don't know."

"Please." Ali tried to look pathetic.

"Oh, all right. Just don't tell anyone I let you do this."

The pilot moved them back from the ship, then switched places with Ali. He showed him how to work the controls. Ali quickly got the hang of it, even moving the craft around tentatively.

"It is a marvel," Ali said.

"It's better than what I was doing back home, I'll tell you that much."

Ali pulled a walkie-talkie from his pocket, careful to maintain control of the hovercraft. "Oh, what did you do then?"

"Drove a forklift in a warehouse."

"Ah."

"That's pretty fun, too, though."

The man went on, apparently satisfied that Ali had learned enough to keep them from crashing. Ali lifted the walkie-talkie to his mouth and spoke in Arabic. Seconds later Ali's seventeen men began clambering over the ladder onto the hovercraft's deck. Ali piloted the hovercraft close and his men climbed aboard.

The operator did a classic double-take when he saw the assault rifles and the black masks. "What do you think you're doing? You can't come here with guns. Look at you, you look like terrorists." He was about to say more, but his mouth clapped shut. He looked accusingly at Ali. "You said they were dignitaries and rich men."

"They are fighting *jihad*," Ali answered easily. "Upon their deaths they are assured endless virgins. They are truly rich."

"I don't care. You and all these…people get off my boat. And you can take your endless virgins with you. Now get up and let me drive."

No one moved.

"I'm afraid my men don't speak English," Ali said, amused. "Thank you for bringing this fine craft to pick us up. And thank you especially for showing me how to operate it."

The sharks got his body, but it was the knife blade that actually killed him.

Minutes later Ali and the Chehili terrorists were approaching the beach of Clipperton Island. "We are committed to this now," Ali said in Arabic. "The man who breaks faith with me will become as that man."

Ali drove the hovercraft, inexpertly, across the beach and up to the helipad. He found the switch that shut the engines off and the air cushion melted away. His men hopped the railing and went to work.

The first target was the satellite dish. Ali assigned its demolition to the two who, days ago, had so effectively destroyed GeneSys's radio repeater on the Revilla Gigedo islands. With the satellite dish down, all of the myriad communications devices—everything from personal satellite phones to major satellite downlinks—would be disabled. And with the repeater destroyed, if anyone attempted to use conventional radio to call for help, they would find themselves unable to do so.

The second target was the transport aircraft. Ali led this attack personally, though it was another of his men who shot both pilots and the mechanic. Others placed the explosive charges. It was gratifying to watch his men execute his plans and use the weapons he had procured for them. The aircraft exploded with delightful fury. Truly the Chehili wind was blowing.

The next item on the agenda was to take over the facility and herd everyone to a central location. Ali led his men through GeneSys's luxurious front entrance. Those inside offered almost no resistance—certainly they were unprepared for an armed invasion. Ali shot a few men randomly, just to ensure the compliance of the others. The whole takeover took less than thirty minutes.

With JIDIOC-P unofficially disbanded, there was no one watching GeneSys's online status.

That was why no one noticed when it simply vanished from GlobeNet.

Eight P.M. came and went. Kaye Hamilton sat with Jordan and Katie in the waiting room beside the GeneSys helipad, awaiting Ethan's transport.

"I want dinner now," Katie said.

"Not with that tone, young lady."

"I'm sorry, Mommy."

"I know you're hungry, honey," Kaye said, hugging her daughter. "Jordan and Mommy are hungry, too." She crossed the shiny tile floor to the counter. "Any word yet?"

The woman in the yellow shirt stifled a yawn. "No ma'am, not in the last three minutes. You'll hear the radio when I do."

"How late do they sometimes run?"

"If the weather turns, they might not fly at all. Those VTOL airplanes don't like strong wind, or so I'm told."

"When will you know? Can't you call them?" Kaye could've called Ethan herself, except that she'd made him leave his phone at home.

The woman shifted. "I haven't been able to reach them on the radio. It could be the atmospheric conditions caused by the tropical storm west of us. Sometimes we can't call the other side of town but we get Hawaii loud and clear."

"What tropical storm?" Kaye asked.

"The one in the area near Clipperton. Actually, the evening

news said they'd just declared it a hurricane. 'Flossie' or something.

"There's a hurricane coming?" Kaye said.

Her voice carried such alarm that Jordan was roused from the game he'd been playing on his laptop computer. He took his VR headset off. "Are they here?"

"It's not coming this way," the woman told Kaye. "They never do."

"What isn't?" Jordan asked.

"Then where's it going?"

"Away from us."

"Where's what going?" Not getting an answer, Jordan went back to his game.

Kaye kept an eye on Katie. "It's not going to hit your island, though, right?"

The woman sighed. "It might. But don't worry, we get about five big storms a year. This one's only a category three so far. The GeneSys buildings are rated to endure a class five. We're equipped with all the best hurricane technology—ventilation, aerodynamics, detection. The buildings actually have the ability to rotate into the wind for maximum safety. There's no danger, Mrs. Hamilton."

"When will you know if the shuttle is coming or not?" Kaye pressed. "My children need to eat."

"I'll try the radio again."

CHAPTER FOURTEEN

Whatever other failings John Hawkwood might have had, inflexibility was not one of them. He who adapted survived. He strode past the hostage petitioners in their line, straight up to the table at the front of the noisy cafeteria. He ignored their bleating. How dare he cut in front of them for the chance to talk to a terrorist? He walked past the masked serf at the table and headed directly toward the cluster of potentates beyond.

The flunky's shouts alerted armed guards, who unslung their weapons and came at him, shouting in some quick language. The masses in the cafeteria hushed, perhaps afraid they would be included in their captors' wrath, perhaps wanting a show.

Hawkwood had no intention of giving them one. He looked toward the terrorist leader and called, "I know a flaw in your plan."

The first guard grabbed him by his windbreaker, forced him to his knees, and brought the muzzle of his semiautomatic rifle to Hawkwood's head. Hawkwood heard the safety click. He thought about the pistol in the holster against his rib cage but decided he wouldn't win this firefight. He stared at the floor and waited. His last vision was going to be of a black smudge on white linoleum.

A quiet command spoken from above removed the gun from his head. He found himself kneeling alone on the cafeteria floor. The guards went back to their card game. A rumble of excitement swept the hundreds of captives, then sunk back into a low drone. John Hawkwood looked up into the black eyes of a young, masked Arab.

"You are not a scientist," the terrorist leader said with a light accent.

"No."

"You are not an administrator."

"No."

"You wear no yellow uniform. Therefore you must be a buyer. I do not shoot buyers today." He turned to leave.

Hawkwood stood. "Don't you want to know the flaw I see in your plan?"

"I have just told you the only flaw: that I do not shoot everyone on this piece of land Allah has forsaken."

Hawkwood followed him as he returned to his chair. He sat at a table that had been detached from the others. Radios, PCS phones, weapons, and GeneSys folders lay on it.

"The flaw I see," Hawkwood said, taking advantage of the fact that no one had escorted him back to the others, "is that your arrival will be detected far earlier than you anticipate."

The terrorist had returned to the documents spread out before him. He didn't look up. "How will this be accomplished?"

"Two ways. First, the aircraft you destroyed will have already been missed. The buyers you spoke of will not call their families tonight or meet their appointments tomorrow. Those new clients scheduled to come out to the island in the morning will find no airplane awaiting them. GeneSys elements in the city will be unable to raise this facility on the radio. I would say you could expect a Mexican patrol craft boarding your ship by noon tomorrow at the latest."

"Mexican patrol craft do not concern me," the terrorist said easily. "Radios and appointments do not concern me."

Hawkwood assessed the man seated before him. Was this machismo or true calm? "I see you are a prudent man," he said. "You have taken this information into account and planned for it."

The terrorist leader opened a new folder. "You claim I will be discovered another way?"

"This way is more subtle," Hawkwood said. "I command a team of computer specialists. We were recently brought here from our headquarters in America to protect GeneSys's electronic borders. The United States government, you see, has gotten it into its head that this good corporation has dealings with certain organizations it considers unsavory."

The terrorist looked up. "Shameful."

"My feelings exactly. It is our job to keep GeneSys's activities hidden from those prejudiced eyes, lest they draw the wrong conclusions."

"They are forever doing so."

Hawkwood nodded. "Even now a whole gaggle of engineers is searching for GeneSys's presence on GlobeNet. One false move from us, one moment of lowered defenses, and a hundred Rambos drop from the sky. That would make things interesting for your handful of brave warriors, wouldn't it?"

The terrorist leader grinned at him. "There is street vendor in your blood."

"My grandfather was a shoe salesman."

"You see? Tell me, son of a merchant, what wondrous elixir do you offer me to save my brave warriors?"

"The defenses we maintain to keep GeneSys hidden must be adjusted every six hours. It has been nearly that now. If my men and I are held in this place when that time expires, we will be visible to those searching for us."

"Impossible," the terrorist said calmly. "I have cut this accursed island off from the entire world. There is no more satellite dish and there is no more radio link. We are in no danger of discovery. You see, I have solved your problem too."

"There is perhaps one thing you may have missed," Hawkwood said, "only because you could not have known about it."

"What is that?"

"We brought our own portable uplink dish to the island with us. It's over on top of the engineering building, where we have set up our equipment."

Ali nodded. "Then you will lead my men to it."

"So you can blow it up? I'm not sure that would be such a great idea—with all due respect, sir."

"Tell me why."

"It's complicated," Hawkwood said. "We have other clients on GlobeNet to attend to. And much of our infrastructure is on the 'Net itself. As I said, it must be adjusted every six hours, but this is not the same schedule for all clients. We must maintain our electronic defenses actively or—"

"Your other clients mean nothing to me."

"I realize that," Hawkwood said quickly. "But all roads lead to Clipperton, if you know what I mean. If the American authorities discover what I have been doing with other clients, they will see where I have been operating from, which is here. Any way you slice it, sir, unless you let me and my men go back to work, American bad guys will come here with guns."

Ali studied him with distaste. "You are a fox. If I let you return to your machines you will call the Americans yourself." He overrode Hawkwood's protest. "None of my men is capable of making sure you do not do so. Therefore you will sit with the other cattle and await our departure. The Americans may discover your other operations, but they are without claws. They will wait and deliberate and go through committee. By then we will be in friendly waters and you will have to grapple with troubles which do not concern me."

John Hawkwood stared at the terrorist leader, noticing for the first time that the files he was going through were scientific records. He seemed to be reading them with some understanding.

Hawkwood felt the first twinges of panic. For all his nonchalance, hysteria was never more than an arm's length away. He felt control beginning to slip. The dangers were real. He remembered his confrontation with that idiot Brainiac. If Hawkwood gave him half a chance, the sky really would fall. He was a capable opponent. They would, no doubt, meet each other again.

"Who is this opponent?" the terrorist asked.

Hawkwood looked up. He must've spoken his thoughts. "An American computer expert who is trying to keep you from getting what you want."

"It has not been my habit of revealing my plans to hostages. What is it you say is my objective?"

"The biological weapon, of course," Hawkwood said. "Why else do all of us sit in here doing squat while a few genetic specialists are escorted in and out under guard? There is no reason for terrorists to seize GeneSys: it makes no political statement, there is no revenue or publicity to gain. They can only have something you need." He shrugged disparagingly.

"How does this American stand in my way? Is he here?" He looked around the cafeteria.

"No."

"Then he is of no concern."

"I suppose you're right," Hawkwood said. "If this man and his team turned off the power to the laboratory freezers, it wouldn't be important. I know the Ebola plague frozen there wouldn't be a problem to the world. We'd all be dead, of course, but the good is that it probably wouldn't spread. Then some of the other diseases kept in there are airborne, from what I understand. The trade winds would carry them far and wide. But what concern is that to you?"

"He could not do this."

"Of course he could."

"You said he was not here."

"He isn't."

They stared at each other. Hawkwood was aware of guards watching him warily.

"Haven't you ever heard of information warfare?" Hawkwood asked. "Don't you remember when the Argentine power grid went down last Easter? Don't you remember the natural gas facility that blew up in New Zealand the year before? The NASDAQ crash of '04? Information warfare, Mr. Terrorist. Computers hooked to other computers all over the world. The good guys have 'em. The bad guys have 'em. Governments have 'em. Companies have 'em. Cyberterrorists have 'em."

"And with this arrangement," the terrorist leader said, "this man may turn off a freezer?" He shook his head in mock amazement. "Truly he is a madman."

"He can turn it off from across the world, is the amazing thing. He can poison the water, turn off the electricity, light the methane storage tanks, and send carbon monoxide through the air ducts. From the other side of the planet."

Hawkwood knew no one could do any such thing, but it tapped into the fear of ignorant people. They always assumed computers were omnipotent and those who wielded them were invincible.

"This man," the terrorist said, "he is so powerful, yet you have been able to prevent him from doing any of these things, yes?"

"That's what I've been trying to tell you. Yes. Unless my team and I are allowed to keep working at our computers, these things and worse would surely happen." He anticipated the next question. "I can assure you I will not call the Americans or anyone else myself. I have reason to avoid contact with most of the governments of the Northern Hemisphere."

"All of these dangers you speak of would vanish like the

winter rains if we dismantled this dish of yours."

"But worse things will happen if you do that." Hawkwood said. He leaned forward. "We will not work for GeneSys forever. I am always looking for men worthy of my services." He swept the cafeteria with his hand. "You have shown by what you have done here—your daring and your thoroughness—that you are such. Tell me, have you ever thought of branching out into computer terrorism? How expensive it must be for you to maintain such a force of men, with their weapons, food, and pay. And how do you know they will not betray you later?

"Why not do it the smart way? Sit in your living room in…wherever it is you came from and do your work from there. Procure money for your cause, make highly visible statements, do damage on a scale unimaginable with traditional terrorism. All safely anonymous, without overhead, and from the comfort of your easy chair. If that sounds good to you, I'm the man to make it happen for you."

The terrorist laughed. "Your grandfather, I know he became very wealthy selling his shoes. You have changed the subject. You are a peculiar man, Mr…?"

"Hawkwood. John Hawkwood."

"You are a peculiar man, Mr. Hawkwood. I occupy your employer's island and feed his employees to the sea creatures, and you offer to work for me. If I enlisted you, I could never sleep in peace again, such a loyal employee you are. Still," he said, glancing at his men, "you make an interesting argument. I will consider it."

Behind them they heard a scuffle. Someone shouted, then yelped in pain.

Hawkwood turned back to the terrorist. "You are so thoughtful to provide a means of hearing grievances."

"It is the least I could do."

"Too bad you're going to kill them all."

"You misjudge me, Mr. Hawkwood."

"No, you won't do it directly. You'll just kill them all when you and your men die of anthrax because you didn't let me protect the computers."

The terrorist leader slammed his fist on the table. But when he spoke, his voice was level. "Very well, go to your computers. You and your men. Protect us from these diseases. Protect us from this superman on the other side of the earth. But—" he held Hawkwood's gaze as if on a skewer—"not one lightbulb will burn out or one airplane fly overhead, or I will shoot you myself."

Even before she'd become a Christian, Tamara Mack had never cursed much. It just wasn't part of her mentality. Whatever words might've eventually worked their way to her lips then were now squashed because of her new relationship with Jesus Christ. But right now she almost wished she had liberty to swear.

It was late Monday night, July 2. Soon after the masked terrorists had seized Clipperton, they had discovered from John Lipscombe the few people necessary to develop their biological weapon. These they culled from the crowd of hostages and ordered to get to work. Tamara had labored in her lab, under guard, until late at night.

Now she wanted to cuss.

She was finding herself unable to create botulin toxin at the purity level designated by the work order. Normally this wouldn't matter. Impure toxin was still deadly. But she needed it very pure so that it would go into solution with the carrier that had been designated. Tamara had heard of impurities clogging fine mist sprayers; perhaps that was an issue here, too.

The previous steps had gone smoothly. She had taken her opening moves from textbooks: temperatures, media concentrations and types, procedures. Though they were published they still had to be checked. She'd actually refined the process on a handful of points. She considered herself the newest expert on how to best grow botulinum bacteria. When she'd arrived at the purification stage it had been with a full head of steam. But there she'd foundered.

The procedure she was working from should've yielded an extremely pure toxin. A researcher had discovered that botulinin was effective in treating muscle spasms. Tamara was using his exact process—which was patented, no less—so it had to work. The only problem was that it wasn't working. She'd repeated the procedure a dozen times, with no better result.

She sat back from the microscope and grabbed two hand-fuls of her hair. Her eyes were dry, her neck hurt, and her right foot was asleep. Then there was the terrible tension. If the pressure she put on herself to achieve excellence wasn't enough, the masked gunman sitting in her lab multiplied it tenfold. She needed a break.

She looked at her guard, seated in a chair with his back against the laboratory door. She didn't know his name. He'd talked to her all the way from the cafeteria to the lab. What he'd said she had no idea. He was young, no more than twenty to judge from his voice. Perhaps she reminded him of an older sister or something, but her blond hair made that unlikely. From time to time he bowed to the ground in deep prayer to Allah. Except for the rifle he carried, he seemed very nice.

He looked up from the paperback he'd brought with him. He said something in his language and gestured with his gun. She supposed he was telling her to get back to work.

"I have to go to the bathroom," she said.

She was afraid she'd have to try to communicate it with pantomime, but he saved her from it. He twisted his fist, made a flushing sound with his mouth, and looked at her question-ingly. Tamara nodded.

He moved the chair and allowed her to lead him down the wide hallway. When they reached the bathroom, he stopped her. He pushed the door open but hesitated. Then he stepped aside and motioned her by.

"What's the matter?" she said. "Afraid of the girls' bathroom?"

Tamara relished the sensation of being alone. She tarried at the mirror, smoothing her tossled hair. How had the young woman staring back at her gone from humble microbiologist to CIA informant to terrorist hostage in just one day? It seemed unreal. Maybe she'd go back through that door and find the hallway thronged with the normal GeneSys traffic.

She stepped into a stall and began unbuckling her belt.

"Tamara," a male voice said softly.

She squealed and rushed through the stall door. "Who's there?"

"It's Ethan Hamilton. I'm in the other stall. I need your help."

The bathroom door opened and the young terrorist came in. He stayed by the sink, taking in the room hungrily. He said something to Tamara.

She noticed both her hands clasped at her chest. "It's…It's okay. I just…" She looked at the closed door of the other stall. "I just…saw a spider. A bug."

He didn't understand. She put finger antennae to her head and pantomimed something scurrying across the floor. He nodded, but seemed unconvinced. Maybe he thought she was telling him she'd seen a tiny bull. He said something that was probably, "Hurry up," and went back outside.

She went into the empty stall and shut the door. "What are you doing here?" she whispered.

"I hid."

Now that she knew who it was, she could picture him. Here was this secret agent on the loose, unbeknownst to the terrorists. Surely he would pull a *Die Hard* and save them all. However, hiding in the ladies' room was an inauspicious beginning.

"They're terrorists," she hissed. "They blew up the shuttle and took over the island. They've killed three people at least.

They shot…they shot my manager, Mr. Thornton. He wasn't doing anything to them; they just shot him. Now I've got this boy guarding me all the time. They make me work on their bomb, Mr. Hamilton! That's what they've come for. Everybody else they've got locked up in the cafeteria. I don't know if they're going to let me eat or sleep or anything. They don't understand that you can't rush delicate work. I'm so afraid! And it's not working. Something's wrong with the process. I need help but they won't let me talk to anyone. They won't let me go back to my apart—"

"Flush, Tamara."

"What?"

"Flush," he said. "Make it sound like you're finishing up."

"But I really need to go! And I can't do it with you in here."

"I'll shut my ears."

"Uh! Can't you just climb out the air vent like you came in?"

"I came in through the door, Tamara."

Tamara tried to picture it. "Isn't that just a little weird? How long have you been in here? And how did you know I'd come to this bathroom? Were you just going to wait here forever?"

"Tamara," he said, "listen for a second. I'm sorry this has happened to you. I'm sorry it's happened to me! I've had more than I've bargained for on this trip, and that's the truth. These are the Chehili terrorists I told you about, remember? Don't push them. On the other hand, you're probably in less danger than anyone else on this island right now because they need you. Do what they ask. I'm going to see if I can use some computers to call the cavalry. Don't worry, these people won't get off Clipperton with what you're making."

"What happens when I'm finished and they don't need me anymore?"

"You're a Christian, Tamara. We're not supposed to fear those who can kill the body but can't touch the soul. God's hand is in this, I firmly believe. Trust him to take care of you."

"I'll try."

"One more thing," he said. "Next time you come to the bathroom, bring food."

"Goodness gracious."

Ethan studied the monitors before him. With everyone confined in the cafeteria, the White Company's whole operation was unguarded. He went from keyboard to keyboard, calling up what each computer had been tasked to do. Each moved him further into incredulity. The White Company was the genuine article.

He found on these computers the means for waging not cyberterrorism but cyber-Armageddon. If he'd known they were capable of this level of mass destruction, he would've planned Operation Hydra much more carefully even than he did. It was like the Allies approaching World War II and suddenly finding out the Axis powers had been in contact with a superior alien civilization who had given them their technology. The fight might still be winnable, but the tactics would have to be drastically redesigned.

He walked around the folding tables at the far end of the dim entertainment room a second time, finding how the systems interrelated. Simply reformatting the data drives wouldn't be enough to stop these people. If he wanted to put them out of business and get the cavalry to come, and he did, then he'd have to do something more extreme.

Setting the room on fire was an option, but then everyone would know someone else was loose in the buildings and they'd go looking for him. Still, it was a good last resort. With the buildings deserted the way they were, he might be able to get into a great hiding place in the next building before anyone arrived. And maybe he could make the fire look like an accident. He decided to take up a temporary career as an arsonist.

But first he'd see about sending a message to his team telling them the situation and another to his family telling them he was safe. He sat at a keyboard and navigated through the system.

There was an unmistakable elegance to the network design. Elements that had never been designed to talk to one another, like network packet sorters and print spoolers from a dozen platforms, were working harmoniously, even adding complexity to the native encryption. It was, in short, a system he would never have been able to crack from the outside. He was honest enough to admit it. But, he reminded himself, he wasn't on the outside.... No, better just to burn it all. The strongest encryption still couldn't defeat elemental flame.

He accessed the communications menu and saw that the regular data channels, through satellite and radio means, had been disabled by the terrorists. That was bad. If he couldn't find a way to get a message out...

He found something: an alternate data channel. Some kind of proxy uplink. He opened an e-mail program and activated its automatic erase feature. That way no one could see what messages had gone out. He shot a quick message off to Jordan, then began a longer one to Mike Gillette.

Out in the hall he heard voices.

CHAPTER FIFTEEN

ifteen teenage boys ran into the entertainment room like brothers racing for the TV remote. Sneakers squeaked in the hall then pounded on the carpet inside the room. They jostled and pushed and taunted. It sounded like recess.

The cockpit Ethan was hiding in shimmied as neighboring ones were occupied. His monitors came on, and he knew the whole system had been activated. If all of them had decided to play, instead of only five or six, someone would've discovered him. His cheek twitched into a smile as he watched the combatants begin to maneuver. It was a highway warfare game. How strong was the urge to take the controls of his own cockpit and play! Instead he had to sit idly by as another player racked up points by destroying his supposedly unoccupied Hummer.

The door to the entertainment room opened again. "All right, children," a man's voice teased, "time to put your toys away and come to the table."

Ethan recognized the voice.

One by one the virtual cars went slack or careened into buildings as their drivers abandoned them. At last he was alone on the virtual battlefield. Ethan wanted to blow all their cars to smithereens, but there was the small matter of the sound still being on.

This isn't a game, Curly. Why was it he had to remind himself of that so often?

Chairs creaked at the other end of the long room. Soon he might attempt to cross to the door and leave. Maybe he could break into somebody's apartment and sleep. It had to be after 11 P.M.

For the last hour a conviction had been growing in his mind—more felt than heard or seen—that the weather had begun to change. Ethan wished Kaye were here. The slightest fluctuation in pressure gave her terrible headaches. He didn't wish the pain on her, but it was a useful poor-man's barometer.

John Hawkwood's familiar voice rose authoritatively. "I have prevailed on the good terrorists not to kill you for now."

The teenagers laughed nervously, perhaps wondering when "for now" would run out. Ethan wanted to peek out and get a glimpse of Hawkwood. Instead he crept to the farthest, darkest end of the long room and waited for an opportunity to cross to the door.

"We've still got to keep GeneSys off the map, so everyone get back to your jobs. Our dish is the only one in operation. The Arabs blew the other one sky high, so those of you who were using the GeneSys dish need to reconfigure. Security protocols on several sites are approaching zero viability, so some of you need to move quick.

"Nobody leaves this room without telling me. And nobody, I mean nobody, does anything non-White Company until this is over. That means no e-mail to your girlfriend, Andy, and no multiplayer Xenon for you, Charidemus.

"Gneisenau and I will run a perimeter check and find out if anything's down. You do the same on your own machines. I want diagnostic reports and security logs in my hands in five minutes. Get to it."

"Sir?" a youthful voice said.

"What is it, Sforza?"

"Are we working for Islamic terrorists now?"

Hawkwood didn't answer at once. "They think we are. But, as always, we work for ourselves. Right?"

"Right!"

It was time for Ethan to get out. Not only because the young men at the tables were engrossed in their computers, but because someone was likely to notice that his e-mail program had been set to auto-erase, since Ethan hadn't had time to undo the changes he had made. Also, if the network wizard was as good as Ethan expected him to be, at least some trace of his message to Jordan would be visible. Ethan wanted to be far away from these people if and when his presence was discovered.

He crossed quietly across their field of view, glad for the darkness at this end of the room. Holding his breath, he reached for the door handle.

The door swung open. Ethan stepped against the wall and let the door press almost to his face. Two masked terrorists, assault rifles at the ready, swaggered by, headed for the tables. Ethan slipped through the door before it shut.

He ran down the corridor, every step expecting to hear the sounds of pursuit. They did not come. When he had put several zigs and a number of zags between himself and the entertainment room, Ethan allowed himself a moment to relax.

What was he going to do now? A good hiding place was priority number one; food was close behind. His lunch had more than deserted him by now. He had failed to contact Gillette and, more importantly, he had failed to put the White Company out of business on the island. Jordan wasn't likely to check his e-mail while on vacation.

He thought of his family, waiting for him at the helipad, wondering where he was, going to dinner without him, going back to the hotel without him. *Father,* Ethan prayed, *let them know I'm all right. And Lord, make that true! Please resolve this situation well. Amen.*

Ethan was in the engineering building. Here was the power hub of the GeneSys campus. All the energy controls were here, all the repair facilities, all the hurricane equipment. Everything needed to keep Clipperton's twenty-first-century inhabitants comfortable. Consequently there were many workrooms and few offices. Storage bays outnumbered living spaces three to one. Ethan imagined that this building might seem deserted even under normal conditions. He found an unlocked equipment closet and went in, feeling his energy sag away.

It was a room formed in the hollow beneath a stairway. The stairs above Ethan turned at a landing and continued up, making his closet very tall by the door, the height of a regular ceiling at the far wall, then, around a partition, shorter and shorter all the way to the ground. Ladders and poles and even a sea kayak stood against the wall at the tall end, while ropes and oars hung from pegs at the short end.

Ethan shut the door behind him and turned on the light to look around briefly. Wedged in the space where the ceiling slanted down to the floor were scuba gear and flotation devices of all kinds. A few heavy buoys and a rope interspersed with plastic balls, like the rope used to demarcate the shallow end at the YMCA pool.

Ethan grabbed a flashlight from a workbench and turned the overhead light off. He pulled a dust cover from a stack of scuba tanks and curled up on it. His ears picked up a strange clicking sound. It was familiar somehow, but his mind was too fatigued to sort it out right now. For some reason he found the sound comforting. His plan was to lie there a moment and think of a way to get some food. Instead, he was instantly asleep.

The guard stopped Dr. Oscar Redding at a closed door. GeneSys's senior geneticist waited silently, knowing a question was useless. Steps echoed from a nearby stairwell. Presently a young Arab man in a black mask joined them in the tile corridor. Redding recognized him as Ali, the leader of the gunmen who had invaded Clipperton Island. Ali said something in their language, and the guard released Redding's arm.

"Good of you to join me, Doctor," Ali said with the light accent Redding remembered from the transposon demonstration weeks ago. "Nice to see you again."

Redding suggested that Ali should visit Hades.

"You are alarmed. I understand. You must believe I had no wish for things to occur as they have. I am a patient man, Dr. Redding. You know how I waited for your company to deliver what I paid for." He put his hands in his pockets, almost managing to look respectable.

"I have learned a difficult lesson in my lifetime, Dr. Redding," Ali said. "The ILA swine taught this lesson to me and I have taught it to my patriots. There are times when a man must go beyond what other men would do if he is to get the thing he must have." Ali paused thoughtfully, staring at the white floor of the hallway. "Sometimes I think that in seeking to eliminate my enemies I have simply become as they are. Do you think such a thing is possible?"

Before Redding could decide how to answer, Ali turned hard eyes on him.

"What could you know of enemies? What is the worst thing that has happened to you? Burned sausage? Soap in your eye?" He looked Redding over from top to bottom, then in one syllable seemed to give his evaluation of Western man: "Bah!" He pushed through the closed door, pulling Redding with him.

Another guard stood in the corner of the small room, his rifle leaning against the wall. In the center of the room sat a chair. And on the chair slumped a man with a yellow GeneSys T-shirt over his head. The shirt stuck to the man's face wetly in places. Ali yanked the shirt off. The man cried out numbly, as if he'd been asleep. Redding gasped when he recognized the battered face. It was John Lipscombe, GeneSys's chief administrator.

"John!" Redding said, going to him.

Lipscombe moaned.

Redding shot a look at Ali. "What did you do to him?"

"He's not permanently damaged," Ali said. "I have grand plans for Mr. Lipscombe."

"He needs medical attention." Redding straightened. "Why did you do this?"

Ali dismissed Lipscombe with a brush of his hand. "I do not like his kind. For months his was the face that told me why my weapon was not yet available. Always he blamed this or that. Smiling like the snake about to eat the rat." Ali lifted Lipscombe's chin. "You should thank me that I have not killed him."

"I demand you let him go," Redding said.

"As I said, I have planned a great destiny for him. Also I will show him what a true leader of men may do. I will bring forth in two days what he has for months failed to produce."

"He has a family."

Even as he said it, Redding's mind dropped to a deeper level. He watched Ali's lips delivering whatever justification he had worked out, but he did not hear. He didn't know why Ali had brought him here to see Lipscombe, but he was sure it was not going to have the desired result. For in this tiny room, with his employer semicomatose before him, Oscar Redding determined to thwart the terrorists. If he could not save children by defeating disease, he would at least save some by defeating Ali.

Just as no one in the United States intelligence community noticed when GeneSys vanished from GlobeNet, so none noticed when it reappeared.

The White Company brought it back online, with defenses at maximum. They sneaked out from their fortress in ones and twos, going about maintaining their dispersed interests.

Redding's guard escorted him to the microbiology wing, Lab #4. Though it was near midnight, Tamara Mack was still at work, guarded by another masked terrorist. Redding had spoken with this young woman several times since she'd come on with GeneSys, but he'd never truly gotten to know her.

"Dr. Redding," she said, shaking his hand. "It's so wonderful to see a familiar face. Are you all right?"

"I'm fine, dear." He found a lab stool and sat.

She misread him. "Have they hurt you?"

"No, child. Not me. Not yet. Tell me, does your terrorist friend here speak any English?"

"Not that I've noticed."

"Good. Neither does mine. That will make things easier. Well then, how goes your progress?"

She pushed away from the counter. "Terrible. I must be doing something wrong. I can't get enough of the toxin purified. I've done it a hundred times, I think, but I just can't make it work."

Redding put a comforting hand on her shoulder. "There, there. Let's take a look at it, shall we?"

He picked up her clipboard and reviewed the process she'd been following. It took him a moment to get back into microbiology gear. It had been some time since he'd done this kind of lab work. After reading half the page he grunted.

"What?" Tamara asked.

He handed the clipboard to her. "It's wrong."

She looked at him dully. "What?"

"The process—it's wrong."

"But it can't be. It's patented. This man uses this process to treat people with—"

"My dear," Redding said, "trust me. The process is wrong. Now, I have no doubt that this man you speak of has perfected the process, and I can see for myself that he owns the patent. Doubtless he inserted errors into the formula to prevent someone from doing the very thing you are attempting."

A light seemed to dawn in Tamara's eyes. "So not just anyone with a microbiology degree could create a biological weapon."

"Correct," Redding said, using his lecturer's voice. "And to prevent rival pharmaceutical companies from benefiting from the process."

"But I thought scientists were supposed to share information."

"My child, when the kind of money biotech companies throw around is involved, the scientific community can jump in the ocean." Redding noted no toxin shortage in his tone. "Now, what we have to do is determine where the errors are and correct them. I have seen one, but doubtless there are others. We will need help. Someone with a background in organic chemistry, I would think. I will tell Mr. Fashir at once."

"Who?"

"Ali al-Fashir. The leader of this Arab rabble. He will jump to your aid when I tell him your work is stalled by this."

Tamara looked at the guards nervously. "We shouldn't be doing this for them."

Redding smiled. "That's what I like to hear. Hold to the pure truth, my dear. You wouldn't believe me if I told you, but it is all too easy to lose it. And then," he said to the air, "I don't think you can ever get it back." He came to himself and rested his eyes on Tamara. "Forgive an old man for babbling."

This time she touched his arm for comfort. "I...I can't tell you everything, but there are things going on that these black masks know nothing about. There may yet be a way out of this for us."

"What are you telling me, girl?"

"I'm just saying that I don't think we have to worry about them getting off the island with this weapon I'm building them."

"You're not planning to do anything foolish, are you?" Redding asked. "Please, child, let me be the fool. You just do as you're told and try not to offend anyone. And don't look them in the eye. Treat them like mountain gorillas. This kind of man likes that."

"Is this advice for dating, too?"

Redding stood up. "You're a good soul, Tamara. Remember what I said. Do what they tell you." He faced his guard. "I'm ready to go."

The terrorist said something that sounded mean. He gestured with his rifle menacingly, bringing it up to poke Redding's chest. The other guard laughed. Tamara gasped.

"Don't worry, my dear," Redding said quietly. "They're only showing off for you. If they shoot me, they'll have Ali to contend with."

At the mention of their leader's name, the guard removed the rifle point from Redding's person. The guard puffed up his chest and leered at Tamara. He said something that sounded lewd, then swept Redding out the door.

In the Northern Hemisphere, hurricanes travel in a northwesterly direction. When they reach the higher latitudes, they turn to the northeast. The winds blowing in the direction the storm is moving deliver the maximum destructive force of the hurricane. Since hurricanes in the Northern Hemisphere rotate counterclockwise, those areas on the north of the storm as it moves northwest and to the south of it when it turns northeast are in for the hardest hit.

At the moment July 2 gave way to July 3, Hurricane Flossie was three hundred fifty miles southeast of Clipperton Island, moving west-northwest at a steady 12 mph. It was a category three hurricane, which meant 111-130 mph winds at the northern rim of the eye. If Flossie turned northeast in the next twenty-four hours, Clipperton would be mostly spared. If Flossie stayed her course, Clipperton would be in trouble.

Already the sea around the little atoll was uneasy.

It would be difficult to describe the joy an eleven-year-old boy might feel awaking in a king-sized bed. He could have turned any direction at all and still had plenty of head and toe room. Jordan Hamilton lay at a diagonal on the hotel bed, just because he could. He stretched, trying to touch the opposing corners of the mattress, and happily failing. He looked at the other bed in the room. His mother and sister were still asleep. Perfect.

Yes, Jordan was concerned about his father's absence at the heliport yesterday, but it had allowed him to have the bed to himself. It had only taken a single, hushed "Hey, Katie, I think I just saw Mr. Fang," to convince his sister she wanted to sleep with Mommy.

Ah, vacation.

Jordan didn't know how this day could do anything but get worse after such a beginning. Should he stay in bed and hang on to the moment, or should he get up and have a few minutes of uninterrupted game time before the day got going? He settled on a compromise. He reached for his laptop and pulled it under the covers.

A message box told him he had e-mail waiting. Surprise, surprise. Jordan always had e-mail. While a game loaded in the background, he read through his mail.

It was mostly low-priority stuff. A few short retorts in a friendly flame war he was conducting with a buddy in South Africa, a price quote on a new game he was salivating over, a note from one of his mother's friends. The last message was from someone Jordan had never heard of: somebody named Charidemus. Mildly intrigued, he clicked on the message.

Jordan,

It's your father. I'm in trouble. Call Mike. Tell him the Chehili terrorists are on Clipperton, holding everyone hostage. Tell him the White Company is here, too. I'm hiding. Okay for now.

Don't return mail to this address! I'll try to get another message to you later.

Dad

"Mom!" Jordan shouted. "Wake up!"

The man looking at Kaye on the vidphone screen was not Special Agent Mike Gillette. "Where's Mike?" she said.

"You can talk to me, ma'am," the young man said. "I'm Colin Bates, personal assistant to the director of Central Intelligence."

"I want to talk to Mike."

"I'm fielding all official traffic for these numbers, ma'am," Bates said. "What can I help you with?"

Kaye told him the situation. She read him Ethan's message. She pleaded with him to get in touch with Gillette and the whole JIDIOC team. He assured her he would pass the message along.

Satisfied she'd gotten the ball rolling, Kaye returned to her children to make the best of a hard situation.

Colin Bates dutifully passed Kaye Hamilton's message on to his superior, DCI Roy Pickett. Somehow the message ended up in the shredder.

Both men began practicing the phrase "I have no recollection of that."

Ethan's bed wasn't quite as cozy as his son's. At first he couldn't imagine why. The room was completely dark. Perhaps it was still the middle of the night. He felt the covers next to him for his wife. His hand struck something metal instead.

"Ouch."

His mind told him there was a flashlight around him somewhere. In that moment it didn't strike him as odd that he would keep one by his bed. Ethan knew exactly what he would be like if and when he ever grew senile: blissfully absentminded. Just exactly how he was when he hadn't had enough sleep. He found the flashlight and switched it on.

He was in some kind of equipment room. It all came back to him then. The terrorists, the destroyed airplane, the White Company.

He shone his light around. The metal he'd struck was a scuba tank. There were about a dozen of them here, standing and lying side by side. He remembered now. This was a storage room for GeneSys's water equipment. His light passed over a stack of booklets entitled *SCUBA for Beginners.*

That's it! he thought glumly, *I'll swim to Acapulco! Through seven hundred miles of shark-infested waters.* He chuckled. *Go back to sleep, Curly.*

The repetitive clicking sound finally breached his awareness. Ethan pointed the flashlight toward the sound. He saw a white wooden frame mounted on the partition dividing the room. His stomach leapt. It looked like… But what would it be doing here? Still, there was a chance. Maybe the building had been wired before they knew what each room was going to house. He stepped closer.

It was what he hadn't dared hope it might be: the communications wiring hub of the entire building. Two rows of narrow plastic trays lined the area within the frame. Multicolored wires meticulously streamed from specific nodes, culminating in great gray shielded cables that disappeared into the ceiling.

Five white computer boxes hugged the wall close by. The clicking he'd heard came from the storage drives doing their thing. Here was the master communications processing suite for this building. Every bit of communications data processed by all the phones, fax machines, and computers in the building went through this little array.

Including the computers in the entertainment room.

CHAPTER SIXTEEN

Gillette here." Mike Gillette took his eyes off I35W long enough to see the face in his dashboard vidphone. "That you, Jordan?"

"Hi, Mike," Jordan said.

"Howdy, Tex. Y'all back home already?"

The boy shook his head. "We're still in Mexico."

"Oh. Great connection." Gillette moved his pickup truck into another lane. "I guess that means you can't go watch fireworks tomorrow night with me and Liz."

"I don't think so."

"Maybe next year. So, what can I do you for, junior?" Jordan started to answer but the special agent interrupted him. "Say, how's your dad?"

"Not so good. Can you tell me what you're doing for him? My mom wants to know."

Gillette looked at the dashboard monitor. "What do you mean, what am I doing for him? Not much we can do for now. He'll be happier out of the spook business anyway."

"Out of it? I thought you'd say he was in it up to his neck."

"What are you talking about, junior?" Gillette's driving seemed to be degenerating.

The boy paused. "Didn't you get my mom's message?"

"What message?"

Gillette had to take the next exit and stop the truck. "What! Go back, Jordan. Tell it to me real slow. You say there's terrorists on Clipperton?"

The boy read something out of the camera's view. "Che-hilly, I think." He looked into the camera. "You sure you didn't get my mom's message?"

"I promise, podner. If Chehili's really there, your dad's in it deep. Read me the whole thing."

Jordan read his father's e-mail message.

"Okay, Jordan," Gillette said, "here's what I want you to do. Is your mom there?"

"Nuh-uh. She took Katie to go get some breakfast for us. I talked her into letting me stay here so I could call you."

"Okay. You tell her I'm on this and that I will definitely turn the big guns on this one. Is there someplace I can reach you?"

"I'll send my number and e-mail address to your computer at work," Jordan said.

"Okay, my address there is—"

"I know it, Mike."

"Oh."

"Mike?" Jordan said, uncharacteristically vulnerable.

"Shoot."

"Is my dad going to be okay?"

"We'll do our best, cowboy."

"Thank you for taking my call, Mr. President."

President Rand Connor faced the vidphone camera from the backseat of his limousine. "Not at all, Mike. It's not every day I get to speak with my Medal of Freedom recipients after the ceremony. Say, what's this Roy's been telling me about our man Hamilton resigning?"

"What did he tell you?"

"He said Ethan decided he didn't like the pressure of the job," Connor said. "I guess I can understand that."

Gillette didn't answer right away. *God,* he prayed, *I kinda need a hand with this.*

"He didn't resign, Mr. President," Gillette said, feeling the pressure inside him seep away. "The DCI put him on indefinite leave. I'm not sure, sir, but I think he wants to get rid of Ethan. I think maybe he didn't like that you installed Ethan in the first place." Belatedly, he thought to say, "If you'll excuse my frankness."

"Quite all right. I'll give Roy a call." The president nodded to someone off screen. "Thank you, Mike. Now, is there anything else I can do for you?"

"There's something else you need to know about Ethan, Mr. President. He's in trouble."

"What kind of trouble?"

Gillette told him about GeneSys and Clipperton and Ethan's reason for going there. Then he told the president about Chehili. He read Ethan's e-mail message. Connor listened intently, but with the carefully neutral expression Gillette had learned to heed.

"Tell me something, Mike. Why are you calling me about this?"

"Mr. President?"

"Don't get me wrong; this is an urgent situation and we will move on it right away. But it seems to me there is someone else you should've called before it got to me. I'm not one to give a hoot about proper channels, Mike—just ask Marie—and I don't know, maybe it's my football days, but I sure can smell out an end-around when I see one developing."

"I came to you, Mr. President, because if I went to Roy he would drop the ball. No personal offense intended, sir, but I believe the DCI has it in for Ethan. I think he would probably act on this, but he might decide to wait a bit too long, or conveniently forget to tell the strike team that Ethan was around and not to be shot.

"The other reason," Gillette continued, "is that this is exactly the kind of crisis you set up JIDIOC to handle. You may not realize it, sir, but Roy has essentially disbanded the team." He saw a quick fire light in the president's eyes. "My feeling is that he's made it just another CIA front. I'm in Fort Worth now, doing basically nothing. I haven't been contacted about any of JIDIOC's ongoing operations for over a week, nor has anyone else on the team.

"I don't mind letting you know, sir, I wasn't completely sold on this counter-cyberterrorism team you invented. I almost turned Ethan down when he asked me to be on it. Besides you, I think Ethan may be the only true believer in it. But now that I see the fix he's in, I see that you had a good idea. Right now he needs more than what any single agency can do. He needs the JIDIOC team, Mr. President. But the person responsible for getting it in gear has dismantled it." Gillette scratched his nose. "So I called you."

The president appeared thoughtful, but his expression betrayed nothing. Gillette became aware of the speaker hiss from his vidphone and the dim sounds of road noise coming from the other end.

"Let me make a phone call, Mike. Stay where you are."

Twelve minutes later, Gillette's vidphone rang. It was the president, still in his limo.

"Mr. President?"

"Well, I'm still not sure, Mike. Roy claims he knew nothing of the situation on Clipperton and has assured me he'll begin taking action immediately."

"Oh."

"I told him not to bother," Connor said. "I told him I wanted you to handle this for the moment."

"Me?"

"Oh, all I really wanted to do was buy some time to do some snooping around, but at the same time make sure things were moving forward for Ethan. You'll do your best, won't you, Mike?"

"Yes, sir. Absolutely, I'll do my best. Count on it."

"Good. For the moment, and until you hear different from this office, I am appointing you acting director of the Joint Intelligence Detail, Mr. Gillette. I hereby order you to assemble the original team and get moving on this crisis. I am vectoring all authority and responsibility to you. If things are as you have alleged, I will deal with Roy myself. Mr. Gillette, you are instructed to report directly to me for the duration of this emergency."

"Yes, sir," Gillette said, overwhelmed. "Thank you, sir."

Connor leaned into the camera. "One more thing, Mr. Gillette."

"Yes, sir?"

"I am holding you personally responsible for letting Hamilton get into this situation in the first place."

Gillette nodded dismally. "I'll get him out, sir."

Ethan had once read someone's theory that crime was rampant in cities because everyone was anonymous. No one knew anyone else; consequently there were no societal restraints. This small island community of only a few hundred people was the perfect test of this theory. He wondered how the experiment had been going.

Not too terribly well, it seemed. The first apartment he came to was locked. So were the second and third. If everyone was so trusting, why did they lock their doors? Ethan was still bemoaning fallen human nature when he broke into an apartment to steal a computer.

He found an adequate laptop in a case by the desk. He also helped himself to a breakfast of candy bars he found in the desk drawer. They weren't Payday bars, but an inferior candy bar was better than no candy bar at all. Sooner or later he would have to find some real food. Nah. To subsist on nothing but candy bars—it was his dream come true. He took the whole stash.

It occurred to Ethan that a life of crime, of plundering and taking what he wanted because he was daring enough to reach out for it, held a certain appeal. At least it did now, with no one in the whole dormitory building to catch him. He felt the seduction of the easy path. Perhaps it was the ocean setting, but this day he fancied himself a pirate. It also occurred to him that this same mentality was what had brought the Chehili terrorists to Clipperton—an island named for a pirate—and allowed them to hold sway.

Ethan pulled some bedding to the floor and wrapped the "borrowed" laptop computer inside, along with the rest of the candy bars and a portable VR headset he found. He hefted the bundle to his shoulder and headed back to his hideout. He vowed to return it all later.

On the walkway between the buildings he was buffeted by a fierce wind. The sky was dark, though it had to be past ten in the morning. To the east it was so dark it appeared someone had forgotten to tell that area that it was daytime. Even on the short walk to the engineering building the wind seemed to increase.

He saw whitecapped waves and thought they must be half again as high as they'd been just the day before on his little walk. Salt spray soaked his clothes and stung his eyes. Unidentified garbage blew around him; airboats left out in the lagoon pulled at their ropes. The wind turbine spun quickly. He thought he detected a slight wobble in the tall corkscrew.

Ethan hoped he'd be able to find food in the engineering building, because it didn't look as if he'd be venturing out of it again for a while.

Ethan plugged his purloined laptop directly into the communications hub in the scuba closet. It was child's play for him. He'd found a spare data cable lying just where he would've put it if he'd been the network designer. The hardest part of the setup was finding an extension cord long enough to reach from the nearest outlet to his computer.

In seconds he was in. He donned the delicate VR headset and entered GeneSys's virtual environment. He saw three-dimensional structures and animated pathways. His trained eyes detected patterns in the data flow and distinctions between automated and human-controlled communications. He sat passively, watching the electronic world go by.

This was his mise-en-scène. He respected his opponents, to be sure, but in here he knew he was a player. Something new and unexpected was about to happen to the White Company. It wasn't time for Ethan to transform into Stupendous Man, not yet. But it was the perfect time for Stealth Boy.

The first step was to determine the enemy's operational stance. What he was up to, where his vulnerabilities were, what kind of intrusion he was prepared to repel. The second step would be to contact the mainland, hopefully through the secondary uplink dish again, to see what resources he could bring to bear. Step three would be full-scale guerrilla warfare.

Ethan felt exhilarated. Now he was a spook in earnest, playing a life-or-death game. He was not done with hiding, neither in the physical nor the cybernetic sense, but he was positively done with cowering.

Mike Gillette rubbed his palms together briskly. "You sure this is going to work, Barnes?"

Captain Kelly Barnes, the U.S. Army's redheaded encryption expert, smiled at him in the large vidscreen monitor. "Relax, Mr. Gillette. You've done this plenty of times before."

"But I ain't never been in charge!"

Major Elizabeth Lee's face replaced Barnes's on the big screen. "You'll do fine, Mike. Would you like me to go over how it works?"

Gillette nodded hungrily. "Thanks, Elizabeth. Lay it on me."

"I'm designating you armchair general. Do you know what that means?"

"I'm guessing it's not football."

"That's correct, sir. For the duration of this call you will have director-level control of all aspects of the transmission: switching, muting, linking, adding and dropping frames, and so on."

"Sanfrantastic."

"Do you have the keypad in front of you?" she asked.

He held up a gray wand about the size of a TV remote control. "Got it."

"Press the number two, the Frame button, and the Take button."

"At the same time?"

"No, one after the other."

Gillette did. "Hey! I can see both of you now."

Lee nodded from the leftmost of the two-paned split screen on Gillette's monitor. "Now hit three, two, Frame, and Take. "

Gillette was in the tiny conference room of the Fort Worth FBI offices. A posterboard-sized flat-screen monitor hung on the wall. The image fractured into four banks of eight white-framed squares. Each of the thirty-two frames was roughly the size of a three-by-five index card. Lee appeared in the top left position, Barnes next to her.

Gillette smiled. "Hollywood Squares."

"Showing your age, Mr. Gillette," Barnes said.

"Har har."

Lee made a sliding motion with her hand. "You should see text at the bottom of every image."

"Got it," Gillette said. "I've got 'Lee' and 'Army' figured out all by my lonesome. But what do 'l,' 'A,' 'L,' and 'O' stand for?"

"I'm image number one," Lee answered. "My audio is on for you. My signal is linked to the other thirty-one stations. And we are all omnipresent."

"That means everybody can see and hear everybody else," Barnes said.

"Don't worry, junior," Gillette said. "I didn't think it meant you were God."

Major Lee continued. "If you want to have a private word with someone, press their number, the Priv key, and Take. Understand, Mr. Gillette?"

"Gotcha."

"Then hit Back to come back to this."

Gillette nodded. "All right, I guess I'm ready."

"Captain Barnes," Lee said, "bring the others online."

"Yes, ma'am."

CHAPTER SEVENTEEN

I t had taken a while but at last the Joint Intelligence Detail, Information Operations and Counter-Cyberterrorism, Provisional team had been reconvened. It was 1 P.M., Texas time, on the third of July. A few team members had gone out of town for the holiday. Twenty-odd faces stared back at Gillette from his large video screen. He cleared his throat.

"All right, people, listen up. As most of y'all know, President Connor has asked me to get things rolling with us again. So here goes. A situation's come up out in the Pacific that needs our special kind of love.

"When we were all out at Langley, Captain Barnes gave us a top-notch briefing on Clipperton Island and a biotech company called GeneSys. Well, what was just a nice show-and-tell back then has turned into a bona fide crisis.

"You remember from Barnes's speech that the Algerian Sirocco Front terrorists—that's Chehili to you and me—had requisitioned a biological weapon from GeneSys. Barnes was doing what he could to hit 'em where it hurt. But then somebody went and built a barbed-wire fence around the place. We decided we needed to get somebody to the island to try to find a contact."

Gillette paused. He stared at the two CIA agents in their

frames. He liked them both, Calvin Coakley, especially. It wasn't their fault what their boss was like.

"I won't go into exactly how it came about," Gillette said, "but for reasons you may be able to figure out for yourself, our former leader, finding himself with a truckload of free time, came down with a sudden and inexplicable craving to see some obscure island in the eastern Pacific."

He let it set a while.

"Agent Gillette?"

"Yeah, Sai," Gillette said to the NSA agent.

"Are you saying Hamilton went to Clipperton alone?"

Gillette felt the same sense of guilt he'd felt under the president's gaze. He scratched his neck. "That's a fact, Sai. Went out there like he knew what he was doing."

"He couldn't wait for a professional?" It was Calvin Coakley, CIA agent-cum-mop-pushing janitor.

One of the DoE agents spoke up. "Maybe he got tired of waiting for somebody to go."

"What's that supposed to mean, Hatfield?" Coakley said.

"Oh, nothing."

"Knock it off, you guys," Barnes said.

Voices rose. Gillette was thankful it was only in the virtual sense that all these people were in the same room together. Things were rapidly spinning out of control. He wanted to scream at a few jarheads and spooks; instead, he prayed.

"Okay, okay," Gillette said calmly. "Everybody pipe down."

There was no sign he'd been heard. Gillette looked at his remote. He selected Major Lee's frame and established a private link. Her pretty Asian face popped onto his screen.

She nodded at him. "Nice meeting, Mr. Gillette."

"Thanks. Listen, is there some way to mute all their audio but let them hear me?"

"Good idea." She told him how to do it.

When next Mike Gillette stared at their faces, all was silent. A few could be seen still yelling, but no one could hear them.

"All right, you jokers, button up. That's better. Okay, we'll wait a minute until Dunbar realizes no one's listening. Hellooo, Commander Dunbarrr."

Gillette saw the naval officer stare at the camera angrily and mouth, What?

"I muted your audio, cowboy." Gillette thought he could get hooked on this kind of power. Too bad it didn't work on the street. "Now that everybody's had their fun, can we put away the turf wars and concentrate on a genuine crisis?

"For whatever reason, and whether he was right or wrong to do so, Director Hamilton put himself in harm's way to pursue JIDIOC objectives. What started as a mission to make contact with a likely informant—a risky enough job, even for a professional—got ugly real quick. Apparently things were going fine, right up until the moment when Chehili took over the island."

Gillette watched their reactions but was thankful not to be interrupted. "If you think that's good, wait till you hear this. It seems our old buddies the White Company are on the island, too." Again he gave them a moment to take it in. "I guess that explains the barbed-wire fence, huh, Mr. Barnes?"

A few team members waved their hands, hoping to be allowed to talk. "One more second," Gillette said. "We've received a single communication from Director Hamilton—an e-mail to his son." He read the message aloud. "Okay," he said when he had finished, "I'm going to unmute everybody."

He pressed the keys on his wand and the 'A' reappeared under every frame.

A Marine officer spoke first. "How did the bad guys get out there?"

"No idea," Gillette said. "Boat or plane, I suppose."

"Kelly," Sai Cho said to Barnes, "who did you say owns Clipperton?"

"France, but Mexico claims it, too. We've claimed it in the past, as well. It's kind of complicated."

"Wonderful."

Dr. Hanover of the National Reconnaissance Office raised his voice. "There's something we need to keep in mind."

"Shoot, Doc," Gillette said.

"Hurricane Flossie. It's southeast of Clipperton about two hundred miles and it's moving northwest at about twelve miles an hour."

"Is it going to hit?"

"It's already hitting," Hanover said. "Winds on Clipperton should be up around seventy-five miles an hour by now. Flossie's a category three hurricane, so if it doesn't veer off, winds on the island could reach one-thirty-three mph."

Somebody let out an amazed whistle.

Gillette scratched his neck again. "Thanks, Dr. Hanover. That does put a spin on things."

"No pun intended, I'm sure," Lee said.

"Huh?"

"Never mind."

"All right. Here's the situation as I see it," Gillette said. "One: Hamilton's out on Clipperton Island. Two: so's Chehili. Three: a hurricane named after the dental floss queen is about to land. Four: we can assume that the Chehili boys are seeing to the completion of their biological weapon. Five: some computer hotshots won't let us do our usual tricks. So let's go around the horn. Who's got anything?"

"Is Hamilton in any immediate danger?" Air Force Captain Gary Reinke asked.

Gillette raised open hands. "You know as much as I do. The message said he was okay for now."

"If it wasn't for the hurricane," Marine Major Fontana said, "I'd say we send in an antiterrorist unit right away. Force Recon or Delta Force or SEALs. But as it is, I'd say we have to wait."

"I concur," Captain McAuliffe of the Defense Intelligence Agency said. "The Air Force has storm chasers that fly with the hurricanes, but paratroop deployments are totally out."

"Who said anything about paratroops?" Commander

Dunbar asked. "SEALs can deploy from subs."

"And who said SEALs would get the call?" Barnes said. "I thought Delta Force took care of business nicely last time."

Dunbar raised a finger. "I've got just one word for you about that, kid: island. Clipperton is a textbook example of a SEAL target. Delta Force and Force Recon are respectable outfits as far as land goes, but when it comes to maritime operations, SEALs win, hands down."

"I agree with you, Commander," Gillette said. "But how do you think you're going to make landfall? Barnes told us in his briefing that a ten-foot surf is normal for Clipperton; what's it going to be during a hurricane?"

"Can you even get in position in time?" It was Jeffrey Larson of the State Department—a nonmilitary person.

"The Navy is a forward-deployed force, sir," Dunbar said. "I'll check with COMSUBPAC. I'd be willing to lay money down that we've got an ASDS-equipped sub less than two days out of this rock. We get a SEAL unit aboard somewhere ahead of the storm, then put 'em right on the beach, hurricane or not. And—" he nodded to Elizabeth Lee—"they're not going in with nonlethal weapons this time."

Gillette nodded. "All right, Commander, it sounds good. What's the earliest the SEALs could land on Clipperton?"

Dunbar reached outside the camera's view and pulled something closer to him. "SEAL Team Nine's the closest. They're pulling R & R at Pearl. And let's see…" His eyes widened. "Whoa, you're not going to believe this. We're closer than I thought. I've got the *George M. Jackson* right in the neighborhood, headed for Panama. The *Jackson's* ASDS fitted. This is terrific."

He did some figuring. "Let's see, a report of approximately twenty armed terrorists… No need for a full SEAL detachment. A platoon would do. Okay, give us two hours to assemble one of Nine's platoons and get them airborne. Then about…ten hours to reach the sub and do a rubber duck. Then another—"

"A rubber what?" Larson said.

"A rubber duck," Dunbar said. "SEAL parachute deployment from a cargo plane to CRRCs—Combat Rubber Raiding Crafts. The sub picks them up and heads to Clipperton at best speed. Figure another six or eight hours at thirty-five knots, surfaced. All told, we have SEALs on the island in eighteen hours." He looked at his watch. "That's tomorrow, the fourth of July, about eight in the morning, Clipperton time."

"Independence Day," Fontana said.

"Dr. Hanover," Elizabeth Lee said, "when will Flossie's winds be greatest on Clipperton?"

Hanover smiled. "Tomorrow morning."

"That's what I thought."

"It won't affect the sub," Dunbar said. "They'll submerge when the seas get heavy. Below the waterline a hurricane has very little effect."

"That landing's going to be a real party, though," Marine Lieutenant Adam Brosnan said. "I wouldn't wish it on anybody."

"They'll be fine," Dunbar said. "And I'll give you another reason the Navy should do this job, Gillette."

"Lay it on me."

"The kid said it in his briefing," Dunbar said, referring to Barnes. "The Navy's had bad luck with this rock. We lost more than one ship and a mess of heavy equipment there trying to get that listening station up in W-W-Two."

"I remember."

"You could say we've got a score to settle with Clipperton Island."

"All right, Commander, you get your wish," Gillette said. "Go on and get it in gear. If you need to go off the air, we'll understand."

Dunbar nodded. His image clicked to black.

"Meanwhile," Gillette said, "what can the rest of us jokers do? Templeton, I don't suppose you can get us any satellite photos of Clipperton until the blow's over?"

"Hurricane?" the National Imagery & Mapping Agency officer said. "What hurricane? Mr. Gillette, I'm not allowed to tell you everything, but I can say that something as trivial as a little cloud cover can't keep us from seeing whatever we want. You might have to get used to some pretty strange color palettes, but we'll get you your photos."

"Sanfrantastic. Get 'em, then."

"Yes, sir."

Gillette was warming to this role. He'd worked for the federal government for almost his entire adult life, but he'd never had access to this kind of muscle. Briefly, oh so briefly, he envied Ethan his position as JIDIOC's director.

"What else can we do?" he said. "Remember, not only is our boss and friend in danger, but there are civilians, terrorists, biological weapons, and a truckload of cloned Hitler babies to worry about."

Major Lee said, "Don't forget the White Company."

Several people agreed.

"We have to assume Director Hamilton will try to contact us again," Sai Cho said. "We'll keep all hailing frequencies open."

Giorgio Vinzetti of the Treasury Department spoke up. "Why don't we work up some things we can give him if he calls?"

"Good idea."

Gillette sat back and listened to them talk. They were beyond the limits of his knowledge now. It only mattered that he had gotten JIDIOC on the road again.

God, that was amazing how you took over like that. Why don't you just take charge of all of it?

It was like Fort Knox in cyberspace. Ethan concluded this after completing his third VR lap around the White Company's computer network. It looked like a maximum security penitentiary. Three rows of electrified fences topped by razor blades. Guard towers every hundred paces. Motion detectors, laser beams, and seismic panels covering every spot of no-man's land. Armed guardbots patrolling at irregular intervals and speeds, led by what appeared to be werewolves on leash.

There were nineteen known vulnerabilities in any networked computer. Everything from the phone lines to the buttons on the keyboard could be hacked. Hawkwood's setup had double and triple protections on all nineteen. It was a mixed-media approach. If you somehow managed to defeat the virtual electric fences, the motion detectors would get you. Ethan had expected no less. In fact, his opinion of Hawkwood would have suffered greatly if he'd found any obvious blunders.

On his inspection, however, Ethan had noticed something odd about Hawkwood's security design. The White Company's computers were geared against attack from the outside world. That was to be expected. It was, after all, to defend against external intrusions that GeneSys had secured the White Company's services in the first place. Ethan was doubtful that anyone, even he, could breach these defenses from the outside.

But what was unusual about Hawkwood's network was that it was also configured to defend against attack from within. The razor-sharp fences curved inward at the top as well as outward. Hawkwood's own computer could be seen sitting like a besieged castle at the center of the White Company's network. A whole new set of defenses, also doubly and triply redundant, guarded the vulnerabilities of his inner sanctum.

Someone doesn't trust his own people, Ethan thought wryly. Immediately he decided that manipulation of this mistrust would be the theme of his attacks.

He turned to the problem of communicating with the good guys back home. With Hawkwood's boys back at the keys there would be no more free rides on the dish. He spotted the 3-D representation of the satellite uplink dish. It was very near Hawkwood's own computer. Ethan could only imagine the defenses that were actively working there now. There was no getting out that way.

All right, Curly. Time to get sneaky.

Ethan had learned the hard way that there was an undocumented twentieth point of entry into almost every computer in use: the weather report downlink. Someone with the know-how could gain entry into even a protected computer by riding the weather updates down the satellite signal. An information warrior could thus plant IOps weapons into any targeted computer.

It was possible that GeneSys had a separate downlink dish just for weather information. Ethan located on his virtual map the computer that handled the weather report downlink. It was not within the White Company's fences, but rather in the GeneSys area—on the "safe" side of the portal to the outside world. He moved through cyberspace to access it.

Ethan had made it one of his soapbox campaigns to make the world safe from weather-report hacking. Last year control of his own car had been seized in this way, and the car had been used to try to kill him. Using this same weather-report glitch, his own "smart" house had been used to attack his family. Now, like a reigning beauty queen, Ethan used his celebrity status to further his cause, raising awareness of the problem and providing the cure: a free software patch, written by him.

But today, as he approached GeneSys's weather report computer, he found himself hoping his cry hadn't been heard way out here on Clipperton Island.

The good news was that GeneSys hadn't gotten the message. The weather downlink computer was sitting as unprotected as a turkey on Thanksgiving morning. The bad news was that the White Company had heeded his warnings. The downlink itself, represented by a small satellite dish atop the computer, was securely defended. His programmer's eyes detected the telltale signs that his patch—his very own code—had been installed.

Way to go, Curly.

This was hardly the end of the road, though. Ethan had designed the defenses surrounding the dish, so he knew how to defeat them. It was possible to send tiny chunks of data through the timing pulse in the signal. It was too small a gap for serious intrusion, but it might be enough to get a message through. He started thinking in short sentences.

He noticed that the computer was receiving no data. Upon closer inspection, Ethan noticed that the dish itself wasn't operating. The way the wind had been blowing when last he'd gone out, it was possible the dish had been knocked over. It was more likely that the terrorists had just gone up to the roof and destroyed everything that looked like it might transmit or receive data.

Ethan pulled the VR headset off and rubbed his face. There had to be another way for communications to reach any spot off Clipperton. With all the satellite dishes either destroyed or under lock and key, he was going to have to get creative indeed.

The thought struck him that there might be a replacement dish sitting in another closet somewhere in this building. He rejected the idea as quickly as it had come. Even if he found one, what would he do? He was no technician. Besides, the wind might just blow it right down.

He surmised that the terrorists had come on the ship he'd seen approaching earlier. Presumably that ship had communications gear that would reach the mainland. It probably even had a GPS system, which meant another accessible GlobeNet link. But how was he supposed to access those options—swim out to the ship? Possibly he could steal a terrorist's radio, link it to his computer, tap into the ship's radio, and somehow surreptitiously transmit something to the mainland. The idea got uglier with each additional "somehow."

There were probably automated communications going on all the time between the complex on Clipperton and their other facility in Acapulco. Every Coke machine and microwave oven on the island had a modem to call for servicing. Artificial intelligence systems monitored thousands of variables on Clipperton, from the scientific to the mundane, and transmitted the findings to the appropriate agencies around the world. Normally, any one of these signals could be harnessed to do what Ethan needed to do. The problem was, with the main satellite dish down, all these calls went unplaced.

What Ethan needed was a way to access GlobeNet from this remote Pacific island without a satellite uplink. At the moment, he couldn't think of any. He put his headset back on.

He almost took them off again so he could pinch himself awake. His virtual presence was still looking at GeneSys's dormant weather downlink computer.

Only now it was receiving data.

"So?" Ali asked.

The GeneSys technician looked up from the computer screen. "I was right. It's a hurricane. Category three. They're calling it Flossie."

The leader of the Chehili terrorists watched the satellite time-lapse sequence on the screen. "Are we in its path?"

"I'd say it's already upon us," the technician said, indicating the dripping rain gear they wore. They'd been on the roof installing a replacement dish. "But yes, we're directly in its path. Even if it turns now it's too late. It's going to hit us with everything it's got."

"When?"

The technician shook his head. "As I said, it's here now. It's only going to get worse. The peak of the storm will be right in front of the eye, which should hit us—" he calculated briefly, "—in about eighteen hours. You'd better get your ship out of here."

Ali laughed derisively. "Your concern for the safety of my belongings touches me."

The technician shrugged. "It's up to you. Anyway, the worst is going to hit us tomorrow morning. We've got to get busy prepping the island."

Ali gestured with his pistol. "What is this prepping?"

"We have to secure the big turbine, lock up the boats, vent and turn the buildings. We have a whole hurricane drill we do."

"You will not do this drill."

"Excuse me?"

"If the people scatter I shall not find them all again. They will stay in the dining hall."

"At least let us vent and turn the buildings. We can do that from a room upstairs. And we need to secure the turbine. If we don't do both of these, you will have much more to worry about than a few missing people." The technician tried to judge Ali's reaction. "Look, this facility was designed from the ground up to weather hurricanes, but only if certain procedures are followed. I'm sorry, but I don't understand your reluct—"

Ali struck him on the side of the head with the grip of his pistol. "It is not for you to know my mind! Go, do this prepping."

It was not a happy meeting when SEAL Team Nine, Detachment Echo, Fourth Platoon assembled at the airfield. A sailor's R & R in Hawaii was not to be interrupted. When Commander Dunbar's order to assemble the platoon reached the naval base, it was ten in the morning, Hawaii time, on July 3. It ended up being a joint armed forces mission just to haul them all in by noon.

Now, after weeks of training for alpine operations in Korea, and only two days into their leave, the men of Fourth Platoon were trundled onto an MC-130 cargo plane and informed that they were about to assault a tropical island.

It's not just a job, it's an adventure.

CHAPTER EIGHTEEN

"I'd have to say it's a good sign," Captain McAuliffe of the Defense Intelligence Agency said.

Mike Gillette watched the zoomed-in infrared satellite image in a window of his wall monitor. It was a strangely colored aerial view of Clipperton Island: all whites and blues and yellows. The seven buildings of the GeneSys complex could clearly be seen rotating, like some architectural synchronized swimming team.

"Since when are moving buildings a good thing?" Gillette asked.

"It means somebody's still alive to turn on the storm system," McAuliffe said.

Gillette looked at his multipaned monitor. Only ten frames were filled now, as other JIDIOC members were off doing mission-related tasks. Major Lee had changed the screen to a twelve-frame view to give everyone a larger portrait. "It could be an automated system," Gillette said. "Don't they have bots to do this kind of thing?"

Lieutenant Brosnan launched into a lecture on the unfeasibility of artificial entities in real-world applications. It sounded like smoke-blowing to Gillette. He knew from firsthand experience just how capable some AI could be. He was about to say so when a message beeped into his mailbox. It was followed immediately by another, then another, then several more. In the space of five seconds, he'd received twenty-five short messages, all from the same source. Gillette clicked the first into a window, not bothering to interrupt Brosnan's lesson.

Mike, tie all these messages together.

Gillette did so quickly. He read the full message.

Mike, tie all these messages together.

It's Ethan. Did you get mail from Jordan? Chehili terrorists on Clipperton. They came in a ship. Blew up airplane and satellite dishes. Employees and clients taken hostage. They're making T. Mack build their weapon. I'm hiding. Can only transmit in 1KB chunks.

The White Company is here. Working for GeneSys. I have access to their computers. Trying to bring them down. Can you mobilize the team? Coming to you through weather downlink. Had to defeat my own defenses to do it. Trying to open longer gap. Have my tools ready to send. Jordan will know.

Data shows a hurricane coming. Dish may not last long. If it stays up, maybe we can use it to go interactive.

Tell Kaye I'm okay.

E.

"Listen to this, everyone," Gillette said. He told the team members how he'd assembled the message, then he read it to them. "Elizabeth, can you send this out to the people who aren't online right now?"

She didn't answer. He noticed her screen was black.

"Major Lee?"

Her face reappeared in her frame. "Sorry, Mr. Gillette. I was taking care of an intruder."

"What?"

"Don't worry, it wasn't much," Lee said. "Yes, I'll forward this to our team members."

"Why did he send me that in pieces?"

"Who knows?" Barnes said. "Maybe he's working with an intermittent uplink signal, maybe he's trying to avoid detection. Could be lots of things."

A new face appeared on Gillette's screen: that of a gangly preadolescent boy. "Jordan?"

"Hi, Mike."

"Jordan, what are you doing here?"

"I want to help."

"Jordan, I know it's your dad—"

"We could use a false carrier," the boy said.

"Huh?"

"To go interactive."

"You heard the message?" Gillette asked.

"No, I read your copy."

"How did you—"

"What do you mean, Jordan?" Lee asked. "Use a false carrier how?"

"Elizabeth!" Gillette said. "Don't egg him on. His mother'll kill me if we let him get involved."

"No, I won't, Mike."

Gillette squinted at Jordan's image. Someone was there with him. "Kaye?"

"That's right." Kaye Hamilton squeezed into the chair next to Jordan. "I'm right here. I understand you never got my message."

Gillette initiated a private link with Jordan and Kaye. Their faces filled his screen. "I never got any message from you, Kaye."

"Well, I sent it this morning. I talked to some young man who said he was the director of Central Intelligence's assistant."

"Do you remember his name?"

"Bates? Gates? Something like that. He said he'd pass it on."

Gillette shut his eyes. "Okay. For now I'll just choose to believe your message got lost innocently. Otherwise I'll get too mad to think. Now, what's this about you letting Jordan get online with us?"

"I want him to help, if he can," Kaye said.

Gillette shook his head. "This is no place for him."

"It's his father, Mike. It's my husband."

"That's the risk we all take in the business, Kaye. Everybody here's got family somewhere. We can't be letting every Uncle Waldo and Aunt Clarice join our investigations."

"Mike."

"No. Forget it."

"Please, Mike."

He shook his head. "Unh-uh."

Kaye's eyes flared. "I'll call Liz."

"Oh, now that's not playing fair."

"Thank you, Mike."

"I didn't say—"

But Kaye had already stepped out of the camera's range. Jordan smiled innocently. "Put me back with the rest of the team, Mike."

"Huh?"

"Use your remote."

Gillette obeyed.

"My dad's message came inside data from that hurricane tracking place, right?" Jordan asked the group.

"That's right," Sai Cho said.

"If he can ride inside their weather updates," Jordan said, "we can, too. We'll just ride it down— Oh, this is better! We'll change the update so it flows through us, through them. See? They send it, we intercept it, drop in our stuff, send it back to them, and they bounce it out to the island."

The few team members present jumped into shop-talk

mode. Gillette had never before heard terms like "packet morphing" and "TCP/GP spoofing" spoken with actual relish. Jordan had energized the JIDIOC-P team.

Gillette should have felt grateful. But he could only shake his head, watching Barnes and Lee and Sai and the other brains interact with Jordan. First he felt responsible for letting Ethan go to Clipperton and get into this mess. Now he was going to put Ethan's son in danger, too. And Ethan's wife had pressed him to do it.

It seemed God had blessed him with the opportunity to learn what it meant to pray with fear and trembling.

Ethan was sure his team would have his IOps software ready. He had only to download it all. But to do so, he'd need more than 1KB at a time. He didn't need much uninterrupted time—maybe thirty seconds or less. But he couldn't get that through the weather report downlink without setting off all kinds of alarms on John Hawkwood's desk.

It was time to start playing with Hawkwood's head.

At 2:30 P.M., Clipperton time, a trio of masked Chehili terrorists brought Dr. Laura Brady to Tamara's laboratory. Laura was every bit as pretty as Tamara, though a little older and with brown hair instead of blond. Perhaps they had mischief in mind. There were probably twenty people on the island with the requisite organic chemistry knowledge to solve Tamara's problem, but they'd chosen a pretty white girl to bring. In an exchange Tamara was only able to guess at, her guard—she'd taken to calling him "my terrorist"—threw cold water on whatever plans they might've had.

It took Laura less than an hour to find the mistakes—two of them—in the purification procedure Tamara had been using. Tamara was convinced that the patent holder had done it intentionally. She half wished she'd been unable to overcome his subterfuge.

The guards took Laura away the moment she and Tamara verified a successful process. It took the presence of a friendly face to show her how much she'd been missing one. Now Tamara could only hope Laura would make it back to the cafeteria unmolested.

The day John Hawkwood had awaited all his adult life had finally come. Someone was attempting to betray him. Someone in the White Company.

For over four hours someone had been testing his defenses. Never enough to trip any alarms. Never on any regular schedule. Just probes, someone looking for weaknesses. Most people wouldn't even have noticed it, but Hawkwood had his alarms' sensitivities set ridiculously high. He had them as high as they could be set without the fluctuations of electricity itself setting them off.

He ran the logs back for the hundredth time and watched the latest such prodding replay. He had it laid out before his 3-D goggles in the form of a cork floating in a fishing hole. He held his face right at water level, watching the red-and-white plastic float. For seconds it drifted in a gentle current, riding the shallow waves. Then it disappeared underwater.

Hawkwood's automated defenses—represented now as a virtual fisherman on the shore—reacted immediately. The rod yanked back. The cork and hook flew out of the water and onto the riverbank. A little pink worm wiggled on the hook.

There were a hundred innocent explanations for this: somebody taking a wrong turn, a transient glitch, a bot automapping the system. But to John Hawkwood, it was a declaration of treachery.

He was almost relieved in a way. It was a game he'd half dreaded, half longed for for years. Now he would get his chance to play, and to come away the victor.

He took his goggles off and looked around the converted entertainment room at the faces of his men. They looked so studious, so intent on their work. But one of them, possibly more, was a Judas.

Hawkwood had to hand it to the guilty one. The places he'd chosen to test the defenses were good ones: lightly guarded, yet only two steps removed from systems manager access. That ruled out a few of his people outright—some were incapable of such analysis. And whoever it was had kept his identity concealed, a feat requiring no small amount of skill, considering Hawkwood's defenses.

Of the people he'd brought with him to Clipperton, only a handful might be capable of such fine work. There were others who had remained on the mainland who might have done it, but they were cut off. It had to be one of the fifteen he'd brought with him to Clipperton. But which one?

The bottom right frame on Gillette's monitor blinked to life. A smug grin. "Hello, Special Agent Gillette."

"Howdy, Director Pickett. How's tricks?"

The DCI's face zoomed to full screen, though Gillette hadn't touched the controls. "Tricks are good, buddy," Pickett said. The grin widened. "Hey, I wonder if you'd like to tell me what you're doing."

Gillette raised an eyebrow. "President Connor asked me to—"

"Don't give me that. This isn't about Connor, it's about you and Hamilton and me, isn't it?"

Though Pickett's smile hadn't vanished, Gillette definitely felt the man's anger. He reached over to the conference room doorknob and locked it. CIA hitmen—yes, at times even the FBI feared they existed—could ruin your whole day. Not that a locked doorknob would do much good.

"All right," Gillette said. "Let's say it is about Hamilton. What exactly were you doing to help him?"

Pickett folded his arms. "Why does he need help in the first place, hmm?"

The DCI's calm irritated Gillette almost past endurance. "Roy, would you mind if we had this conversation later?"

"You sound just like Hamilton. My, how cozy. People had told me about you two, but I didn't want to believe them."

Gillette didn't take the bait.

"Guess who I got a visit from today," Pickett said. "The president. Yes, he came right into my office, actually."

"Oh."

"He said you'd told him I was using the Joint Intelligence Detail as a front for CIA activity. Did you tell him that?"

"Weren't you?"

"Absolutely not. Since I relieved Hamilton I have been in close contact with the NSA, the Air Force and Army, the departments of State and Treasury, and even the FBI. There are, aren't there, people at the FBI besides yourself?"

"Yes."

"There are even other FBI agents on this fancy team, or have you forgotten Max Cobb?"

"You're telling me you've been in constant contact with Max?" Gillette said. "That's funny, because when I talked to him fifteen minutes ago he said he hadn't heard from you since Lang—"

"As I said, there are others in the FBI besides yourself."

Again Gillette checked himself. "Roy, I'm sorry your feelings were hurt when I went over your head. I know that must've been embarrassing for you. For that I really am sorry. But Roy, to me it looked like you weren't moving quickly enough on GeneSys, if you were moving on it at all. I realize this might not be so, but it looked to us—not only me—like you might be dragging your heels because of Ethan's involvement."

Pickett sounded hurt. "That's simply not true, buddy. I'm

deeply concerned about this. As soon as Rand told me about it, I jumped into action. But for some reason the president didn't want me to act. You don't think Connor's the one who's dragging his heels, do you?"

"I talked to Ethan's wife recently," Gillette said.

"Moving in on her while the hubby's away, huh? Pretty bold. Go for it, cowboy."

"She said she contacted your office about this long before President Connor even knew about it."

"Oh, really. Hmm. I'll have to check my messages."

"She said she talked to your assistant, Bates."

"Did she? All right then, that explains it. Colin's been out of the office for a while. I'm sure he was going to tell me at his first opportunity."

Gillette almost laughed. He didn't know what it was, certainly nothing in Pickett had changed, but somehow Gillette was hearing him differently. Now the DCI simply sounded ridiculous. Gillette saw in that moment what Roy Pickett was, a fearful man in a job too difficult for him, managing to look good only by making others look bad. In an act that surprised even himself, Gillette was moved to pray for him.

"All right, Roy, thanks for calling. Bye now."

John Hawkwood had turned the audible alarms off. He didn't want the traitor to know he'd been discovered.

When the subtle probing came this time, Hawkwood was ready. He'd switched back to the penitentiary motif. As soon as the silent alarm told him someone was again testing his defenses, Warden Hawkwood sprinted off to investigate.

Hawkwood circled the triple fences surrounding his own computer. He caught a glimpse of movement as he rounded the second corner. He charged. A flash of color disappeared around the next corner.

"This is crazy."

He looked at the virtual representations of his men—some guarding the towers, some patrolling, others in buildings. Normally he would call on them to help him chase the intruder. But he couldn't risk it now. Better not to let anyone know he was on the prowl, in case the traitor had accomplices. He doubled back, hoping to meet the intruder coming the other way.

At first he didn't recognize the high-pitched whine. He stood there stupidly, scratching his virtual head, looking out over the prison compound. Then his spatiated speakers drew his attention to the source of the sound. It was an alarm on his private computer.

"Security breach!"

His men ran to him, both in virtual reality and in the entertainment room.

"Where?"

"What's the location?"

"What's happening?"

"Should we shut it down?"

"Mr. Hawkwood, we need coordinates!"

Hawkwood cursed. He had been lured out of position. He ripped the VR helmet and gloves off and fumbled to access his security control panel on his computer screen. "Five! Server five. Somebody's gained access. Gneisenau, take it off line!" He rushed to where his men were unhooking cables.

Gneisenau, a red-faced teen with tightly curled brown hair, dropped the cables. "There. It's done."

Hawkwood stared at his men, chattering and cursing and laying blame. Under his gaze they quieted down. He noted with satisfaction the fear with which they regarded him. "I want to know two things," he said as if he were inquiring about the results of a tennis match. "What was done and who did it."

The White Company dispersed quickly and Hawkwood went back to his computer. One of the benefits of being a cruel disciplinarian was that no one dared say, "Why weren't you at your post when the alarm went off?" Despots get to make mistakes for free.

When he sat in his chair, he saw he had a new e-mail message waiting for him. He called it up, thinking he'd find the first report about the incident.

Why did you bring us here?
Some of us don't work for you anymore. At the time of our choosing, we will dispose of you. Who is loyal to you and who is not?
The game begins.

Hawkwood shot a look out over his men, searching for the telltale glance from someone who knew about the message. They all seemed to be intent on their work. The hypocrites.

Several minutes later, he watched as three of them formed into a small huddle out of his earshot. They conferred. At a word, all three looked at him. Then they approached.

Hawkwood reached a hand beneath his windbreaker to the automatic pistol he carried at his rib cage and un-Velcroed the strap. Then he folded his hands on the desk before him. When the cabal reached his desk, he actually smiled.

"What can I do for you gentlemen?"

To his mild disappointment, they laid a sheet of paper on the desk. "It's a preliminary damage estimate, sir."

They stood over him, awkwardly awaiting instructions. In the end, they peeled off to their posts.

His heart knocking in his neck, Hawkwood forced himself to read their assessment. Knowing only the part they knew, their guesses were good. High probability of random packet deflection; lower probabilities of cable failure, component failure, or false positives due to elevated sensitivity settings on security filters.

They said a break-in attempt was not a possibility, since their defenses were at full strength. The breach had been an internal one, they felt, not one originating from GlobeNet.

Further, the report writers didn't think anyone had been trying to break communications out, either. No one except the members of the White Company would have the skill to even attempt a breakout. For that reason, they considered that a non-possibility, too.

Hawkwood looked around the room. Each of the three report writers had spoken with at least one other person since the delivery of their report. He understood now why governments sometimes prohibited group meetings of the citizenry. What could they be talking about except revolution?

He turned back to the report. It detailed what the report writers felt were the best- and worst-case damage scenarios. Best case: nothing whatsoever happened during the security breach. It was a bug or some transient power fluctuation. Worst case: they were doomed. All security protocols had been down for a full seventeen seconds, virtual millennia in the information age. If an information warrior had been at work, he could have done any amount of damage. They had only to wait to see the results.

Hawkwood crumpled the paper. Why did he think he could trust anything they wrote? One or all of them had turned against him. Why would they give him a report that incriminated themselves? No, they would wait until he was incapacitated in some way before revealing themselves. He felt the pistol with his elbow. He just had to be sure he didn't get incapacitated.

"Mr. Hawkwood, sir?"

Hawkwood looked up at the skinny teen approaching his desk. "What is it, Culbertson?"

"Sir, a minute ago I did something out of an old habit. I forgot for a second what was going on because, you know, of how hard I was trying to figure out what went wrong. Because server five was kind of my responsibility and all, so I—"

"Culbertson, I'm aging."

"Right, Mr. Hawkwood. Sorry. Anyway, I think you should know: the weather dish is back up."

"What!" Hawkwood spun to his computer and accessed the onscreen communications panel. He cursed. "Everybody go to full EMCON," he said, standing. "The dish is back up."

One disaster after another. Hawkwood sat down heavily. He checked the weather satellite's downlink log. The dish had been up for almost four hours. It had been up at the time of the security breach.

Ethan was sitting pretty. Though his surroundings didn't suggest it—perched on a life preserver in a dank storage closet—he was loaded. The seventeen-second lapse he'd enjoyed in the White Company's defenses was about six seconds more than he'd needed. As he'd hoped, Mike Gillette and the JIDIOC team had placed gobs of IOps goodies in an online cache should he call. Now Ethan was equipped with everything he needed for waging full-scale, high-stakes information warfare.

But it was too early to strike again just yet. Better to lie low for a while. Let the poison work in Hawkwood's mind. Let him make the mistakes.

Ethan leaned back against a cold scuba tank. He could feel the building settling and shifting under Flossie's leading winds. Perhaps it was more than that. A moment of vertigo was followed by another. He thought he might pass out. Then he thought he might throw up. He heard a sound like Godzilla's battle scream. Then a deep bang. Behind it all he thought he detected a chugging motor. What seemed like a squadron of shrieking banshees swept into the building.

Something fell to the floor with a crash, sending equipment clattering across the concrete floor. Ethan shined his flashlight, thinking the creature from the black lagoon had stepped into his closet. Instead he saw the sea kayak askew on the ground. Scuba gear fell from pegs behind him.

That's it, Curly. You're being blown into the ocean.

The vertigo stopped. The more prominent sounds fell away,

leaving only the supernatural howl of the wind.

Ethan checked his computer. Everything was fine. He donned his VR headset and went under. A flapping alert flag on a GeneSys node caught his eye. He activated it. Text appeared in the ether before him.

Rotation Successful
Dynamic Automated Reaction Systems (DARS) Online
Very Large Vertical Turbine (VLVT) Secured
All Buildings Aligned Optimally
Date: 07/03/07
Time: 8:13 PM

Several other details followed, including wind speed, barometric pressure, and distance to the eye of the approaching hurricane.

Ethan shook his head. Buildings that spun like weather vanes. At least it was a better explanation for the vertigo than the revenge of a bad candy bar. Speaking of which, he had consumed his entire stash. He never thought the day would come when he'd be sick of candy. But that day was today. He really needed to get some better food soon.

But not now. If the ground would just agree not to move for a while, he could get some sleep. In a few hours he would go out in search of food. After that it would be time to pay Mr. Hawkwood another virtual visit.

Ethan pulled his copy of *With Christ in the School of Prayer* from his pocket and settled back to read.

Ali al-Fashir was not a cruel man. For his fellow man he held admiration, even affection. Only one group did he despise. With the rest he was at peace.

He stood outside a nursery looking through a Plexiglas window. He saw the pink and brown babies and the nurses he'd let care for them. These were not especially unusual babies—no clones or chimeras. They were test-tube babies, to be sure, but in vitro fertilization was a stable process even in Algeria.

What made them GeneSys material, so he'd been told, were an assortment of extenuating circumstances: they were babies that had been frozen as embryos for decades, babies conceived from the eggs of deceased mothers, genetic "children" of same-sex couples, and so forth.

Ali rested his face against the glass, feeling its coolness penetrate his mask. He couldn't help thinking of his own baby sister. Had this place existed then, and had he commanded the resources he did now, would he have been able to somehow bring her back? And would he have become the man he was now if he'd had access to a company like GeneSys then?

Someone cleared his throat. Ali turned to find one of his men with a message. The biotech sorcerers reported a major stage completed. Ali turned again to the nursery. A nurse was holding a tiny body to her shoulder, rubbing gently. From this angle it could have been any mother with any baby.

No matter what he did, he could never bring his mother and sister back. What did anything matter?

CHAPTER NINETEEN

Some seek the will of God in an inner feeling or conviction, and expect the Spirit to lead them without the Word. Others seek it in the Word, without the living leading of the Holy Spirit. The two must be united. Only in the Word and the Spirit can we know the will of God and learn to pray according to it. In the heart, the Word and the Spirit must meet.

Ethan laid aside *With Christ in the School of Prayer* with a tiny moan.

To know the will of God. It was his heart cry. To always know exactly what God wanted him to do. To have certainty when all he ever seemed to have was ambiguity. Here was a man, this Andrew Murray, who was telling him he could know it.

Murray said the path to this knowledge was simply listening. Quieting the mind, muzzling the "gimme" prayers for a moment, and simply giving ear to the still, small voice of the Holy Spirit. How did the Holy Spirit speak? In the words of God, of course. Scripture.

How beautiful it sounded. Ethan thought of all the sincere Christians who had taught him over the years that such a thing was impossible, that God didn't speak in a living voice anymore.

It wasn't the first time Ethan felt that mainline Protestantism, in its fear of the Holy Spirit, had given away something crucial—the mystical dimension; the astonishing, playful Spirit of Jesus—in exchange for a stolid Bibliology.

Ethan wasn't ready to accept any so-called revelation that went beyond what the Bible said, but he might be willing to give Murray's listening prayer a chance. He settled back against a pile of life preservers and determined to try it. He relaxed, he focused, he silenced his racing mind.

It proved harder than he'd expected. His mind wanted to flit like a hummingbird from topic to topic. Certainly he had many things on his mind: terrorists, information warriors, hurricanes, hunger. Every time he managed to shift his brain into neutral, he heard his daughter's voice singing "Twinkle, Twinkle Little Star." Nevertheless he persevered. "What should I do, Father?"

An image appeared in his mind: a bald old man. Some personified voice of authority, perhaps. He turned to Ethan and shushed him severely. "Be quiet now," he seemed to be saying. "Listen." Ethan obeyed.

It was some time before he realized he'd received an answer to his question. A new song had popped into his head. Not popped; more like surfaced. It was a Scripture memory song he'd learned long ago. "The steps of a good man are ordered by the Lord, and he delights in his way. Though he fall, he shall not be utterly cast down, for the Lord upholds him with his hand."

The song had entered his mind as if placed there by someone else, like a slide being dropped into a projector. With the verse came an instant application. "I'm in charge of what's happening to you," God was telling him. "You just keep taking steps and I'll direct them. Don't worry, I will uphold you with my hand."

Ethan felt like shouting. His heart was buoyant, as if filled with helium. The God of the universe had spoken to him. To him! How many times had that quiet voice gone unheeded? How many times had the resolution to his dilemma been right before him, if only he'd listened?

It was a revelation the likes of which Ethan had experienced very few times in his life. What a strange time and place to meet God! On the other hand, what better time or place?

The balance of power had just officially shifted into Ethan's corner. No, it hadn't just shifted, it had been there all along. The difference was that now Ethan knew it. He was entering the fray confident of a foreordained victory. God was upholding him with his very own hand. It changed everything. For the first time in years, perhaps for the first time since he'd become a Christian, Ethan faced a major struggle in his life with an almost scandalous assurance.

"I will not allow you to do this," Dr. Redding said.

Ali al-Fashir looked at him, bemused. "You build it for me but you do not wish me to use it?"

"Use it on someone else. Far away from here."

"I will test it before I leave this place." Ali gestured at the video image of John Lipscombe, who was sitting in the same death chamber in which the monkeys had died. "He is the one I choose to test it on. Forgive me, Doctor, that I do not take GeneSys at its good word, but I have been disappointed too many times not to know better."

They were in an elevated control room in one of the lab buildings. A semicircle of television and computer monitors spread before them. Here someone with the know-how could tap into what was going on in every laboratory on the island, even to the point of seeing what every microscope was looking at.

Redding folded his arms defiantly. "No one will help you."

"No?" Ali turned to one of the two guards in the room. "Go find someone in a yellow shirt and shoot him."

"Wait!" Redding shouted. "You wouldn't."

Ali sighed deeply. "Dr. Redding, do you not know what I am? I am a terrorist. We terrorists are desperate people, so I am told. We kill to make political statements. We kill for attention. Do you believe one such as this would hesitate at killing one of your minor employees?" He shrugged. "I will simply keep killing them until someone agrees to help me test out my weapon. Or you could help me kill one man and in so doing save dozens."

Redding clenched his jaw. "This is the grand destiny you had planned for him?"

"It is."

"He has a family."

"So you have said. Do you know, such things do touch me. Do you believe that?"

"If they touch you, then why not let them sway you?"

Ali waved a naughty-naughty finger at him. "This world is a hard place, Doctor. You only make it harder by trying to act like it's not so. Now—" he turned again to the monitors—"is my weapon set for testing?"

Redding looked up. "A sample of the toxin has been pre-pared for test release, yes. You do know that you won't see the effects for up to three days. I thought you were planning to be gone by then. So this man will die for nothing."

"What is the phrase you Americans use? Hmm....ah, yes: humor me."

"I will not help you, Ali," Redding said firmly. "And don't bother trying to frighten me with your guards, either. You know as well as I do they don't speak English."

Ali chuckled. "Ah, forgive my deceit." Then he turned to his guards and spoke in Arabic. One of them left. Ali turned back to Redding. "I told him to find a woman who had a young family." He gestured to the room's television control panel. "We will be able to watch the executions from this room, will we not?"

Redding's punch glanced off Ali's jaw, but the terrorist fell down from sheer surprise. The other guard beat the old man's back savagely. Ali finally called him off.

"Get up," Ali said. Then he said something to the guard, who hauled Redding to his feet.

GeneSys's senior geneticist was bleeding from a head cut and holding a bruised rib.

"I am surprised at you, Dr. Redding. A man of your advanced age and learning should know better than to go around striking madmen."

"Don't…shoot anyone," he said with difficulty. "I will help you."

"Oh, I don't know if I can catch Aziz in time." He clucked. "He's a bit hard of hearing, I'm afraid."

"If anyone dies…I won't help."

Ali shrugged. "As you wish. Anyway, I only sent Aziz to bring me some water."

The guard carried Redding toward the door. The geneticist turned back. "You should have killed me, Ali."

"All in good time, Doctor."

Because 90 percent of the GeneSys facility was currently uninhabited, and because it was late at night, any electronic activity whatsoever caught Ethan's eye as he sat in his virtual hideout. Someone had activated cameras and other specialized computer systems in the laboratory space. Ethan tapped into the live feed.

He saw a man tied to a wooden chair in the center of a glass-walled room, a hood over his slumped head. Another man approached him. He seemed to be in some pain. Ethan turned up the microphone volume.

"John, it's Oscar," the standing man said.

The sitting man stirred but didn't speak. Perhaps he was gagged.

"John, Ali wants me to test the weapon we've made for him. He wants me to test it—He wants me to test it on you, John."

The seated man sat very still. The occasional twitch of his

head suggested he was not asleep.

"I told him I wouldn't do it, but he says he'll kill our people one at a time until someone agrees to do this to you."

The standing man was holding his side and there was something that might have been blood on his forehead. He cast a hateful eye at the camera. It wasn't a look intended for Ethan; nevertheless he cringed under it.

A new voice cut in. "Take his hood off."

"Why?"

"I want to see his agony. If this weapon you have made me doesn't cause terrible pain, Dr. Redding, your task is not finished."

"I've told you the effects are not instantaneous," Dr. Redding said. "You will see nothing when he is exposed to the toxin."

"Then you will increase the dosage. Take off the hood!"

Redding took the mask off. Ethan didn't recognize the seated man.

"Very good," the lightly accented voice said. "Proceed with the test."

Ethan had heard enough. He accessed the GeneSys power grid and located the appropriate laboratory. "Let's see you run your test without power, Mr. Chehili."

It occurred to Ethan as he flipped the switch that he had officially resumed JIDIOC's mission on Clipperton: to prevent terrorists from obtaining biological weaponry. The events that had transpired to make such a thing possible were impressive. Had he not come to this island, had he not been away from the main crowd when the terrorists arrived, had he not stumbled upon this closet, had he not acquired his IOps software, he wouldn't have been poised to save this man's life and continue the JIDIOC mission.

The steps of a good man...

"Sir?"

John Hawkwood took the VR helmet off. "What is it?"

"I don't know if it's important," the prematurely balding teenager said, "but some of the rooms in building four just lost power."

"Which rooms?" Hawkwood demanded, already raising his helmet again.

Ethan released control of the GeneSys power grid. The power stayed off in the selected rooms, but he needed to get away from the scene of the crime. He backed away from the grid's online representation—a radio shack. Seconds later an artificial body flew from the White Company's penitentiary toward the shack.

Hello, Mr. Hawkwood, Ethan said to himself.

Now that he had his suite of IOps software, Ethan felt in charge again. It was a dangerous feeling, likely to give him a false sense of security. But it just felt so good to be empowered.

Ethan set about changing how things in the GeneSys network appeared to him when he looked through his purloined VR goggles. In virtual reality, everything was configurable to one's liking. True to his medieval heart, he elected to portray the White Company's computer complex as a castle guarding a mountain pass. The castle protected a pastoral, thatched-roof village—the GeneSys network. The newcomer, whom Ethan's software now depicted as a man-at-arms, ran to the village watermill (until recently a radio shack) and began tinkering with the gears.

Things could get tricky if Hawkwood—if it was indeed him—decided to turn the power to the labs on again and leave a guard. Having two sets of Black Hats to contend with, the high-tech White Company and the low-tech Chehili terrorists, made things infinitely more intricate. Having to protect a man Ethan could see only through the occasional camera feed while himself remaining hidden sent it off the register.

Ethan decided it was time for a little misdirection. Hawkwood had shown on more than one occasion his propensity to jump to trouble spots, leaving other sites unguarded.

A quick check of the castle's inner ward revealed that Hawkwood had intensified the defenses arrayed against his own people. His computers recorded every move they made. He was responding to Ethan's manipulations nicely.

Hawkwood zipped from the watermill back into the castle.

Ethan conjured up a simple bot and mapped a data signature he'd copied from one of Hawkwood's men onto it. He sent it into the mill. If Hawkwood had set any traps, the bot would set them off and the path of blame would lead straight back to the White Company. The bot returned untouched and undetected. Ethan erased it just to be sure.

Then, at full stealth, he visited the mill himself. Power had indeed been restored to all the rooms, but there were no active camera feeds. Perhaps the test had been postponed. He stationed a new bot in front of the displays and another to guard the perimeter.

The bots he was using were simplistic programs. Nothing on the order of what Ethan had dealt with against Yoseph and Alternate Realities. They were more elementary even than the guardbots he used to have protecting him in cyberspace. They were single-task artificial intelligences, rather like a purple rabbit named Thumper he'd once known.

He placed two more of these on alert to tell him whenever anyone sallied forth from the castle, heading either into the village (GeneSys) or to the mountain pass (GlobeNet).

A chime drew his attention to the weather downlink. The bot he'd left watching it reported that something had changed.

Ethan displayed the weather report in a pane he conjured into the air before him.

The hurricane was nearer. A twelve-hour time-lapse animation showed the storm picking up speed. Clipperton, picked out in bright blue, vanished under Flossie's leading arm. Projections put the worst of it ashore in nine hours, 8 A.M.

It didn't concern Ethan. He was confident of the buildings' ability to withstand the storm. If anything, Flossie would either sink the terrorists' ship or prevent them from leaving for a while. Every hour that passed brought help closer. Or so Ethan hoped.

"It's a nice weather report," he said to his bot, "but why did you call me? What changed?"

The software agent, a generic biped model, pointed at a line of text scrolling by at the bottom of the pane.

New storm being tracked: Hurricane Curly.

"Hurricane Curly?" Ethan said dryly. "I don't think so."

He selected the text, expecting a chopped-up e-mail message. With the White Company's security protocols back up, all messages would have to go back and forth in 1KB chunks.

Instead, he materialized in a plain virtual room he recognized instantly. A wire-grid floor stretched to the artificial horizon. Stylized figures stood in rows as in a group photo at a costume ball. He saw soldiers, sailors, candlestick makers, and more. All with real-video faces.

"Greetings, Brainiac," someone said.

Ethan recognized the voice. "Mike?"

"In the flesh," he said. The voice came from a caricatured cowboy. He stood in the back row, presumably because the ten-gallon hat stuck up so tall. "Well, sort of flesh."

The other members of the Joint Intelligence Detail, Information Operations and Counter-Cyberterrorism, Provisional team greeted Ethan in turn.

"How are we doing this? There's way too much data going on here to fit in signal pulses."

"You'll have to ask the brains," Gillette said.

Ethan looked at the rocket scientists and nerds. "Well?"

"Don't look at us," one said.

"What's that supposed to mean?"

They pointed to a paunchy figure in a massive sombrero. It was the only person in the artificial room with a computer-animated face. "Who are you?"

"Hi, Dad."

"Jordan! How——? No, sir. Get out of here this minute, young man."

"But——"

"Does your mother know you're here?" Ethan drove the hombre toward the edge of the room. "It's after eleven. Are you in the hotel room? Keeping Katie awake?"

"Dad! If y——"

"Go on, Jordan. I want you out of here."

"Hang on there, Tex," Gillette said. "Whoa, Bessie. Kaye knows he's here. In fact, she's the one who kind of blackmailed me into letting him be here. Right now I'm glad she did, since Junior here's the one who made this little powwow possible. He figured out how to… Tell him what you figured out how to do, kid."

"I defeated your weather-report patch, Dad. Sorry."

Ethan didn't know whether to be furious or to laugh. "Is your mother there now?"

"She's taking a bath. But Mike's not kidding. She wants me to help out."

"Are you guys okay? How's Katie?"

"She's fine, Dad. Uh, don't you want to have this meeting?"

"I…That patch was supposed to be foolproof."

"I'll show you what I did later. I know how you work, remember?"

Ethan looked at his son. "You're Hurricane Curly, aren't you?"

Jordan swept off his sombrero in an elaborate bow.

"The name was my idea," Gillette said. "I remembered you

used to call yourself that. I figured it would get your attention."

"It did," Ethan said. "Wow, seeing you all here makes me feel like I'm back home. Wait a minute. I thought Roy disbanded you guys."

"The director of Central Intelligence," a redheaded soldier boy said with mock seriousness, "has been instructed to take some well-deserved vacation time while his status is reevaluated."

Ethan was glad his virtual face didn't let his smile show. "Oh."

"I was put under presidential edict," the cowboy said, "to get this posse saddled up again. So here we are."

"Did you get our delivery?" a rocket scientist asked.

"It was perfect, Sai. I'm in business now, thanks." Ethan moved away to address the whole group. "Let me tell you guys what my situation is. I'm hiding in a closet. There's a hurricane about to blow us into the ocean. The biological weapon is ready, I think. The chief terrorist wants to test it out on a hostage and is threatening to shoot others from the cafeteria. Far as I can figure, Hawkwood's only brought part of the White Company to Clipperton. Maybe you all can look for the other part? And I'm fresh out of food. I'm hoping somebody's about to tell me the cavalry's on its way."

"It's not the cavalry," a sailor figure said, "it's the United States Navy. I won't give details on this line, but let's just say that if you hear shooting, keep your head down."

"I'm good at that," Ethan said. "All right, here are my goals for us: I want to prevent this weapon from leaving this island; I want Chehili put out of commission; I want the hostages saved; I'd love for GeneSys to mysteriously go out of business; and most of all I want the White Company taken down. I want Hawkwood personally apprehended and all his people, here and wherever else they might be, sent to jail. Now, how can we do these things?"

Ethan hadn't realized how good it felt to command this elite force. He'd been so nervous in the early days. But now, suddenly reinstalled as their leader, he understood how much he'd missed it. It also struck him, hearing himself list off objectives, that he was good at it.

"The Algerians and the hostages are as good as taken care of," the sailor said. "We'll get Hawkwood and the others, too."

"We won't be able to find the White Company's stateside headquarters without help." Ethan recognized Elizabeth Lee's voice. "We need Hawkwood to contact them."

Ethan considered it. "I'll see what I can do. You just be watching."

"Always, sir."

"Mike," Ethan said, "you be in charge of making sure everybody has a chance to contribute. Let's make this a whole-team effort."

"Gotcha, podner."

"All right, sportsfans, let's get to it. It—it's nice to be back with you all."

"Don't you worry," Barnes said. "We'll get you out of there safe and sound."

"Good to hear it."

The JIDIOC crew began popping off line.

"Hold it, José," Ethan said to his son.

"Yeah, Dad?"

Ethan waited until they were alone. "Good job setting this meeting up."

"Okay." Even in cyberspace Jordan squirmed under praise.

"You are in the hotel room in Acapulco, right? That's what your choice of costume is telling me, isn't it?"

"'Course, Dad. Our tickets aren't for four more days."

"Oh, right. What day is it, anyway?"

"In about an hour it will be the fourth of July. Wednesday. Hey, Dad," Jordan said, "what's it like in a hurricane?"

"Loud. Actually, son, I'm trying not to go outside. I can feel it shake the building, though."

"Whoa, cool. Do you think you'll get picked up and thrown

like a Frisbee and maybe land in Guam or something?"

"I hope not. Jordan, can you give your mother a message for me?"

"Uh-huh."

"Tell her I love her and that I'm being safe. As safe as I can with bad guys running all over the place and a hurricane about to throw me to Guam."

Jordan giggled. "Okay."

"Give your sister a hug for me."

"Forget it."

Ethan smiled. "It's good to hear your voice, son."

"You, too, Dad."

"We can't hold position in this wind any longer," the ship captain said over the radio.

"Stay where you are," Ali said. "We only need a few hours more here. We'll come aboard with our package at first light and we can leave then."

The radio transmission was badly distorted. The captain was shouting. "We'll capsize or run aground! We can't stay."

"You will stay."

"We'll run ahead of the storm and turn south. We'll be back in twenty-four hours."

"Stay where you are or, as Allah is my witness, I will have your heart for my dinner."

The radio squawked. For a time the captain did not answer. When he did he seemed calmer. "Very well, Ali. We will stay. I will keep her steaming into the wind. Your hovercraft will not make the passage. The cyclone will flip it like a tortoise. I will be here to see it. Then I will go home."

CHAPTER TWENTY

While Tamara went into the ladies' room, her terrorist sat out in the wide hallway, trying to stay awake.

Tamara checked all the stalls but found no one. She pulled half a sandwich out of her coat pocket and unwrapped it. "Hey," she whispered to the ceiling, "Ethan, I brought food again."

She'd brought food after every meal since their first ladies' room encounter. Her terrorist must've thought she'd developed some kind of bladder condition, considering how many trips she made.

But Hamilton had not returned. She decided to leave the sandwich on the back of the toilet. She would come back in the morning and, if it was still there, flush it.

She lingered in the stall. She didn't want to go back to her lab. Somehow, she wasn't quite sure how, she had completed the hated work order. Though she normally took pride in completing difficult tasks, this one shamed her. The only thing worse than working on a biological weapon for terrorists was handing the finished product over to them. Who could tell all the consequences of what she had done here?

Lord, how did this happen? What should I do?

She determined to destroy all the notes she'd taken along

the way. Someone else might repeat this procedure, but it wouldn't be from copying Tamara Mack.

Fourth Platoon's trans-Pacific flight from Hawaii was uneventful. The fourteen men slept as much as they could. Increasing turbulence marked the end of the ten-hour flight.

When the submarine had been contacted and sighted, the MC-130 dropped to wave-top height to perform a nighttime "rubber duck" maneuver. Fourth Platoon parachuted out behind their Combat Rubber Raiding Crafts, then climbed inside them.

The USS *George M. Jackson*, one of two submarines in the Pacific equipped with the Advanced SEAL Delivery System (ASDS), gathered the SEALs up and headed southeast for Clipperton Island at flank speed.

Andy Culbertson read the message that had appeared in his e-mailbox.

> Culbertson,
> Now that our defenses are in place again, get a message out to our other location. Update them about our status. Have them send an activity log. I want to see if everybody's doing what they ought while the cat's away.
> Hawkwood

As night warden of the computer at the very front of the White Company's defenses, it was no surprise that the message would come to him. Andy looked across the entertainment room to his boss's desk. Hawkwood wasn't there. Perhaps he'd joined the others, who were trying to get some sleep. It was after two in the morning, after all. But that meant he must've sent the message some time ago—why hadn't it popped into his box until now? *Oh, well,* he thought, *maybe it's the storm.*

Andy composed a message to the Indianapolis HQ, but before he sent it, he took the opportunity to bundle with it a private message of his own. His beloved Cindy had been without him for almost two weeks now. She might not even recognize Andy's name anymore. Best to keep his presence fresh in her memory. He wouldn't be on this rock forever, after all. He encrypted both messages and fired them off.

"Good news, Dave. We have a winner!"

Mike Gillette found Kelly Barnes's face on his large monitor. "What is it, Mr. Barnes?"

"Sir, Romulan Warbird uncloaking off our bow."

"Speak English, boy."

"The White Company, sir! The Clipperton group. They've just sent a message to their buddies. Some other message, too. Looks personal."

Gillette leaned forward. "We got 'em? Where? Where are they?"

Barnes glanced at his monitor. "Indianapolis."

"Send it to me, Mr. Barnes," Gillette said, already dialing his vidphone. "Give me everything that might help us find them."

"You got it, sir." Barnes's voice took on a quasi-British accent. "Our first catch of the day."

On board the USS *George M. Jackson,* platoon commander Lieutenant Morris "Buck" Sanders read Fourth Platoon's orders. "Operation Sea Fire. Approach Clipperton via ASDS. Neutralize Chehili terrorists. Apprehend White Company computer technicians. Avoid civilian casualties. Extract via ASDS to USS *George M. Jackson.* Tactical note: Hurricane Flossie."

Platoon Chief Petty Officer HTCS Patrick Logan looked incredulously at his commanding officer. "That's some tactical note."

"Stow it, Logan," Sanders said. "Nighty-night, SEALs. Try to get some more shut-eye and read your briefings. We've got about six hours of hurry-up-and-wait time. I told you this would be better than Honolulu, didn't I?" He checked his watch. "I want team leaders at my bunk at oh-five-hundred and gear prepped for inspection at oh-five-thirty. Dismissed."

Andy Culbertson's first hint that something was wrong was Hawkwood's shout of rage.

"Culbertson!"

I'm dead, Andy thought, trying to remember what evil thing he'd done for which he was about to be crucified. Hawkwood had been in a foul, suspicious mood all night. All he'd needed was someone to pin it on. Andy stood as his boss approached. *I am seriously dead.*

"Don't try to run, cockroach," Hawkwood said. "You're on an island."

Andy held his ground. "What did I do?"

Hawkwood looked at the teenage boys waking up around him. "Who's in it with you, huh? Sforza, I bet. Zizka?"

The ones named pleaded their innocence.

"It was the girl, wasn't it?" Hawkwood was back in Andy's face. "I took you away from your—" he made an obscene gesture—"didn't I? So you get me back, huh? But you bring us all down. You bring yourself down." He pushed Andy backwards against an equipment table. "What's the matter with you? Don't you even want to deny it? Go ahead. You've earned a big gloat. I'm sure you've rehearsed one. Let's hear it."

"What did I do?"

Hawkwood laughed mirthlessly. "Watch him, gentlemen. He's good. You are accused of treason. Of breaking EMCON and sending private e-mail to your woman. Of betraying our position to those who would prosecute us. And all for the love of a dame."

Andy walked to his computer and printed out Hawkwood's e-mail. "Is this what you're talking about?"

Hawkwood snatched the paper. He read it aloud, beginning scornfully, ending dully. "Where did you get this?"

It was Andy's turn to laugh. "You sent it to me."

"No, I didn't."

"Our brilliant leader," Andy said, his sealed doom giving him boldness, "sent me e-mail telling me to update our headquarters in Indianapolis. You can read the message yourself. Then, when I do it, he attacks. All I can say is that you guys better be careful before doing what he tells you, because you might go to the wall for it."

"I never sent this message," Hawkwood said, mostly to himself.

Andy shrugged. "It came from your computer, it's signed by—"

"No, it didn't." Hawkwood marched to his own computer and typed. Instead of countering Andy's accusation, however, Hawkwood fell into his chair and cursed. "How'd you do that?"

"You know," Andy said calmly, "I used to want to be just like you."

Culbertson's dig went unheard. Hawkwood was intent upon the information on his monitor. He was tracing the mysterious message.

It really had gone through Hawkwood's computer. That was the strangest part. It bore a relatively simple routing log—from his computer to the local network, from the network to a router, from the router to Culbertson's computer. It was absolutely certain that this message had originated at Hawkwood's computer. Except of course that it couldn't have. He'd only been away from the keys long enough to go to the men's room.

Someone had posed as John Hawkwood in order to convince Culbertson to break the communications silence. But why? Was someone trying to frame Culbertson? Surely not— what would he gain? Or was someone trying to expose the White Company's location to the world watching on GlobeNet? Again, why? If someone on this team wanted to destroy Hawkwood while remaining anonymous, why would he wait until he'd dragged everyone to Clipperton, thus radically reducing the number of possible suspects to hide among? It didn't add up.

John Hawkwood rubbed his eyes vigorously. There were only two possible solutions: either Hawkwood sent this message himself (which he was sure wasn't true) or someone on his team had sent it.

Hawkwood looked at them now. These fifteen he'd picked to bring to Clipperton because of their abilities, certainly, but especially because of the loyalty to him they'd displayed over the months. They were the cream of Hawkwood's crop. He really must be paranoid to suspect any one of them. But there weren't any other options.

Hawkwood's head cocked. Yes, there were.

The USS *George M. Jackson* arrived on station to the west of Clipperton Island at 6:49 on the morning of July 4. At a depth of forty feet, the Pacific Ocean was calm, though the surface was in chaos. The men of Fourth Platoon, Detachment Echo, SEAL Team Nine stood by their ASDS minisub, awaiting orders to assault the island.

The Advanced SEAL Delivery System was essentially a small submarine. The advantage of this vehicle over its predecessor (the SEAL Delivery Vehicle, SDV) was that eight men—roughly half a platoon—could ride together, without harm from the occasional shark, all the way to the egress point, and there disembark simultaneously. The SDVs—essentially self-propelled pallets—had carried only two men and had left them exposed to the environment.

Though the powers that be had sunk billions of dollars into developing the ASDS vehicle and outfitting four submarines as mother ships, many SEALs despised the little subs. The fact that it required two trips to ferry an entire platoon was a regular complaint.

Fourth Platoon's commanding officer, Lieutenant "Buck" Sanders, stood at a map table with the *Jackson's* intelligence officer, considering infrared satellite imagery of the GeneSys complex.

"Where are they?" Sanders asked.

The intelligence officer, Lieutenant Kevin Archibald, drew a circle around one of the buildings standing like ships in formation in Clipperton's lagoon. "Sir, the on-site contact has the civilians here, in the cafeteria. People are pretty much staying inside due to the storm, but via satellite we've also been able to detect limited movement to and from these three buildings as well. You'll be coming in from the southwest." He pointed. "Here."

"What's this?" Sanders indicated a white blob to the north of the island.

"The Algerian tanker, sir," Archibald said. "She's listing pretty badly in the wind. Skipper's trying to keep her dead into it, but we're staying clear of her."

"What's she doing out in this?"

"Getaway car, sir."

"Very good. Now," Sanders said, "can we shoot at anything that moves, or do we have to check fire?"

"Best check fire, sir."

Sanders swore.

"I can give you a tip, though," Archibald said. "If it carries a weapon, you can shoot it."

"That we can live with."

"Hey, look! It's Forrest Gump."

Everyone laughed. The man whose picture stared out at them from Hawkwood's computer monitor did resemble the gumbo millionaire.

The members of the White Company, Andy Culbertson included, sat around Hawkwood's desk in a casual semicircle. They were going through the digitized freeze-frames of the latest batch of guests, looking for anyone suspicious. It was just before 7 A.M.

Hawkwood had told them his theory that it might be a stranger to Clipperton who was causing their security breaches. The idea of a mysterious adversary who was not of their number had had the effect of solidifying them and swelling morale. That no such phantom had yet been proven to exist was considered an irrelevant detail. In a sense, they needed to believe in him. Now all they lacked was pizza. Even John Hawkwood seemed relaxed.

"And here's Vice President Gwent," the young man called Gneisenau said. "'Duh, where's my pantyhose, boys? Oh, sorry, Donna, are these yours?'"

They laughed, perhaps more heartily than the joke deserved. Few of them had slept more than a handful of hours. Hawkwood turned to the next photo: a picture of a thin, thirty-something white man with a slightly receding hairline.

The teenagers were quiet, each one trying to come up with something clever to say. Finally someone said, "Hey, I know that guy."

"Yeah," Andy Culbertson said, "it's your boyfriend, Ward."

"No," Ward said over the laughter, "I'm serious." He sat up. "That guy was in this room day before yesterday. Remember him, Sforza? Over there by the cockpits?"

"Was it that guy?"

"Yes!"

Hawkwood brought the guest's name onto the screen.

Ethan Hamilton.

"What's wrong, Mr. Hawkwood?"

They still sat in their semicircle, but all levity had vanished. Hawkwood sat unmoving, a hand to the side of his head. A few other White Company members had cursed and walked away.

"I don't get it," Andy Culbertson said. "Who is he?"

"It's Hamilton, dude," Sforza said. "Ethan Hamilton."

"You're gonna have to tell me."

"You ever hear of a guy called himself Patriot?" Gneisenau, Hawkwood's second-in-command, said. "Kind of a superhacker."

"'Course!" Andy said. "Who hasn't?"

Gneisenau pointed at the monitor. "This is the guy that brought him down."

Andy's eyes locked onto the screen. "That guy? Looks like a dweeb."

"May be, but he's a kickin'-tail-and-takin'-names 'Net jock."

"Remember last year when that AI just about wiped every-body out?" Sforza asked.

"I don't live in a total hole, dude," Andy said.

"Remember the name of the guy who stopped it?"

Again Andy's eyes popped to the screen. "Don't tell me."

"And he's here, man. On the island! Doing us in."

The robot drone plane Iroquois circled lazily within Flossie's twenty-mile-wide eye. Though it could not appreciate it, the view was magnificent. A monstrous thick spiral of dirty white cloud, evocative—to a human, perhaps—of the Milky Way.

At the designated time, Iroquois released a dropsonde. The

instrument pack, descending on a parachute, measured temperature, air pressure, wind direction, and humidity within the eye. The dropsonde relayed the information back to computers aboard the unmanned hurricane hunter, which sent it on to the National Hurricane Center.

Since 1943, when Army Air Corps Colonel Joseph Duckworth and his navigator had made their first, impulsive flight into a hurricane, people had argued about the wisdom and benefits of so-called hurricane hunting.

Some said that satellites and improved radar made such flights superfluous, leaving only the dangerous elements. They pointed to the four hurricane hunter aircraft that had been claimed without trace by previous storms. Others said that a satellite could never deliver the up-close-and-personal data that a plane in the eye could. The rapid strengthening of a hurricane just before landfall, for instance, was almost always first spotted by hurricane hunter aircraft.

With the advancement of AI, both positions could be pleased. Now robot planes penetrated the eye wall, getting firsthand data, but without risking human life. The only losers, perhaps, were the pilots whose hunger for danger had to be sated elsewhere.

The data from the dropsonde continued to come in. Winds had climbed to 135 mph. Barometric pressure had fallen to 27.7 inches. At the NHC, Flossie was upgraded to category four.

Category four hurricanes uproot trees with ease and turn them into missiles traveling one hundred fifty miles an hour. Boats are flicked away like crumbs of food. Mobile homes are puffs of wood blowing by.

The Iroquois calculated the probable dome size caused by the current air pressure. The low pressure at Flossie's center sucked up a mound of water under her eye like water in a straw. If Flossie ever hit land, she would carry this water for miles inland, creating a twenty-foot storm surge. Storm surges could raise the water level four feet in four seconds. They caused nine out of ten hurricane deaths.

The software that operated Iroquois had no algorithms to feel compassion for anything in Flossie's path. It only circled patiently, releasing the occasional dropsonde.

John Hawkwood sent his adepts through the crowded cafeteria with a printout of Ethan Hamilton's photo. Though he was fairly certain they wouldn't find him here—surely Ali wouldn't allow his hostages to sit at computers and jack into the network—not to look here would be foolish. Hiding in plain sight was just what Hawkwood would do in Hamilton's position.

His men came back with nothing. A few guests and one GeneSys tour guide recognized the picture, but all said they hadn't seen him in days. One suggested he might've been shot in the terrorists' initial attack.

Hamilton could be anywhere, Hawkwood realized. Communications lines between all the buildings were interconnected. All someone would need was a computer and a phone jack. With everyone locked up in here, there were hundreds of computers and phone jacks available.

Hawkwood led his boys back through the torrential rain to the engineering building.

Ethan was almost bored. He hoped his forged message to Andy Culbertson had given his JIDIOC team all the clues they would need to find the White Company's hidden fortress. The Navy was on its way. He was monitoring every lab on Clipperton for another execution attempt. He was the only human on this floor of a large building—a floor to which there was no reason anyone would go. There was danger, certainly, but it seemed remote. Right now there wasn't much for him to do.

His computer told him it was seven in the morning. According to the weather satellite, which was giving static more and more, Hurricane Flossie's worst winds were only an hour away. The building creaked rhythmically and the venting howled, but beyond these the storm seemed to have no power to reach him. He'd found sandwich and soda machines on the top floor of the building and a stash of coins in a desk, so he was well nourished. This was the way, Ethan decided, to ride out a hurricane.

Nothing much to do but wait. He spent his time reading or practicing the listening prayer he'd learned from *With Christ in the School of Prayer.* The rest of the time he dozed. His borrowed computer would alert him if anything changed.

CHAPTER TWENTY-ONE

amara Mack sat next to Dr. Redding in the cafeteria. She had turned the purified botulin toxin over to a team of technicians who were now mass producing it into fifty-gallon drums, suspending it into the mist solution, and bottling it into Thermos-sized aerosol canisters. It was out of her hands now. Her terrorist stood at Ali's table, waiting for an audience.

She looked around the dining hall. It looked like an indoor refugee camp. Makeshift walls of tablecloth marked off certain sections for dubious privacy. The windows showed only gray light. Rain pelted the transparent shielding almost horizontally, giving the impression that the whole building was being driven through a car wash.

In the cafeteria, Tamara noticed, normal social hierarchy had been laid aside. Junior mechanics could be seen to hold sway among groups of PhDs. Custodians and expert biologists had become fast friends. It was an admirable society, she mused. One in which strength of character counted for more than titles or pedigrees.

Tamara had been excluded from its formation because of her special role in the terrorists' drama. She wondered what strength of character she had and where it would've placed her. She looked at Dr. Redding beside her—visibly sore and bandaged, but stable. At least now she was on friendly terms with this brilliant man. Should she thank Ali for that?

"Doctor," Tamara said, "what have we done?"

He looked at her a long moment before speaking. "You are so young. Too young to be touched by this. I at least was an old man before I'd built my first weapon of mass destruction." He stared into space. "You know, over the years I secretly hoped that one of these things I built for men like Ali would find its way to Australia and be used on Mortimer McCall."

"What did Mr. McCall do?"

"Don't you know, my dear? Don't you see what we do here? This is McCall's little black box. Have you ever seen GeneSys's charter? No? I have. McCall's name isn't on it. When all this is over," he said, indicating the terrorists, "we will all be ruined and GeneSys will be gone. But McCall won't even be touched."

They sat sullenly for a while. The building swayed slightly beneath their feet.

"I have arranged a surprise for them," Redding said.

"For who?"

"Them." He nodded toward Ali. "A nice little surprise."

"What have you done?"

He pointed with his chin. "Do you see the water they're drinking?"

Tamara saw a sweating pitcher on Ali's table. "Did you do something to it?"

"Do you remember last spring when we announced the discovery of the genetic disposition to violent behavior?"

"The Hate Gene, sure. But wasn't that pretty much discredited? No offense, sir."

"Not completely," Redding said. "It was more complex than we'd realized—it's a combination of about twelve genes, actually—but the fundamental discovery was genuine. Even though the Hate Gene was disproven, its treatment remains infallible."

"I don't think I ever heard about the treatment," Tamara said.

"No, you wouldn't have. We didn't dare announce it in the wake of the public relations fiasco."

"Dr. Redding, what have you done?"

"Let's just say that in about two days, everyone who drinks that water will be about as violent as Quakers."

Tamara inhaled. "You didn't." She almost giggled. "But two days. Won't that be too late?"

"Not if they head off in that tub of theirs."

"Won't they just give the canisters to somebody else who will use them?"

"It's just one dose, my dear. The effects won't be permanent. But if we're lucky, they'll pull into port and start picking daisies instead of setting off canisters. If we're very lucky, they'll get picked up by the authorities and their weapon seized."

Redding silenced the objection on Tamara's lips. "My child, I have done what I could. My conscience is at rest, for the first time in many years. Not that we'll be around to appreciate their distress." He sighed deeply. "Have I ever told you about a patient I once had? A little boy by the name of Gabr—?"

"Dr. Redding, what do you mean we won't be around? You don't think…"

"Come, come, girl. They are making good their getaway on a slow ship. They won't reach their destination for weeks. If they leave anyone alive here they know we will send someone to the mainland by boat. Their ship will not be safely away in time. No, they cannot afford to leave us behind. Our days—perhaps our hours—are numbered." He patted her leg. "We have done what we could, eh?"

The man who had been speaking with Ali walked away, and her terrorist moved forward. Ali looked over at Tamara while he listened. It sent a cold spike through her arms and down to her fingers. He said a single word to her terrorist and looked down at his papers. Her terrorist did not meet her eyes when he approached and took her by the arm.

Oh dear Jesus, Tamara prayed, *help!*

Someone was thinking about Ethan's wife and children, and it wasn't Ethan.

John Hawkwood stared, in GlobeNet, at the Hamilton family's travel itinerary. He flew through cyberspace tracing their path backwards from Acapulco to DFW International Airport to Tyler Municipal Airport to their home. He made tentative probes into the house computer's defenses but found them predictably robust. Then he zoomed back to Mexico and found the hotel where Mrs. Hamilton was staying with her two children.

Hawkwood tapped a finger. It wasn't every day one tested one's mettle against a legend. He would have to think of an appropriate opening salvo. He went over in his mind the story of Ethan Hamilton and Patriot, the event that had secured Hamilton a place in the GlobeNet Pantheon. Perhaps something there would inspire him.

Something did.

The ASDS pulled away from the *George M. Jackson's* wet dock at oh-seven-thirty hours, on the first of two planned trips. Eight SEALs from Fourth Platoon, Detachment Echo, SEAL Team Nine rode in the minisub, equipped for underwater insertion. In addition to the diving gear, each carried a full array of waterproofed weapons, electronics, and explosives. They were the world's premier unconventional warfare force, moving in to do what they did best: antiterrorism. Operation Sea Fire was under way.

At a depth of forty feet the sea was stable but unusually murky. The sailor piloting the ASDS saw little marine life and no predators at all. At the specified spot, the SEALs left the ASDS one at a time and began swimming to shore using bubbleless scuba gear. When the last diver was out, the pilot turned the minisub toward the *Jackson,* where he would take on the remaining SEALs. The plan was to assemble inside a designated GeneSys building, then move on the cafeteria.

As the divers ascended, the sea became trickier. The hurricane had raised sea level in the area enough to carry the SEALs over the treacherous coral reefs skirting the island. That was the good news.

The bad news was that there was very little island left. Waves, under the occasional wind gust in excess of 150 mph, swept all the way across the island without stopping. The atoll's freshwater lagoon was gone, marked only by a slightly calmer place on the storm-driven ocean.

The GeneSys buildings broke the waves prow-first, like iron ships somehow immune to the rolling of the surf. At this moment they were the only fixed points in the visible world. The water level was still rising, consuming the buildings' sea legs. Waves brushed the undersides of the buildings. If the eye of the hurricane passed anywhere close by, the dome would raise the sea level even more.

A fair weather plan might've had the SEALs hitting the beach at night and simply climbing up the target building's pilings. As it was they were hitting it in the morning, there was no beach, the pilings were immersed, and a hurricane was driving waves onto the buildings themselves. No matter. They were SEALs with a mission to accomplish. Somehow they would make it happen.

Ali al-Fashir gripped the walkway's steel railing. Though his parka and black mask covered all but a tiny hole over his eyes, his face was drenched. The wind wanted him. It shoved him back and lifted at his legs. The world was losing its color. Green trees and tan beach and red land crabs were all draining into something that might have been blue.

He could not see the ship, though he was looking right toward it. No dark silhouette, no running lights. Nor could he hear its churning engine or waves breaking over its bow. Silhouettes of a few bent coconut palm trees, the veritable symbol of hurricanes, were all he could see.

The hurricane, which had thus far been Ali's accomplice, extending the time before any government could try to intercept him, was proving an opponent. He desperately wanted to leave this island now that he had his precious weapon, but there was no way to get to the ship.

He fought his way back inside. He would have to wait out the storm. After it passed, perhaps it would still hinder any pursuit while providing his ship cover for their escape.

The advantage of virtual reality, thought Special Agent Mike Gillette, was that when you wanted to save the world you didn't have to get up from your easy chair to do it.

Gillette was aboard an American Airlines flight headed for Indianapolis. The captain had turned off the No Electronics light, and Gillette was unpacking his mobile computer. It took a minute to figure out the travel VR headset. It was lightweight plastic folded along about a million metal hinges. He finally asked the little girl in the seat next to him for help. He placed the headset on and plugged in.

A few misfires later, Gillette was in contact with Major Elizabeth Lee, and through her, with the whole JIDIOC bunch.

"Good morning, everybody," he said.

The travel headgear didn't afford the same feeling of immersion that a normal helmet did. Gillette was instantly aware of how loud his voice was in the crowded airplane cabin. He wondered briefly how many times people had listened in to his supposedly private conversations. He leaned against the window and covered the mouthpiece.

"What's news?" he said.

The delegates of each of the United States intelligence agencies gave their status reports.

In his setup Gillette had selected a teleconference format called Theater in the Round. He instantly regretted it. He stood in a virtual room surrounded by the JIDIOC team members. Every time someone spoke, he had to spin around looking for the speaker. By the time he found the right person, someone else was talking.

"So what y'all are telling me," he said, "is that we're not doing much."

"There's not much more we can do," CIA agent Dean Berry said. "The Navy's taking care of the situation on the island. We're all here to offer whatever support they might need. You're handling the Indianapolis hit yourself. Besides that, I don't know what needs to be done."

Several others concurred.

"Somebody can give me an address in Indianapolis, for one thing," Gillette said. "It's a big place, I hear."

"We're working on it," Captain Kelly Barnes said. "But they're not going to be easy to find. The address had the Club on it," he said, referring to the nickname of an especially effective encryption routine.

Gillette finally located Barnes in the virtual room. "What about that personal message you said came with it?"

"We're working on that," an NSA agent said, causing Gillette to spin again. "It's encrypted, too, of course, but not with the Club. We think we're close."

"Good," Gillette said. "Maybe we can lean on whoever it was sent to to find a hard address for the HQ. Get it to me as soon as you have anything."

"Will do."

"Now, I cannot believe there's nothing more the great American spook force can do in this situation. Come on, people, let's do this right."

CHAPTER TWENTY-TWO

Kaye Hamilton terminated the long distance vidphone call. Her parents had agreed to get the prayer chain going again. How was it that Kaye always found herself in this situation, getting people to pray for her husband who was out trying to get himself killed? If Ethan were a little more timid, they wouldn't be having this problem. The yes-but-he's-so-heroic argument didn't do much more than infuriate her these days.

"What'd I do?" Jordan said.

Kaye looked at her son, who had lowered his VR goggles from his head. "What, honey?"

"You humphed," the boy said. "You only do that when you're mad. What'd I do?"

"Oh." Kaye walked over to the king-sized hotel bed, where Katie was still sleeping. "I didn't realize I'd said it out loud. Never mind."

"You're thinking about Dad, aren't you?"

She lay back on the bed. "Always."

"Me, too."

Someone knocked on the door.

Jordan stood up. "I'll get it."

"Check through the chain first, honey."

He did. "Uh, Mom, there are some policemen or soldiers or something outside."

Kaye sat up. "Maybe they've heard something. Let them in."

Three Hispanic men in police uniforms walked into their hotel room. One, a trim man with a mustache, spoke. "Señora Hamilton?"

"Yes, that's me."

"Come with us, por favor?"

Kaye put on her shoes. "What is it? Has the storm passed?"

"No."

The policemen spoke in Spanish a while. One laughed. Katie woke from her nap frightened. Kaye held her. The first officer turned back to Kaye.

"Señora, *sus niños y usted* come with us."

The laughter had unnerved Kaye. "Why?"

The officer showed her a piece of paper.

"I don't read Spanish," she said.

"No? I will translate." He looked at the document. "The city of Acapulco, the state of Guerrero, and the great nation of Mexico would like to invite you for a prolonged visit of the most excellent San Juan jail."

"What!"

"For trafficking illegal drugs."

Kaye stood. "What! That's crazy!"

"Tsk tsk. Señora Hamilton, your government does not think we fight drugs in Mexico. Perhaps now they will believe. Come. Your crimes are very serious."

"This is crazy!" Kaye sat down heavily on the bed. Katie whined. "I'm not going with you," Kaye said.

Jordan, who had been collecting his portable computer, made a break for the hallway. The two other policemen went after him.

"Your children," the first officer said, "will be held at a juvenile facility nearby. When your husband returns, he will also be charged with drug trafficking."

"This isn't happening," Kaye said, stunned.

The policeman produced very real handcuffs and dangled them in front of Kaye's face. "You want me to use these?"

Jordan was carried in, biting and flailing. "Someone did this to us, Mom!" he said. "By computer. Just like Patriot!"

"Omigosh," Kaye said dismally. Then she stood and allowed herself to be led to a Mexican jail.

Hawkwood chuckled softly. He was watching the police's computers. Kaye Hamilton's arrest status went from At Large to In Custody. "Let's see you dig yourself out of that one." Sending Hamilton's family to jail wasn't Hawkwood's usual style, but he felt it was appropriate. He wondered if Patriot's mother was still in the Jamaican prison.

"Zizka," he said to one of his teenage employees, "call up schematics of this building. Find the phone room and cut us off from the other buildings."

"Gotcha, Mr. Hawkwood, sir."

When Zizka got to the door, the two Chehili guards didn't want to let him go. Zizka tried to explain by pantomime. In the end, one of the guards just accompanied him on his errand.

It was 9:45 A.M., Eastern time. Most of the JIDIOC team members hadn't gotten much sleep. Now they were showing it.

Major Fontana and Giorgio Vinzetti were having an almost-civil disagreement. Larry Templeton of the National Imagery & Mapping Agency tried to restore order. "Okay, Fontana, Vinzetti, what's this about?"

Vinzetti answered. "Major Catastrophe here thinks we should nuke the whole island."

"That's not what I said."

"Then why don't you explain it to us," Vinzetti said.

"What I meant," Fontana said, "was that we should use the

weapons we have in place to resolve this situation."

"What did you have in mind, Major?" Elizabeth Lee asked.

"Vesuvius, ma'am."

The virtual room fell silent. The Vesuvius network of military satellites was a sore issue for the U.S. military in general and the Army in particular. The Army operated the Vesuvius orbital arms platform, the existence of which, until an incident last year, had been imminently deniable. Nine months ago Vesuvius had been subverted by hostile forces. The Army had been forced to admit to the world not only that a chain of satellites capable of nuclear, chemical, biological, laser, and accelerated particle warfare was in place, but also that it had almost been used against humanity on a global scale.

"The public wants to think Vesuvius went away," Vinzetti said. "You use it now and it'll all come back in your face again."

"Who's going to tell them?" Marine Lieutenant Brosnan said.

Lee spoke carefully. "Command does not want Vesuvius in the public eye, that's true. But it has not gone away. It remains our primary platform for antisatellite operations and theater-wide deterrence. If the situation warrants it, I have authorization to request target extirpation."

She held up an artificial hand to silence interruptions. "In my opinion the situation hasn't called for this. Nevertheless I have alerted Command to our status and they have Vesuvius on heightened readiness."

"Which means?" someone asked.

"Which means it can power up and fire in under seventeen minutes," Captain Kelly Barnes said.

"From what I understand," Fontana said, "Vesuvius's lasers can cut right through roofs, concrete, bulkheads, and even the armor of a main battle tank, yet are still accurate to within six inches. Is this information correct?"

"That's classified, Major."

"We could be using that thing right now to pick these people off from orbit," Fontana said. "Nobody has to get in front of a gun."

"It won't work," Vinzetti said, almost singing.

"Why not?" Larson of the Department of State asked. "It sounds logical to me."

Vinzetti walked between the cybernetic bodies of the JID-IOC-P. "I'll tell you why you can't use Vesuvius. They're in the middle of a hurricane, for one thing. If you start drilling holes in the roof you take away their protection from the storm. Two, these are scientific buildings with sensitive electronics and substances with narrow temperature tolerances. You start punching holes through the building and who knows how many freezers you'll unplug. Then there's all the innocent people you'll skewer."

"Very well, Mr. Vinzetti," Lee said, "thank you for your opinion. When Director Hamilton or Agent Gillette next comes online, I'll be sure to pass your feelings on."

They sat in silence a while.

"What about TEMPEST?"

"Who said that?" Lee asked.

"That would be me," Air Force Lieutenant Daniel Suggs said.

"Tempest?" Lee said. "Danny, isn't that—?"

"Yes," Sai Cho said. "And it would be better if we didn't talk about it."

"I'll talk about it," Suggs said. "TEMPEST is the NSA's technology for reading the passive radiation generated by electronic devices and reconstructing it into data."

"Huh?"

"They can read what's on your computer monitor while sitting in a van a mile away," Suggs said. "You type it in on your computer and it appears on their monitor, presto! By now they can probably do it from orbit. What do you say, Sai? Want to help out the uninformed here?"

"It is true you may be uninformed," Sai said.

"They can also read what's on your storage devices," Suggs said, "but for that they have to get closer. Or can you do that from orbit now, too, Sai?"

Sai didn't answer.

"How's that going to help us?" Lieutenant Brosnan said.

"We want to bag the White Company, don't we?" Kelly Barnes asked. "With this technology—if it's really viable—we could read every word they're typing, even download the contents of their storage drives. We'd have everything we need for prosecution. Isn't that right, Agent Cobb?"

"Very likely," the FBI agent said.

"Sai," Major Lee said, "is any of this true? Is TEMPEST what they say, and can we use it?"

Sai didn't answer.

"It's probably all true," a Department of Energy agent said. "But he's not allowed to say. Nor is he allowed to let any of you see it. So, no, Major, we can't use it."

Elizabeth Lee shook her head. "This is getting us nowhere. Probably every agency represented in this room has resources that could be called upon to enhance this operation's chance of success, but no one's willing to play nice. A bunch of schoolchildren is what you are. If and when Director Hamilton does come back, I'm going to recommend that JIDIOC be disbanded permanently. Why don't you all go back to your cubicles and wait for word that it's over? In the meantime, I only hope the Navy commandos and Agent Gillette can resolve this situation without any help from us."

The area immediately around the eye of a hurricane—called the eye wall—is the place of greatest difference in air pressure. Thus it is the place of highest winds. The elements from SEAL Team Nine were attempting to infiltrate the GeneSys facility while enduring Hurricane Flossie's eye wall. It was not going well.

The waves had the SEALs completely at their mercy. The

ASDS had ventured too close to the surface and been thrown against Clipperton's coral wall. The minisub had broken apart, spilling commandos into the water. Lieutenant Commander Buck Sanders had no idea where his men were. He felt himself pulled along in a powerful current.

Atop one ferocious breaker Sanders saw an image that imprinted on his mind. The world had turned a deadly monochrome blue: dark blue objects—bodies?—floated nearby in light blue water beneath a wall of medium blue cloud. The objects bobbed heavily amid the wreckage of the ASDS.

How could he tell his platoon to abort? Were these men lost? Sanders kicked away from the surface, heading for calmer water. If he had to knock on the hull of the submarine with his knuckles, he was going to get the rest of his men into the water or get approval to scrub the mission.

He never got the chance. A wave picked him up like a baby rattle and flung him against the prow of the nearest building.

The last things Sanders saw were hundreds of crabs sheltering in the building's pilings, watching him with malevolent, otherworldly eyes.

Tamara's terrorist kicked open a door to an apartment. He had dragged her across the treacherous walkway between buildings, never releasing his grip on her arm. She'd struggled once, and he'd hit his head on the railing. Now he was in the foulest mood she'd ever seen him in. Gone was the kind boy reading his paperback novel. In his place was an animal. An animal who wanted something.

He tore Tamara's wet parka off and shoved her onto the bed.

Ethan stopped short as he rounded the corner. Men were in his closet.

An Arabic-looking man in a black mask stood in the doorway,

an assault rifle at his side. Someone else was inside the closet. A flashlight beam shined and reflected. Ethan heard English.

He squeezed his eyes shut. Moments ago he'd been asleep in that room. Only a full bladder had averted his being discovered. Yet this was just as bad. His computer was in there, still on. His information warfare software was there for anyone with an ounce of IOps savvy to see. He'd left the Hurricane Curly line wide open in case a message came through. Not only had he left himself open for disaster, he'd left his team vulnerable, too.

A teenage boy emerged from the room at a run. "Mr. Hawkwood!" He ran up the stairs toward the entertainment room. The gunman followed him.

Ethan ran down the concrete hall toward the closet. Midway to the door the teenager appeared again at the bottom of the stairs. They froze, staring at each other. Ethan saw recognition dawn in his eyes.

"You!" He held a palm at Ethan. "Stay right there." The teenager called up the stairwell. "Hey, Saddam! Get down here."

Ethan ran, heavy footfalls slapping the floor behind him.

PART THREE

He loads the clouds with moisture;
He scatters his lightning through them.
At his direction they swirl around
over the face of the whole earth
to do whatever he commands them.

JOB 37:11–12

CHAPTER TWENTY-THREE

The Rock exulted in the storm, laughing at the hurricane like a maniac. Like Álvarez. Intoxicated by violence and rape. It soared into the black sky audaciously; Satan's very spearpoint.

The tempest shrieked, powerless to master the tower of trachyte. The great wind had come to drive the Rock into oblivion. Too late it realized it had been by it summoned.

Ethan was in the Otherworld. Maybe it was hell. A nightmare of deafening shrieks and jet engine wind. Spray sandblasted his face. Titanic waves slammed him into the railing like a cat stunning a mouse. The edge of the universe had come at last and his spirit was about to be sucked into the void.

In desperation he had run through the only door through which his pursuers would not follow him. He had evaded capture by venturing onto the walkway between buildings.

Ethan's world had shrunk to a fifteen-foot sphere. Waves materialized out of the blue ether and hurled him into the metal railings anew. There was no more division between sea and sky. All was water and wind. The elements had united to purge themselves of him. He clung to the downwind set of railings, preferring to be crushed into them rather than be ripped loose from the upwind set. He was losing grip on his sanity—how quickly it could go. To have been rational at this moment would have been insane.

In the breaks between waves he slid himself toward the dormitory building. He took that building's reality by faith, since his salt-stung eyes told him the walkway ended in just fifteen feet. For all he knew the storm had peeled the entire GeneSys campus up like an old scab.

He braced for the next wave, but not quickly enough. It shoved his head into a vertical pole. Darkness encircled his vision. He almost lost his grip on the railing. Another wave threw him into the rail. His ears popped as the atmospheric pressure dropped.

Just let go, a voice told him. *You can't hold on, not against me.*

A small shark lay on the concrete beside him. Ethan wondered how long it had been there. He wondered if it had been the one speaking to him. It spasmed, and Ethan saw that its eyes had popped out.

Another wave hit, throwing the shark's body into his. His face lay against its smooth skin. Then the water dropped them to the walkway and the shark slid away. Ethan edged farther into the blueness.

He was conscious of being cold, of his clothes hindering his progress, of more points of pain in his body than he'd ever felt at one time. Nevertheless a part of him was exhilarated. He felt radically alive. This storm was the keenest experience of God's raging power he'd ever known.

A whitecapped breaker tossed him against the top railing. The sea was rising suddenly. Water no longer seethed off the walkway between waves. He felt the concrete beneath him begin to bend.

Then suddenly he was running. A wet body enveloped him. Rubbery like the shark. There was a metallic scraping sound, almost ringing. Something held him fast. A wave hit and Ethan thought he was doomed because he wasn't holding on to anything. But when the crest passed, he found himself still being pulled on through shin-deep water. He heard the metallic ringing again and it seemed to him it was impossibly loud. A huge blue shape coalesced ahead. Leviathan, perhaps. Ethan was pulled relentlessly toward its jaws.

Crashing and blowing. Water and spray and a bright metal hinge. A rude shove. Then softer sounds of the storm, as if coming from outside. Dry carpet.

"Help me!" a voice said. "Help me shut the door!"

Ethan wasn't alone. There was a man with him, dressed in black. The figure dropped a rifle and a pack of gear onto the carpet and struggled to close a door. That must mean he was inside somewhere? Yes, a hallway. How pleasant.

A cold splash shocked him around. "Close that door!" he said, as if the other man were intentionally holding it open. Ethan had to go back outside one step, but together they swung the door shut and managed to both be inside afterward.

The other man collapsed on the carpet. Ethan realized he'd glimpsed the clean-shaven face when they were out in the storm. He saw blood on the man's hands and on the steel cable that snaked out from some kind of utility belt. There was a long knife strapped to his ankle. He shrugged a strange-looking air tank off his back and lay against it.

"Are you all right?" Ethan asked, out of breath.

The man nodded. He looked at his hands briefly, then let them drop.

"Where'd you come from?"

The man must've thought he'd asked his name, because he said, *"George M. Jackson."*

"Thanks for pulling me in, George."

An angry shout came from down the hall. Ethan rolled to his knees, ready to run. A woman screamed.

John Hawkwood paid no attention to his employees chasing Hamilton around. Let him go. Now he was in possession of something far more valuable. He knelt before Hamilton's laptop like a yegg before a safe. "Well, well, well," he said. He found the VR headset and put it on.

Hawkwood flew around the virtual castle environs, familiarizing himself with the layout. He whistled softly when he found Hamilton's IOps arsenal. With such a stockpile he could've brought the White Company to silicon meltdown. So why hadn't he?

Hawkwood took the headset off and sat on his heels. His stomach ulcer wouldn't tolerate too much more roller-coastering. First he'd been secure behind his cybernetic walls, then Algerian terrorists had arrived, then he'd been smacked on the head trying to get permission to work again, then he'd been betrayed by one of his own, then that was proved false, then he'd found himself squared off against a notorious do-gooder, then a hurricane had hit. What was next, space aliens?

A beep in the headset on his lap caught his ear. He put it back on. A message hung in the air before him: Hurricane Curly update.

"Hurricane Curly?" He clicked on the Goto button.

Tamara was ready to give in. Her terrorist was relentless. No one would come to rescue her. She was getting tired of fighting. Soon he would overpower her and there would be nothing she could do. Why not just let him do his business and be done with it?

He sat atop her back on the bed, a knee sharp in her ribs. He had struck her on the side of the head and on her jaw. Now he leaned into her ear and said something in Arabic that sounded obscene. She struggled feebly and he laughed, sensing the end of the chase.

O sweet Jesus, Tamara prayed, *I can't fight anymore. I'm sorry.*

She lay still. He flipped her over and tore at her shirt. She tried to fight him, but he backhanded her face. A ring bloodied her cheek. He pulled again at her clothes.

Then he seemed to leap off her. He flailed to catch his balance, and in that instant Tamara realized he was being attacked. He fell against a writing desk, toppling picture frames and pencil jars. She saw the back of someone's head and noticed that the newcomer was sopping wet. They shoved each other clumsily, neither looking like he fought hand-to-hand with any regularity.

Tamara rolled off the bed into a corner against the wall, dragging the bedcovers with her. She didn't know who was attacking him—it might've been someone else who wanted her first—but for that moment, the enemy of her enemy was her friend.

"Ethan?" she said then, recognizing the wet man.

He didn't answer. He was being slung into a wall. Her terrorist's black mask came off and Tamara beheld a face like a boy's. His hand pulled away from Ethan's head with a fistful of hair.

She and her terrorist noticed his rifle at the same moment. She lunged for it, but he jabbed her face, sending her into a blind fall onto the corner of the mattress.

"Watch out!" she managed to shout. "He's got a—"

BANG.

The bullet struck Ethan in the sternum. Or maybe it was the leg. How could he be sure? He had pains all over his body. A hurricane had used him as a punching bag; what more could a piece of lead do? Still, he'd always thought getting shot would hurt at least enough to tell where the bullet had entered.

The terrorist's body collapsed on the carpet. Tamara shrieked and scrambled away.

Ethan blinked. He couldn't find any blood on his own body. "What happened?"

The man he'd called George walked into the dormitory room, gave Ethan a glance, and flipped his assault rifle to safety. "Everybody okay?"

Ethan stood up, feeling a new bald place on the side of his head. "I guess."

Tamara ran to Ethan and held him tight. She buried her face in his chest, despite his wet clothes, and sobbed deeply.

Ethan's wits were slowly returning. He looked over at the man who'd saved his life. It was clear he was a soldier—but where had he come from? "You want to tell us who you are?"

The man retrieved the terrorist's rifle, hefted it, checked the ammunition, and clicked the safety on. "Platoon Chief Petty Officer HTCS Patrick Logan, Fourth Platoon, Detachment Echo, SEAL Team Nine."

Ethan gently pried himself from Tamara. "You're here! Great." He stepped out into the hall and looked both ways. "Uh, don't you guys usually come in sets?"

Logan looked strange wearing a wetsuit in a carpeted apartment. "It was a problematic landing," he said.

"I can imagine," Ethan said. He introduced Tamara and himself.

"I know who you are, sir," Logan said, wiping a thumb across his nose. "We were fully briefed."

Logan reached into a pouch at his side as if just remembering he'd put a puppy in there. He pulled out sleek night-vision goggles and tried them on. Satisfied, he replaced them in his pouch. "I need to assemble with my team." With that he disappeared through the door.

Kaye Hamilton recognized her name. It was the only part of the guard's utterance she understood. She sat up from the bed in her jail cell as the female guard slid the barred door open.

It was a nice jail. The nicest, in fact, in which Kaye had ever been incarcerated. She supposed that this plain white room with a sink, a toilet, and only one bed was reserved for affluent criminals. Or Americans.

The guard beckoned to Kaye. Perhaps it was time for her to be shot. She straightened her bright green one-piece and followed the woman out of the cell. She was led to a room in which her own clothes were hung on hangers. The guard said something, indicating Kaye should change clothes.

Afterward, Kaye was led through successive checkpoints and finally ushered into an office. A white woman Kaye had never seen was there. She smiled and extended a hand to Kaye.

"Mrs. Hamilton, I'm Margaret Novicki, the United States' consular agent in Acapulco."

"You're who?"

"I was contacted by our Washington office. It seems someone in the FBI was trying to find you at your hotel. The hotel told him you'd been arrested. Calls were made." She opened her palms. "And here I am. If you're ready we can go. I have a car outside."

"My children—"

"Are already in the car. They're fine." Novicki opened the jail door for her. "Happy Fourth of July, Mrs. Hamilton."

Ethan caught up to Logan at the door to the walkway. "You're going out there?" Ethan asked.

Logan eased open the door. Immediately the wind ripped it from his hand, swinging it outward. The storm screamed like demons fleeing the abyss. Logan was knocked backward by a 150 mph wall of water.

Ethan crawled across the wet carpet toward the opening. Only occasionally could he see the surface of the walkway. He caught Logan's arm as the soldier tried to move past him, but Logan yanked Ethan's hand free and continued into the gap.

"Look ou—!"

The door slammed inhumanly fast, as if flicked shut by a giant finger. Logan only had time to snatch back his foot from the threshold. From somewhere Ethan heard the shrill banshee whistle of air pressure equalization venting. Tamara joined them in the hallway.

"I think you can pretty much forget assembling with anything," Ethan said.

Logan snatched a walkie-talkie from a Velcro pocket at his thigh. "Mother Superior, this is Fullback, over."

Ethan and Tamara slouched against the wall. Tamara was bleeding on her cheek and her jaw was already bruised.

"Fullback calling Home Team, anybody home? Over."

Logan swore at the silent radio. It wasn't the endless string of profanities Ethan had expected every sailor to be good at, but rather a single, efficient malediction. He put the radio away.

"What's wrong?" Tamara asked.

Logan shrugged.

"Maybe nobody else made it," Ethan said.

"You think a little wind could take out a whole platoon of Navy SEALs? You been watchin' too many movies, sir. We'll hear from them sooner or later." He sighed. "I need to contact the *Jackson*. Is there a radio?"

"You need to contact who?" Ethan asked.

"The USS *George M. Jackson*," Logan said, poking a thumb over his shoulder. "A submarine. I need to tell them our mission's a wash."

"I thought you said they could still be all right," Tamara said, alarmed.

Logan turned his eyes on her but didn't comment. He turned back to Ethan. "Is there a radio?"

Ethan leaned his head against the wall. "Sure, plenty of them. Problem is, the bad guys have them all. I don't know, maybe they'll let you borrow one if you ask real nice."

Logan twitched his nose. "Other options? Radios in vehicles? Radios not in the central comm rooms? Fax machines? Anything they might not have thought of?"

"I just had a perfect link to the States," Ethan said morosely. "In the other building. I had tapped into the White Company's network and even held a teleconference with my people."

"Why didn't you say that before?" Logan said. "Let's get to your computer."

"Two problems with that plan," Ethan said. "One, it's over in that building." He pointed. "Two, one of the two groups of bad guys on this island found my little hiding place. I had to run. That's how I ended up on that walkway when you dropped in. I didn't even have time to disconnect the computer."

Logan rubbed a finger in his ear vigorously. He repeated his single curse.

"Would ham radio work?" Tamara asked.

Logan and Ethan both looked at her, dumbfounded.

"Uh-huh," Ethan said.

"The creep down the hall from me was into all that." She shuddered. "He kept asking me out."

"Did he have a full setup, ma'am?" Logan asked.

"I don't know. He had lots of gadgets. Used to brag about who he'd called. 'Ooh, Tamara, made a new friend in Brazil,' he'd say. 'I think she wants me.'" She shuddered again. "Creep."

Ethan and Logan exchanged glances. "Lie to me a little, Tamara," Ethan said. "Tell me his apartment is in this building."

"It's upstairs."

CHAPTER TWENTY-FOUR

"S orry to speak like this," John Hawkwood whispered into the headset microphone, "but this room echoes and I'm afraid they'll hear me."

Twenty real faces atop virtual bodies stared at him in the artificial room. The standard naming convention applied here, Hawkwood was happy to see. When he pointed at someone's figure, that person's name would appear over his head. A few names appeared whimsical—Hedgehog and Spidey and Obi Wan—but the others appeared to be actual names—Cobb and Vinzetti and Barnes. Hawkwood recorded them all.

"Understood," a woman named Lee said. "We can hear you just fine, Ethan."

"Nice to see you all," Hawkwood whispered.

There was a moment of silence. Hawkwood wondered if he'd already blundered. Then one of the figures, Barnes, said, "You're wondering where everybody is, aren't you?"

"Where are they?"

"Well," Barnes said, "Gillette's still en route and Suggs's daughter got sick at school. Between one thing or another we're down six people. Every agency's represented, though."

"That's fine," Hawkwood said softly.

Normally the name Gillette wouldn't have meant anything to Hawkwood, but hearing it in conjunction with Ethan

Hamilton's made alarms go off in his mind. He decided to do a little probing.

"If Gillette's not here, who's here for the FBI?" He said it with a lilt on the end, as if in jest.

"I'm right here, boss," a man said, a little querulously.

Hawkwood pointed at the figure, bringing up the name Cobb. "Oh, sorry, Mr. Cobb," he whispered. "When's Gillette due to arrive?"

"Plane touches down in twenty minutes."

"Okay."

The Lee woman spoke again. "What is your status, Director?"

Director? Hawkwood shook his head. *Hamilton, you dog.*

"Director?" Lee said.

"I'm sorry, what was the question?"

"Your status."

"Right. Fine, fine. Well, I'm hiding out in this closet here. Still watching everything our wicked friends are up to."

"How's the hurricane?" someone asked.

"Loud," Hawkwood whispered.

"See any SEALS? They should've landed by now," a man dressed like Popeye said.

Everyone was watching him and waiting for an answer. "Oh, the seals? Sure."

"They're there? You've seen them?"

"Well, not exactly," Hawkwood said, barely remembering to keep his voice disguised.

"You've heard their weapons, though?" Popeye said.

"I don't think so."

"Then how do you know they're there?"

"No," he whispered, "they haven't landed yet. It's only just after eight now. Maybe they don't get up so early. I...I just know they're as good as here, that's all I meant. Look, why don't we get on with it? I'm fine. The SEALs aren't here yet. Now, before I get captured, why don't you tell me what you called to tell me."

Hawkwood listened as one by one the thirteen agencies of the United States intelligence community briefed Ethan Hamilton, or so they thought, about how they were going to rescue him from Clipperton, neutralize the Chehili terrorists, and seize the nefarious White Company. It was a chilling inventory. Midway through it, Hawkwood had made two deductions: one, this was the U.S. government's anti-cyberterrorism force, against which he'd squared off before, and two, Ethan Hamilton was its director.

While someone from the Marine Corps droned on about C4I, Hawkwood explored the computers at the other end of this conference call. The system was pitifully undefended. Nothing that would stop anyone with half an ounce of sizzle. And why not? This was supposedly a secure connection among members of one big, happy family. Still, Hawkwood would've left better defenses up between computers, if for no other reason than to discourage interagency snooping. As it was, Hawkwood drifted in virtual space from computer to computer, funneling everything of note back to his storage drives.

He half listened to a briefing from an agency he'd never heard of. And as he did so, a glorious plan began to coalesce in his mind.

The only thing better than eliminating JIDIOC altogether would be rendering it impotent. What if he could make it his tool? Let it keep its doors open for business, let the lawmakers feel they were doing all they could to fight acts of cyberpiracy, even toss the team a bone every now and again to make them think they were making progress. But play them like a drum.

With the information now in his possession—agency procedures, chains of command, lists of passwords and back doors—Hawkwood had it in his power to play a fabulous game. He imagined a cyberutopia in which he could break any law and steal any prize with no interference from the U.S. intelligence community. If you know your enemy, Sun Tzu had said, and you know yourself, you need not fear the result of a hundred battles.

Hawkwood's attention was drawn back to the briefing. Someone new had appeared in the artificial room. The newcomer's voice sounded like that of a preteen boy, though he looked like a fat Mexican peasant. He approached Hawkwood.

"Hi, Dad."

Hawkwood thought it might be a trick. Then again, this was Ethan Hamilton, the man whose son Jordan was almost as renowned as he was.

"Hi, Jordan," he whispered.

"What's wrong with your voice?"

"I think there are people close to my door."

"Oh. Hey, Dad, guess what? Mom and Katie and I were in jail. It was cool."

"What? How did that happen?"

"They said Mom was a drug smuggler! You should've heard 'em. They said, 'We don't need no stinking badges,' and everything. Boy, was Mom mad. Me and Katie stayed at this kids' jail, so we didn't see any murderers. But Mom saw a real live mass murderer: Audelia de la Machete or something. She's lucky."

"How did you all get out?"

The boy hesitated. "What's wrong with you, Dad?"

"I told you, I'm trying to be quiet because of the people outside the door."

"It doesn't sound like you at all."

It might've been Hawkwood's imagination, but he thought he saw Jordan's animations freeze for an instant. It was probably just a trick of the distance or some distortion caused by the hurricane, because the boy was right there again as if he'd never left.

"When are you coming home, Dad?" Jordan asked.

"Soon, I hope. Jordan, I have to go now."

"Sure, Dad. The sooner we get off the sooner we can get back to Fort Worth, huh?"

"Right."

"I bet Cuddles misses us."

"I'm sure," Hawkwood said. "Okay, bye everybody."

He logged off. When he took the headset off he found his hair damp with sweat. He carried Hamilton's laptop upstairs to the entertainment room, already planning his first heist.

"That's not my dad."

Several members of the JIDIOC team had already logged off. Among the few who hadn't left yet was Captain Kelly Barnes.

"What are you talking about, Jordan?" Barnes said.

"We don't live in Fort Worth, Kelly," Jordan said. "We live in Tyler."

"So? Didn't you used to live in Fort Worth?"

"We don't have any pet named Cuddles."

"He's under stress," Barnes said. "He forgot."

Jordan shook his head. "I checked his TCP/GP. Dad always scrambles one digit. This time all four were scrambled."

"He's being extra cautious," Barnes said, sounding less certain. "Who could blame him?"

Jordan persisted. "He also didn't sound too surprised that we got arrested. My dad would've been plenty mad. But all this guy wanted to know was how we got out. Almost like he'd put us there, huh?"

"Now you're totally guessing," Barnes said.

"You heard his voice, Kelly. That wasn't my dad. My mom's right here. She listened to the whole thing. She says the same thing. In fact, she was the one who figured it out first. That's why I went and checked his TCP/GP."

"Really?" Barnes said. "Your mom thinks it wasn't him?"

"And don't tell me he was scared of people outside the door," Jordan said. "He talked loud enough last time. Trust me, Kelly, whoever that guy was, he was not my dad. Check your registry. I'll bet you a large Cici's pizza you've been snooped."

"Okay, Jordan, just to humor you."

Jean-Paul Dechateauvieux was the third eldest boy in the family. In all, he was the seventh eldest child of nine. He often wondered if his parents were determined to make Dechateauvieux as common a name as DuBois.

Jean-Paul's other brothers were handsome and quick. Jean-Paul was neither. Even his youngest brother, six-year-old Olivier, could outrun him if the race stretched longer than three steps. Bless him, all his life Jean-Paul had been chubby. He was smarter than them all, but it was no consolation; it only meant he could easily comprehend what little favor he held in his family.

His Oncle Nicolas was the only member of the Dechateauvieux family who shared his lot. Nicolas was not overweight now, but he swore he'd been positively rotund when he was Jean-Paul's age. They were both shockingly smart, a fact that brought them together even as it set them apart from the rest of the family.

It was Nicolas who introduced Jean-Paul to the world of ham radio. Nicolas had somehow missed the Internet revolution when he was young, though it would've been a perfect match for his saber-toothed wit, and now Jean-Paul had shown little interest.

"CQ CQ CQ," Jean-Paul said in French. "DE JG7UHA K." He listened for a reply to his general call to any station. None came. "HA2LNE DE JG7UHA. Are you there, Oncle Nicolas? K."

It was 11:15 A.M., Eastern time, Wednesday, July 4. It wasn't a big Canadian holiday. Most of Jean-Paul's family had gone to the park to watch the more athletically inclined Dechateauvieuxs play football, which the Americans called soccer. Jean-Paul had been left at the house to care for a sister who was sick in bed. He couldn't have been happier with the arrangement.

"HA2LNE QRZ JG7UHA. Oncle Nicolas, *écoutez!*"

Jean-Paul heard a signal trying to come through. He fine-tuned his frequency dial until he'd isolated the transmission. It was a man's voice, speaking urgently in English. Unlike his brothers, Jean-Paul excelled at foreign languages.

"QRS QRS. BK. DE JG7UHA. Name is Jean-Paul. QTH is Quebec. QSA 5. GA. K."

The voice was unsure. "Ah, I don't know what you're saying out there. Sorry, I don't speak ham. This is Platoon Chief Petty Officer HTCS Patrick Logan, United States Navy. Who's this? Over."

The United States Navy! Jean-Paul's Oncle Nicolas had once reached a Swedish destroyer in the North Sea. Jean-Paul was hoping to best him. He introduced himself, without ham prosigns, then couldn't resist asking, "From where do you call me, Officer Logan?"

"Jean-Paul, I am transmitting from Clipperton Island in the eastern north Pacific Ocean. Are you telling me I've reached France, Jean-Paul? Over."

"France? Mais non! Only Quebec." Jean-Paul wrote the island's name down. He would have to look it up later. But the eastern north Pacific! Was that farther than the North Sea?

"Jean-Paul, I have been trying to raise Mexico but have failed. Somehow we have reached you instead. Over."

The twelve-year-old nodded judiciously. "The atmosphere, it is the hall of the spirits," he said, quoting his uncle. He'd always wanted to say that to someone else. "Atmospheric conditions make the games with our poor transmissions. There is perhaps a storm near to you."

"We're weathering a hurricane right now," the man said. "Over."

"Aha, you see? A hurricane, you say? But how splendid."

Jean-Paul was certain his uncle had never spoken to anyone in the midst of a hurricane before.

"Jean-Paul, I need you to do something important for me, over."

"Oui, d'accord. You have only to say it."

"I need you to make a few calls."

"Do you know how many computers there are in the Indianapolis area, Special Agent Gillette?"

Gillette placed his white Stetson on his head. "No idea, podner."

The FBI agent who walked beside him through the Indianapolis International Airport was Chris Probst. He was a foot taller and about a hundred pounds heavier than Gillette.

"If just half the people in the city have one," Probst said, "that's almost four hundred thousand computers, not counting people with two or more each."

"That's a mess of computers, Special Agent Probst."

"It is. Now, we'll give you all the help we can spare, but I don't mind telling you you're not going to find anything."

"No?"

"Not in a million years. Ever hear of an old story about a needle in a haystack?"

"Sure," Gillette said. "Have you ever heard the one about a camel going through the eye of a needle?" He'd been reading that story on the plane.

"That's just about as likely as finding one certain group of computers in greater Indianapolis."

"You're missing the point, cowboy. The point is that the things you and me can't do at all can be done nice and easy by my God in heaven."

Probst looked as if he'd just stepped in something. "I read the bulletin on you guys, saying how we have to be polite and tolerant of our Buddhist brother agents."

"Buddhist ain't the same as Christian, Special Agent Probst."

"Maybe, but it's all in the same category to me." Then he told him exactly what category that would be.

They walked for a time in silence. Finally Gillette said, "You do have your strike team standing by, though, right? Tell me you do."

"I do, for all the use it'll be. They had to be pulled from a training mission in Fort Wayne for this."

"They can train anytime. The real thing don't come around as often as they show it on TV."

"It won't come around this time, either."

"Tsk, tsk. You of little faith. Friend, you got to have two things to make it in this life: Christ in your heart and—" he produced a piece of paper from his jacket—"a surprise in your pocket "

"What is it?"

"It's the address of the young lady who's going to tell us where the bad guys' hideout is."

"Honey, what are you doing at the Hotel Club del Sol? Did you change hotels?"

"I'm here with the woman who got me out of jail."

Ethan turned the volume up. "Say again?"

"The consular agent. She got me out of the Mexican jail."

Ethan was acutely conscious of Tamara and Logan in the room. "What did you do?"

"I didn't do anything! But believe me, after it happened I was mad enough that I could've killed someone. It's probably good they had me locked up."

"Kaye! What happened?"

"We don't know, Ethan. Jordan thinks that your Hawkwood person gave me a false criminal history."

"What? A Mexican jail?"

"This one wasn't like the movies at all. It wasn't bad. For a jail."

"What happened to Katie? Is she all right?"

"She's fine. We're all fine, but I think I'm going to go back to our hotel and sleep for a few years."

"Good idea. But first I need you to contact my team. Tell them my computer was discovered and I'd left the Hurricane Curly channel wide open."

"Hurricane what?"

"Just tell them, Kaye. Tell them they better zip it up tight, because Mr. Hawkwood's going to give them a call, if he hasn't already downloaded the entire intelligence community's database."

"I'll do it," Kaye said. "Jordan's in contact with them on his computer."

"Good boy."

Kaye hummed a sigh. Ethan knew it was a cooing she made when she wanted to comfort him. "Are you being safe, honey?"

"Not for a while, Kaye. I'm sorry. Not until we're off this rock. But I'll tell you one thing, I've never felt more in the arms of God than I do right now."

"Okay." Seconds of static-filled silence passed. Finally Kaye said, "I love you."

"I love you, too. Kiss Jordan and Katie for me. And stay out of jail!"

When Ethan turned off the radio, Tamara and Logan were watching him. Tamara had a clean bandage on her face, and Logan had treated his hands.

"My wife was in a Mexican jail," Ethan said.

"We heard," Tamara said.

"Come on, Hamilton," Logan said, "see what you think of this plan."

CHAPTER TWENTY-FIVE

Ali al-Fashir was a happy man. He had taken a terrible risk coming out to this island. He, the bulk of his Chehili patriots, the largest of their three loyal ships, and the entire future of the movement lay bundled in one place, just asking for a single blow to take them out entirely. It violated everything he had learned about operational safety.

Nevertheless it had been gratifying to be the ones in power for a change. Too long he and his men had been the victims. Now, on this island, he was master; his men, lords of all they surveyed. The sheep cringed at the wolves' approach.

Most delectable of all was that now his vengeance was at hand. Ali took away the mental stops and allowed the horrible images to flow. His mother dead on the floor, his unborn sister cut from her womb. Soon he would release them to their eternity. But not until they were borne on the backs of their murderers.

He stared at the wooden crate on the table before him. A dozen aerosol canisters, filled with botulin. Soon this womanish storm would pass and his final journey would begin. In two weeks, he and eleven other Chehili patriots would drive a dozen vans into a dozen ILA villages.

It was unfortunate that many children would suffer and die in the attacks. Ali was truly sorry for that. But with one mighty stroke the plague of Algeria would be removed and over a million innocent Muslims would be avenged. Sometimes it took killing to stop the killing.

Ali gazed a moment through the glass wall before him. Dr. Oscar Redding and John Lipscombe lay on the concrete, a depleted canister on the floor beside them. Their suffering had been marvelously intense. He'd been able to hear their screams even through the thick glass.

Ali al-Fashir was a happy man.

Few things filled a conference room like crisis. Virtual conferences were no exception. Major Elizabeth Lee had watched the numbers dwindle at every consecutive JIDIOC meeting. Now, with the rumor out that their computers had been grievously cracked, Lee's multiframe screen was packed.

"Gentlemen," Lee said, "allow me to tell you what we know. Forty-five minutes ago, in our last transmission through the National Hurricane Center, hostile operatives penetrated our system and collected an alarming amount of intelligence."

The members of the Joint Intelligence Detail broke into babble once more.

"How did they get in?"

"What about our encryption?"

"All our operations are blown!"

"I knew the NHC was a bad idea."

"Think about the operatives! Their identities are exposed."

"That idiot Hamilton."

"Forget their identities—what about ours!"

"Are we in danger?"

"I'm bringing my kids to the base."

"Good time to quit, anyway."

Lee brought her microphone up to some speakers. A piercing feedback squeal made everybody yelp, but left them quiet.

"You people stow your tongues and listen," she said. "Yes, this is a serious breach. In a short time this meeting will be over and you can take whatever precautions you think reasonable. For now, let's concentrate on what's happening on Clipperton Island. As most of you know, we received word from Director Hamilton via ham radio linkup. He gave us— What was that? Someone have something they wish to share?"

No one answered.

"Very well, then. I trust," Lee said, searching their faces, "that any of you who blames Director Hamilton for this security breach will be searching himself for blame, too."

"What'd we do?" someone asked.

"Yeah," Commander Dunbar said. "Seems to me if Hamilton had been just a teeny bit more careful none of this would've happened."

Others grunted approval, though they were careful not to reveal themselves.

"And it seems to me," Agent Coakley said, "that if somebody hadn't decided to play secret agent none of this would've happened."

A stronger grunt of agreement.

"Don't stop there," Lee said. "Why not say that this whole interagency situation is Director Hamilton's fault? And without him we wouldn't have been on the same channel together in the first place and this intruder wouldn't have gotten his intelligence."

"You said it, sweetheart, not me," Dunbar said.

"The problem with that," a new voice answered, "is that this team wasn't Hamilton's idea." President Rand Connor's face appeared in a new frame. "It was mine."

They mumbled shamefaced greetings.

Connor smiled gently. "Major Lee, I understand we have something of an intelligence disaster on our hands."

"Yes, sir. It appears that way."

"And I detect that some of you feel Ethan Hamilton is to blame for it?"

No one answered.

"If anyone is to blame in this matter it is me," Connor said. "This interagency group you're all a part of was my idea from the ground floor up. It seems to me—wouldn't you agree, Mr. Coakley? Commander Dunbar?—that radically new things are rarely perfect on their first try."

"Yes, sir."

"Joint intelligence is nothing if not new. Someone once told me that you have to break a few eggs to make an omelet. I trust all of you have learned from this little episode with the intruder and are taking measures to ensure it doesn't happen again. We'll take good care of you and your loved ones, rest assured.

"Talking about the omelet puts me in mind, if you'll excuse the breakfast food pun, of Francis Bacon, who said, 'He that will not apply new remedies must expect new evils.' There are new evils out there, are there not, my friends? This group represents one of my fondest hopes for a new remedy. Now, what are you people doing to get my boy Ethan off that rock?"

"I was just telling the others," Lee said, "about the ham radio call we received from Director Hamilton. The reason we were vulnerable to the enemy infiltration was that the director's hiding place was discovered while he was away from it. Doubtless he should've taken precautions against such a discovery, just as we each should've had better safeguards locally. Director Hamilton is safe for the moment, but has been effectively eliminated from the IOps picture, unless he can find a way to log on again.

"Before I terminated the link with the National Hurricane Center, I learned that the eye of Hurricane Flossie will most probably pass directly over Clipperton Island. It may be that we can use this to our advantage. Without a viable computer link our traditional IOps strategies will not help us. Perhaps it's time to do as our commander-in-chief has suggested and come up with a few new remedies. Mr. President, do you have anything else you'd like to add?"

"Only this," Connor said. "I know you people have your differences. You've got traditions of hostility toward one another that, in some cases, reach back to the founding of our nation and beyond. Each agency represented here has a fine, proud history.

"But pride isn't always a good thing, is it? Usually the only time people put aside their differences is when they're faced with a common foe. Well, look at the foes we face in the twenty-first century. Look at the foes we face on this Pacific island! World-class terrorists with biological weapons, high-tech criminals who have put you and much of America's intelligence machine in jeopardy. It's a tremendous challenge—the stuff of legends, ladies and gentlemen. I know you'll make me proud."

Connor's frame blipped to black.

The eye of Hurricane Flossie passed across Clipperton Island at 8:32 A.M., local time. Barometric pressure plunged, killing countless fish. The wind dropped to a meek breeze and the air became sweltering. Oddly, the sea remained savage, its level at the highest Flossie could make it in the open ocean.

Clipperton itself remained underwater. Only the Rock, appearing now like Poseidon ascending in the surf, could be seen of Clipperton's natural features. The GeneSys buildings glistened in the hot sun, wet from Flossie's rage and the still-violent sea.

And three people made desperate crossings.

Mrs. Duke was as pleasant as she could be. Mike Gillette would have rather asked for milk and cookies than give her the ol' FBI scare, but it came with the territory. They stood at the door of the Dukes' single-story home, squinting in the Indiana sun.

"No, I'm sorry, Mr. Gillette," she said, "she didn't say when she'd be back. Her boyfriend took her out this morning at eight. I don't know what could be taking her two and a half hours. Would you like me to call her?"

Gillette and Special Agent Probst both nodded. "If you don't mind, ma'am," Gillette said.

"Please come in," Mrs. Duke said.

She led them into a living room full of mismatched middle-class furniture. Gillette took his Stetson off.

"Cindy's her own person, if you know what I mean. Have a seat, won't you?" Mrs. Duke produced a phone from a pocket and pressed a button. "She's always coming and going. She...she's not in any trouble, is she?"

"No, ma'am," Agent Probst said, looking ridiculously large in a low-backed chair. "We just need to ask her some—"

"Here she is now," she said.

Through the windows Gillette could see a blue convertible pulling into the driveway. A young man drove; a pretty brunette rode close beside him.

"I'd better call her in," Mrs. Duke said. "She's likely to sit out there until noon."

"That's all right, ma'am," Gillette said. "It's a fine day. We'll just talk to her where she is." They went outside. "Cindy Duke?"

The girl shielded her eyes against the sun. "Maybe." Her tone, her clothing, and the music pounding from the car's speakers gave the unmistakable impression of rebellion.

The agents showed their badges. The young man turned his radio down.

"Little lady," Gillette said, "I wonder if we might ask you a few questions."

"Let me guess," Cindy said, "you're not from around here, are you?"

Gillette tipped his Stetson. "Is there someplace we could talk alone?"

"About what?"

"Cindy!" the driver said. The teen's appearance matched

hers, but he at least knew how to play nice. "They're the FBI. Find out what they want to know."

Cindy pulled away from him. "Stay out of this, Pike." The look she turned on Gillette was defiant. "What am I accused of?"

Gillette and Probst exchanged curious looks. "Only what you'd expect," Gillette said. "If you'd just step over to—"

"Whatever Dolly McKay says is a lie," Cindy almost shouted. "That guy was dead when we found him. He had track marks all the way up both arms. Sleeping under the bridge…"

Pike nudged her.

"…wasted all day, puking all night…"

"Cindy," Pike warned.

"…stinking, filthy, rat man. He could've died from any one of those or all put together." She seemed to come to herself. She looked at Gillette innocently. "Why, what did Dolly tell you?"

Pike shook his head. "Smooth, Cin. Real smooth."

Probst was writing in a notebook.

"Actually," Gillette said, smiling, "we haven't talked with the young lady in question."

"Way to go, Cin," Pike said, then proceeded to swear fluently.

Cindy's eyes were wide. "You haven't?"

"But don't get me wrong," Gillette said, "I'm sure someone will now."

Probst walked to the rear of the car and wrote down the license plate number.

"So what do you want to talk to me about?" Cindy said, her tone sweet and helpful now.

"If you don't mind, your friend Pike will have to excuse us."

"Why? He's in on everything else."

Pike swore some more.

"All righty then," Gillette said. "I want to talk to you about Andy Culbertson."

She looked up at him warily. "What about him?"

"Yeah," Pike said, interested, "what about that punk?"

"You leave Andy alone," Cindy said.

"Oh, now you're defending him? I thought you said that was all over between you two."

"It is. Now will you just shut up?" Cindy turned to Gillette. "What about Andy?"

"Mr. Culbertson is part of a computer outfit called the White Company. Ever hear of it?"

Cindy was perfectly still for a five-count. Then she looked like a trapped cat. "I have to go now." She looked at the passenger-side door longingly, but Gillette stood there. She pushed at Pike. "Let me out."

Pike all but tumbled to the driveway. "Hey! Watch it."

"Miss Duke," Gillette said, watching Cindy round the front of the car, "I'd rather do this real polite-like, but if you want to play tough I'll be back this afternoon with a court order. Then you will answer my questions."

Cindy opened the door to her house. "I'm not talking to you."

"Tell me about the e-mail Andy sent you last night."

SLAM.

"Nice work, Special Agent Gillette," Probst said. "You managed to scare off your only lead."

Gillette leaned against the car sullenly, feeling a new blister on his heel.

Pike got back into his car. "That twerp sent my Cindy e-mail yesterday?"

"That's a fact." Gillette headed back to Probst's car. "Come on, Chris. Let's go ruin the DA's holiday."

Pike ran after them. "I thought Culbertson was out of the country."

"Can't comment on that, son."

"She told me she hadn't heard from him in weeks." The two agents got into Probst's car. Pike knocked on Gillette's window, and Gillette lowered it. "What's it worth to you?"

Gillette looked at him shrewdly. "What're you offering?"

"If I was to, you know, help you guys out, then, say, some other case came to trial, like maybe about some dead old street dude, would things, you know, maybe go easier for me?"

Again the two agents exchanged looks. Gillette squinted at Pike. "It's a distinct possibility. Whatcha got?"

Pike stood up and sighed. He looked at the house uncertainly. Then he leaned close. "Try the Paul Building."

CHAPTER TWENTY-SIX

Platoon Chief Petty Officer HTCS Patrick Logan, the entire known remnant of Fourth Platoon, Detachment Echo, SEAL Team Nine, opened a metal panel in the hallway. "This is it." He turned to the young woman with him. "You ready?"

Tamara Mack blew out a sigh. "I think."

Logan adjusted his robes and mask, which he'd taken from the dead terrorist. He took a moment to feel under the robes for the knife at his ankle, the pistol in his holster, and the night-vision goggles on his belt. He slung the strap of the terrorist's rifle over his shoulder and pounded himself once on the chest. As long as he still lived, Operation Sea Fire was viable. He looked at his watch. It was oh-nine-hundred hours—SEAL Team Nine's lucky time.

"Ready." He looked at Tamara. "Give me to a hundred."

"Okay."

He strode to the cafeteria door and stepped inside.

Ethan had his dry clothes on now. He'd carried them across the walkway in a large freezer zip bag belted to his chest. Now the wet clothes were hidden, the dry ones from someone's apartment were on, and the zip bag, newly perforated, was carrying something else entirely.

While Logan and Tamara were over in the cafeteria taking on the terrorists, his job was to incapacitate the White Company. For this he had concocted another complicated plan. So many things that could go wrong—no, should go wrong. He heard Commander Dunbar's admonition in his head: Keep it simple, stupid. Nonetheless, Ethan had to admit to a wee bit of pride in his idea. It might not work on every member of the White Company, but he was pretty sure it would've worked on him when he was their age.

Ethan checked the hallway once more. Still nothing. He hefted the remote control in his hand, then sat back against the wall to listen to God. His body still ached from the beating he'd taken crossing the walkway the first time. Now he'd gone across again during the eye—though the winds had been calm, the sea hadn't been. What was this penchant for abuse?

Almost as soon as he'd shut his eyes, a Scripture memory song popped into his mind. "Cast thy burdens upon the Lord and he will sustain thee. He will never suffer the righteous to be moved. As for me, I will call upon God and the Lord will save me."

Amazing. The voice of God again. If that wasn't a promise that God was in control of this very moment, he didn't know what it was. He vowed that if he survived this ordeal he would go out and purchase many more Scripture memory recordings.

He pointed the remote control down the hallway and pushed Play. Nothing happened. Ethan pressed the button again. Had he not just received assurance of God's control, panic would've begun its quick ascent, but now he simply kept pushing the Play button, knowing that if this didn't work, God had some other solution in mind.

Ethan was almost startled by the sound of his own voice, though he shouldn't have been, because it meant that the player had finally obeyed its remote.

"Hey, guys!" Ethan heard himself say in what he hoped sounded like an adolescent voice. "You've gotta come see this! Now that the storm's died down the terrorists have brought all the chicks onto the roof of their building and they're making them strip! Come on up and see!"

Ethan shut his eyes. This was the crucial moment. If the fifteen teenage boys in the White Company—and their two guards—didn't take the bait, things were going to get much more complicated. He strained his ears for the sound of hormones getting the better of reason. What if they hadn't heard? Would he have to sneak back over there and crank up the volume?

The disc player, concealed above a ceiling tile, went on in Ethan's voice. "Mr. Hawkwood, you'd better come too. I think there's a dead body floating around out here. What should I do?"

Patrick Logan counted twelve armed terrorists in the cafeteria. A clump of five at a table, twos and threes here and there, singles scattered around. They certainly weren't expecting any resistance. A few had their assault rifles more or less ready, but most had laid them down altogether. He deliberately lowered his rifle to a slack position, trying to look as negligent as the rest.

He walked through the dining hall, totally ignored by the hostages. Some were still sleeping. He loathed their passivity. If there'd been a man among them, he'd have gotten these people to rise up against their captors. They had to sleep, didn't they? They had to eat. They had moments of vulnerability that could be exploited. But these people had taken to captivity like dairy cows. Logan debated the merits of risking his neck for a group such as this. Still, he had a job to do. It also occurred to him that he had on his hands the chance to carve for himself a place in Navy SEAL legend if he could pull it off. And so he edged closer to the clump of five at the table.

Hurry up and get to a hundred, woman, he thought. *I'm ready.*

"Where are you all going?"

If the men of the White Company heard their master's call, they didn't show it. It certainly didn't slow their tumbled exodus from the entertainment room.

Hawkwood stood up wearily. If there really was a dead body out there, they would need his help. They might be 'Net wizards every one, but when it came to common sense they were genetically challenged.

"Come on, Ward," Hawkwood said. "You, too."

"But…"

"I know the thought of seeing naked women doesn't excite you." Hawkwood shrugged. "That's your business. But I may need someone to help me up there who isn't drooling at the mouth."

"Yes, sir."

As he led the last of his employees into the hall, John Hawkwood couldn't shake a nagging thought. He hadn't recognized the voice that had called them all out there. Or rather, he had recognized it, but he couldn't exactly place it.

Tamara Mack stood in the carpeted hallway outside the cafeteria, just as she had hundreds of times before. Inside she'd had memorable moments: a surprise birthday party, an especially good gourmet pizza, a prayed-for opportunity to witness to a friend. It had been one of the happier rooms in her mostly happy time as a GeneSys employee, though it was essentially a plain, utilitarian place.

She wondered at how mundane spots could become immortalized if something spectacular happened there. The grassy knoll, Cemetery Ridge, and the plains of Kitty Hawk came to mind. And now the GeneSys dining hall on Clipperton Island. Whatever happened in the next few minutes, it would never be the same.

...ninety-nine...one hundred.

Tamara opened the breaker box panel. She saw a double column of switches over two feet long. She began flipping breakers two at a time. For a pulse-quickening moment nothing seemed to be happening. Maybe this was the wrong breaker box! She had no clue where another might be. She flipped switches feverishly.

Finally the compressor in the water fountain near her fell silent. Then lights down the hallway went out. She had about half the switches left. Flip, flip, flip. She thought she could hear sounds of surprise from the nearest cafeteria double door.

There was no question about the next thing she heard. Someone was coming down the hall. Someone speaking a language that was not English. She shut the panel as quietly as she could and bent over the water fountain. Just as three terrorists came around the corner: two guards and Ali.

Patrick Logan, the newest Chehili terrorist, stood frozen, ready to pounce. His hand was under his robes ready to pull out his night-vision goggles. But the light outage that had begun on the far side of the cafeteria hadn't swept across the room.

Logan could feel the moment slipping away. Terrorists were milling around, leaving the positions he'd marked in his mind. The blood rage he'd summoned when the lights started to go was hot in his brain. It demanded release. *Just strike anyway!* it screamed at him. *Surprise will be enough!*

But he knew it wouldn't be. He might take half of them out before the others could react, but react they would. They would open fire in this crowded room of civilians. And they wouldn't stop until every bullet was expended or every hostage dead.

He reined in the rage and moved toward the double doors to see what was wrong with Tamara. *Remind me again why it is I never work with civilians?*

Ethan peeked around the corner of the entertainment room, ready to run. The White Company computers sat on the tables, humming their electric harmony. Everyone was gone.

Unbelievable.

He felt as if he were entering a haunted house as he approached the tables. There was an almost palpable presence pushing him away, laying curses on his immortal soul. *Steady, Curly.*

He set his oversized zip bag—with its squirming contents—in a chair and sat at the first terminal. He knew he didn't have time for anything fancy, so he opened a base-level interface window and typed in the command to irrevocably erase the computer's entire storage array. It was one of those commands that wasn't supposed to exist but which technicians at storage drive factories found useful. When the first computer was busy erasing itself, Ethan moved to the second.

Ali commanded his guard to release Tamara's hair. Without so much as an apology he said, "Where is Ahmed?"

Tamara recognized the name of her terrorist. *Dead on the floor,* she almost said. She clutched the front of her blouse as if holding it shut and called tears to her eyes. "He's sleeping."

Ali translated and his men laughed. "You came here through this accursed storm by yourself? Do you miss captivity so much that you would risk your life to return to it?"

Tamara tried to look defiant. It wasn't hard. "The winds have stopped."

"So they have." Ali studied her shrewdly. At last he said

something to one of his guards, who took her by the arm toward the cafeteria.

Away from the breaker box.

Ethan could feel Hawkwood's computer calling to him. *Come try me, big boy. Show me what you've got.*

He pushed the urge away. There were still a handful of computers to erase. But the most important information would be on Hawkwood's computer. And anything he did to these lesser units could be easily undone if he ran out of time before getting to it.

He looked toward the door, unsure. He'd only been in the room sixty seconds, but it felt like half an hour. Surely he was an instant away from discovery. And he would have to go toward the threat to get out the door and safely around the corner. But he heard nothing. Apparently his ruse had worked better than he'd hoped.

Try me, hotshot.

He sat down at Hawkwood's computer.

Logan saw the terrorist bring Tamara through the cafeteria doors. Her eyes found his, then she was shoved onto the floor. The terrorist kicked her perfunctorily and left the way he'd come.

Logan almost smiled. He wondered if there had ever been a strategy in the history of military endeavor that had worked exactly according to plan. It brought out the fight in him.

He headed for the hallway.

Ethan couldn't believe what he'd found. Hawkwood's computer stood wide open to him. There were no defenses in evidence. Of course its master had just been sitting here and there would be no barriers to him, but Ethan had expected defenses to activate after a certain time-out had elapsed. Hawkwood had left his organization just as open to attack as Ethan had left his.

Ethan's fears had been on target. Here was data that Hawkwood could only have plundered from JIDIOC computers. Here were explicit references identifying Ethan Hamilton as Brainiac. He knew he should just erase the whole storage drive as he had with the others. But there was so much more here. Enough hard evidence to send John Hawkwood and his cyber-mercenaries to jail for a month of Christmases. He needed the data on this drive.

Ethan chewed a thumbnail. If Elizabeth Lee and the others were as sharp as he knew they were, they would've detected Hawkwood's break-in and cut themselves off completely. So no funneling this data to a JIDIOC computer. Fortunately, Ethan knew of another option.

He looked at the door. Still no sound coming from that way. Either these hackers weren't as smart as they thought they were or his lie had turned out to be true.

He accessed the White Company's satellite dish and started uploading the contents of Hawkwood's storage drives to Ethan's home computer.

That's when John Hawkwood stepped into the room.

They both froze. Ethan like the fox caught in the chicken coop, Hawkwood like the farmer with his shotgun.

"You," Hawkwood said.

Ethan swallowed. *Got greedy, didn't you, Curly?* His eyes swept the room for another exit.

Hawkwood shut the door firmly. "I always seem to find you in my most vulnerable locations, don't I? What am I going to do with you?"

Ethan glanced at the computer screen beneath him. The transfer wasn't more than a quarter finished. He could think of two options: push the computer over and run for it, or stall for time.

Ethan laughed lightly. "Don't you think this is funny?"

Hawkwood approached. "Hysterical."

"Ah-ah!" Ethan put his fingers on the keyboard. Hawkwood halted. "You know very well what would happen if I just typed a certain thing at a certain place." He typed leisurely then held a finger over the Enter key fiendishly.

"You were going to tell me what was funny," Hawkwood said.

"It's just that each of us has what the other one wants."

Hawkwood edged closer. "You want out of here before the terrorists get back with their machine guns."

"That would be nice."

"And what do you have that I want?" Hawkwood unzipped his windbreaker.

"Don't play dumb, Condottiere," Ethan said. "Or should I call you…" he read from the monitor, "John Coulter Millerd?"

"How do you know that name?"

"What kind of name is Millerd? Dutch?"

"What, not white enough for you, Ethan Hamilton?" Again Hawkwood took a step forward. "You know, we've really gone and done it now."

"What'd we do?" Ethan said innocently. The transfer was about halfway finished.

"Now we know each other's true identity. If either of us gets off this island, the other will be finished."

"That does present a problem," Ethan said. "But I have to say I'm sick of this place, so I don't think I'll be the one staying." Ethan thought he heard voices in the hallway.

"No, I'm afraid you *will* be the one staying."

Ethan detected something in Hawkwood's tone. His eyes, which had glanced toward the door, snapped back to Hawkwood. Who now pointed a pistol at Ethan's midsection.

"Look at them!" Captain Kelly Barnes said, pointing at his monitor. "Like frogs in a flashlight."

So long as the eye of the hurricane remained over Clipperton, the members of the Joint Intelligence Detail, Information Operations and Counter-Cyberterrorism, Provisional team needed no infrared imaging to enhance their view. The Vesuvius camera they were using revealed the very peach fuzz on the faces of the teenagers far below.

They could see seventeen young men on the roof of one GeneSys building. Two were masked and carried rifles. The others were adolescent white males. All seventeen stared into the sky as if they'd seen a UFO. The building upon whose roof they stood seemed to be an island in and of itself; no land could be seen around it.

"That microwave beam is remarkable," Major Lee said.

Earl Hatfield of the DoE smiled. "We aim to please."

"How long until the backside eye wall hits?" Lee asked.

Larry Templeton of the National Imagery & Mapping Agency answered. "Approximately four minutes, ma'am."

"Very well. Sai, how's the download going?"

The moment the transmission had left Clipperton Island, the JIDIOC team had intercepted it. When they'd seen it was headed to Ethan's home computers, they'd taken action. If this was an attack on their director's home, they were prepared to defend his cyberspace. But as they'd monitored the content of the transfer, it had quickly become clear that this was a delivery from Ethan. They'd begun saving copies of the information themselves, but with full filtering on this time.

"We're sending it directly to two printers," the NSA agent said, "as well as to every diverse storage media we could get our hands on. There's rumor of an intern downstairs swapping floppy disks."

Lee smiled. "Was anything chopped off the front end?"

"A little, but we can pick it up later from Ethan's copy. Besides," Sai said, "what we've got is plenty juicy."

"And if Mr. Hawkwood pays us a visit again?"

"Won't happen, Elizabeth," Sai said. "TEMPEST is online now. I'm watching everything that gets typed on every computer on the island. If anything looks suspicious, I'll just pull the plug."

"Very well," Lee said. "Please tell your superiors we appreciate access to TEMPEST."

"Will do, ma'am."

"Mr. Hatfield," she said, "how long will these men remain in this condition?"

"As long as we can keep our beam on them," Hatfield said. "We haven't ever tested it out during a hurricane, but my hunch is it will disrupt the signal significantly."

"So when the eye goes, they go?" Lee asked.

"Yes, ma'am."

"Very well. Mr. Hatfield, has the Department of Energy worked out a way to deliver any kind of suggestion to them?"

"Not yet, Major."

Lee nodded. "Well, we'll just have to hope delaying these men here will be of some help to Director Hamilton. Mr. Larson, I understand we have both Mexican and French warships headed toward Clipp—"

A new voice interjected. "Excuse me, ma'am."

"Yes, Mr. Coakley?" Lee said to the CIA agent.

"Well, Major…" He seemed reluctant to speak. "I think we may be able to help out with that."

"With what exactly?" Lee said.

"With the suggestion thing."

"I'm listening."

"I can't explain it all, Major. It's not that I'm hiding anything, ma'am. It's just that I'm not at liberty to say."

"I understand, Mr. Coakley."

Coakley sighed. "I can tell you that it involves dental fillings."

Lee raised an eyebrow at Coakley's image on her monitor. "I see. So, you're hoping that these teenagers take care of their teeth as poorly as most do?"

"Exactly. It probably won't work on all of them, but it should get a few."

"Very well, carry on with it."

Coakley looked sheepish. "There's something else."

"Please tell us quickly," Lee said.

"We're going to need to piggyback the DoE's beam to do this."

None of the JIDIOC members moved. They all knew what it meant for the CIA to ask for the DoE's help after the debacle with Operation Hydra. All eyes centered on the two agents from the Department of Energy.

"Well, Mr. Hatfield," Lee said, "what do you say?"

The DoE agent hesitated only a moment. "Tell him to bring it on."

Flip, flip.

The last breakers tripped, Patrick Logan donned his night-vision goggles. The advantage was his, but only for a moment. He parted the double doors and waded into the cafeteria with perfect, if computer-painted, sight.

He heard terrorists shouting instructions in Arabic. They were afraid. The hostages cried out. Then a woman's voice rose above them, speaking in English.

"Everybody get down on the ground. American soldiers are here, so get down!"

Everyone in the cafeteria who understood English dropped to the floor, leaving only the terrorists and a handful of foreign GeneSys customers on their feet. Logan decided that maybe all civilians weren't idiots after all.

One of the terrorists began feeling his way toward the breaker box. Logan drew his knife.

CHAPTER TWENTY-SEVEN

Y ou don't understand," Ethan said to Hawkwood. "Your gun can't scare me because I've already made my choice. I knew I was probably trading my life for the chance to stop you. But, knowing what you do, I think I've saved thousands of people. Seems like a good trade to me."

Ethan scared himself. He shouldn't be able to speak about his mortality so flippantly. Didn't he have a little girl at home who would have trouble remembering her daddy after he'd been gone a few years? Didn't he have a son who needed him? Didn't he have a soul mate he never wanted to leave? But that was just the perspective that allowed him to speak so boldly. He never would be separated from Kaye. Not for eternity.

"Did you know I'm a Christian, Mr. Millerd?"

Hawkwood fired the pistol into the wall. "Don't call me that."

"Oh, sorry." Ethan knew his tranquillity was driving Hawkwood to distraction. "But did you know?"

"Yes, everybody knows you're a Bible thumper, Hamilton. Shut up about it."

Ethan noticed that the upload was finally complete. He paced away from Hawkwood's computer toward the chair that held his freezer zip bag. "The thing about being a Christian," he said, "is that you're immortal until God decides it's time for you to die."

Hawkwood raised the pistol to point at Ethan's face. "Lucky for God he's got me to help him make that decision. It's too bad you and I didn't meet under different circumstances, Hamilton. You're not half bad in there," he said, pointing to the computers, "and that's not something I say to many people. I think you and I could've been friends." He shrugged. "Oh, well. Easy come, easy go."

Ethan threw the contents of the large zip bag at Hawkwood and dove under the table. Hawkwood fell to the floor, writhing. Ethan would have liked to stay to watch, but voices in the hall made him find his feet and break for the door.

Crawling over John Hawkwood's body, frenzied by hunger, were twenty red land crabs that Ethan had plucked from the pilings of the building.

"Don't worry, John," Ethan said over his shoulder, "they only eat things that are organic."

Logan went about his task with a ferocious efficiency. It almost didn't seem fair, his ability to walk up to blinded men and cut their throats. It wasn't fair that one man should have to take on twelve armed terrorists in a single attack, either. Never fight fair, the SEAL maxim went. Win at all costs.

Ferhat and Chadli were headed to breakfast. They had escorted Ali to the rooftop and were now approaching the dining hall.

"If that cook has not done what I told him to," Ferhat said in Arabic, "I will make him regret it."

Chadli laughed. "If you do anything to the only cook on this island it will be you who regrets it. Besides, he makes excellent soup."

"Soup! I'd rather—"

Chadli shushed him. "Look. Where are the lights?"

They had rounded the corner onto the hall leading to the

cafeteria. Windows in the double doors revealed that the dining hall was in utter darkness.

Ferhat pulled his mask from his eyes and peered through the window. "Did Houari find a projector?"

Chadli noticed a metal panel on the wall, partway open. "Do you see a film projector, Ferhat?"

"No."

Chadli started flipping breakers.

Ethan ran blindly. He crossed the entertainment room and shot out the doorway at full gallop. If he encountered people now, they were going to meet a charging bull. Ethan had struck his blow against the White Company, and now he was running for his life. He'd been willing to sacrifice himself for the many Hawkwood would hurt, but now that he'd been given half a chance, he was thinking only of himself.

He found himself at the hallway junction. Amazingly, he'd met no one in the hall. Had he imagined the voices? He was all but free now. Once away from here he could just go find a hole to hide in until the cavalry—er, the Navy—arrived.

The door to the stairs burst open. Members of the White Company stumbled into the hall. Ethan heard something like moans echoing in the stairwell behind them. He took the other hall.

In Milton's *Paradise Lost,* Pandemonium is the capital of Hell. When the lights flipped on in the GeneSys cafeteria, pandemonium was on Clipperton Island. Hostages screamed, trying to get away. All over the cafeteria clumps of frightened people careened into other clumps.

Tamara was shoved into a table, then catapulted over. She narrowly avoided smacking her face into the linoleum. She started to get up but felt something slick on her right hand.

When she saw what it was, she added her scream to the bedlam. All around the dining hall lay the bodies of their captors.

Tamara had observed an autopsy once as part of her education. She'd thrown up then, too.

A flash of black caught her eye. She saw Patrick Logan pushing people out of his way. He'd discarded his disguise and now wore only his wetsuit. He brought an assault rifle to his shoulder. People screamed all the more, jostling him. Tamara thought she could hear him swearing. He climbed onto a table, aimed toward a doorway, and shot.

Ferhat fell back under an explosion of broken glass and splintered wood. When he hit the floor he did not get up.

Chadli looked through the remains of the double doors and saw the hostages in an uproar. He also saw a figure dressed in black looking at him over the sights of an automatic weapon. Their eyes met.

Chadli dove for cover. He saw a muzzle flash from his peripheral vision. Bullets impacted where he'd just stood. Unlike poor Ferhat, when Chadli hit the floor he was still alive. He sprinted toward the roof access.

The Paul Building was seven stories tall. It was a 1950s monument to ugly brown architecture. The few tenants it had left were mostly cut-rate insurance companies and ambulance-chasing lawyers. It was one of the least desirable places to do business in all of old Indianapolis.

Two four-man squads searched the Paul Building floor by floor. Special Agents Gillette and Probst stood with the rest of the FBI strike team in the ground floor lobby, waiting for the search squads to find something. They wore black FBI shirts, vests, and/or caps, their badges clearly displayed. Everyone carried a firearm of some kind.

It was a regular business day at the Paul Building. All the companies inside were open. Gillette hadn't wanted to warn anyone, lest the black hats were among those warned. Civilians who entered the lobby took one look at the FBI gunmen and hurried past.

The agents watched the search proceed on a computer-generated 3-D map of the building, beaming from a laptop on the counter. When one of the search squad agents used his radio, a yellow pointer hovered over his blue icon on the screen.

"We're at the east wall," one said.

"Affirmative," another agent answered. "Both teams proceed to the sixth floor. Assemble at the stairway door and await my signal."

On the screen the blue icons snaked up the stairs.

Probst folded his arms over his chest. "Rest easy, gentlemen," he said to the agents in the lobby. "Never fear, this won't end up being a bust. We're here with the famous Mike Gillette. Cowboy for Christ. Hey, by the way, Gillette, didn't I hear about another strike team you led? Out in Phoenix, wasn't it?" A few of the other agents snickered. "I hope your instincts have improved," Probst said.

Gillette had overdrawn his patience account. Probst had been jibing and heckling and obstructing all day. Surely the good Lord would forgive a man if he just had to let the ol' hay-maker loose. He gazed at Probst evenly. The war of eyes lasted several seconds until a radio signal gave Probst the excuse to look away.

"Alpha team in position."

"Ten-four. Beta team in position. Go on my mark. Three, two, one, mark."

On the 3-D map the blue icons spread out from the stairways. Gillette imagined coffee mugs spilling all over the sixth floor. After fifteen silent seconds, the search leader spoke.

"Negative. The floor is clear. These people are legit. Both teams head upstairs."

Probst's beefy smile was back. "Only one floor left, Mr. Gillette."

No one in the White Company had ever seen John Hawkwood in a compromised position. Indeed, no one had ever seen him in any position but on top of whatever had come their way. Now he was lying on the floor, covered with land crabs.

The teenagers came inside the entertainment room dully, as if sleepwalking. A few gawked at their illustrious leader. It wasn't until a crab attached itself to a teenager's tennis shoe and started feasting that anyone came to.

"Hey," the teenager named Gneisenau said, shaking his leg. "Shoo."

Hawkwood shouted at them. "Get these things off me!"

As a few White Company members complied, four more rushed into the room as if chased. The terrorist guards came in, too. They were without their guns and seemed to have forgotten they were supposed to be separate from Hawkwood's group.

"Is he here?" one White Company member demanded of those in the room.

"Who?"

"Álvarez! Is he in here?"

"No."

That seemed to relieve the newcomers mightily. One broke into sobs.

"What's wrong with you?" Hawkwood said, standing.

"Álvarez is looking for us!"

"Who?"

"Álvarez! The lighthouse keeper. He's in the building somewhere."

Hawkwood threw a wiggling crab against the wall. It hit the ground and skittered under a table. "There is no lighthouse, you idiot. Now shape up. We've got to catch someone."

"We saw someone running away just a minute ago,"

Gneisenau said. "Who was it?"

Hawkwood looked at them as if they'd all had their brains extracted. "Hamilton! It was Hamilton."

They looked at him dimly. A few appeared to be trying to recall the name.

"Is he in league with Álvarez?" one of the newcomers asked.

"What is this about Álvarez?"

"He's here?" someone said, jumping into a game cockpit to hide.

Hawkwood wondered if body snatchers had taken over his team. They were all under some kind of mass hallucination. "Yes," Hawkwood said deliberately. "Yes, Hamilton is in league with Álvarez."

"I knew it!"

"If you catch Hamilton," Hawkwood said, "Álvarez will go away."

The thought clearly appealed to some of them. Others were skeptical. "What if it just makes Álvarez mad?"

"Get out of here and find him!" Hawkwood shouted. "I'll make it worth your while if you catch him. Take the goons with you. Shoot Hamilton if you get the chance. Now get out of here. And stop talking about Álvarez!"

It didn't take many gunshots to tell Ethan that his choice of hiding places wasn't going to cut it. Now that people with guns were actively searching for him, the second floor break room seemed altogether dumb.

He ran to the stairwell and went down, a radical idea taking shape in his brain.

John Hawkwood didn't have any more crabs on his body. But he wouldn't believe anyone who tried to tell him that. Every few seconds his hand would streak to a new place on his body or in his hair, looking for whatever was tickling his skin.

Interrupted by such scratching, it took him three times as long to type the simple message. He was composing what was going to be the last message he'd ever send to his Indianapolis headquarters. He was telling them to bug out.

As soon as he sent it, those JIDIOC lowlifes would be able to pinpoint the Indianapolis HQ's exact location. But he owed it to the men he'd left behind to warn them. Besides, they would have precious minutes to destroy as much incriminating evidence as possible.

Hawkwood had spent months designing that Indianapolis base. Years refining its systems. It had served him well for so long. And now he was losing it, thanks to that whining brat Hamilton.

As soon as he'd returned to his computer, Hawkwood had discovered Hamilton's last file transfer: what it contained and where it went. The White Company was finished, at least for now.

Hawkwood finished his message to Indianapolis and sent it out. He leaned back in his chair and rubbed his temples. It was too bad about that base. But perhaps it was time to move on. Right then Hawkwood began designing an improved headquarters. Located, perhaps, in Algiers.

Ali knew he should step back inside. The eye of the hurricane was finally passing on. When it did the fiercest winds would return, with no gradual buildup this time. The clear sky was being edged out by a wall of angry blue cloud. Nevertheless Ali savored the relative calm a moment more.

He'd come to the roof just to experience the eye of a hurricane, but he'd been treated to several additional surprises, all pleasant. He'd found that, for once, the sky over Clipperton was not filled with seabirds. Where they'd been blown to, he didn't care. For once, the air didn't stink of ammonia. For once, the only sound was the surf. If it didn't take a hurricane to bring about these conditions, Clipperton would be a tourist paradise.

The best surprise, though, had been the appearance, just minutes ago, of his tanker. He'd been unable to reach the captain by radio, but the important thing was evident—the ship was still afloat. A few hours of wind and he'd be on his way home.

The low door leading from the roof flew open and one of his men hurried up.

"Chadli," Ali said. "Allah has been kind. Our oceangoing friend has made it through the storm."

"Ali! Soldiers are here!"

"What!"

"Soldiers! In the dining hall. Ferhat is dead. The people have risen against us."

"What? You saw them, the soldiers?"

"Yes!" Chadli glanced behind him anxiously. "One shot at me and is probably coming this way."

Ali couldn't hear him over the sound of his crumbling revenge.

His whole plan revolved around secrecy. They had destroyed the communications dish and the only aircraft capable of reaching the continent. They had confiscated all personal communications devices—no mean feat in 2007. They had struck seven days before the next scheduled supply ship. They had worn masks so as not to be identifiable later. They had done everything to keep their activities hidden from the world.

Ali saw his mother and his poor sister. Now their deaths would go unavenged. He raged at the injustice. Their murderers would go free. How could he be crushed so cruelly twice? He was sinful before Allah, no doubt, but was he so evil as to deserve such a fate?

A hammer blow of spray struck his body, almost knocking him down. Ali ran for the door. If his life's purpose was not to be reached, neither would many others reach theirs.

Tamara stared at Dr. Oscar Redding and John Lipscombe through the glass wall. At their lifeless bodies on the ground.

She had killed them.

Tears nearly kept her from seeing the lab table bearing Ali's crate of canisters. She heaved the crate into her arms, finding it heavier than she'd expected. She had to get it to her lab, where she could deplete the canisters safely. With the few terrorists left alive occupied with Patrick Logan, she might be able to undo what—

Ali blocked the doorway.

"What are you doing?"

Tamara lumbered at him. The crate was too heavy to carry all the way, but she didn't dare put it down.

He wrested it from her grip and shoved her to the floor.

Tamara twisted her knee violently when she fell. She squinted at Ali through bleary eyes. "You can't have those."

Ali put the open crate on the floor and loaded his arms with canisters. He left the room without a word.

Tamara attempted to get up but her knee wouldn't hold her.

"Alpha team is at the east wall."

The search squad leader's voice issued from the tiny speakers on the laptop. "Ten-four. Hold position. Lobby, you guys copy?"

Special Agent Chris Probst spoke into the built-in microphone. "That's affirmative, Bill. You guys come on down for sausage balls and punch."

"Roger, on our way."

Probst turned to the rest of the FBI strike team gathered in the lobby of the Paul Building. "All right, boys, that's it. It's officially a bust. Bad Guys two, Mikey's Raiders zip." He shot an I-dare-you look at Gillette and began herding the strike team toward the door.

Mike Gillette felt chewed up and spit out. He couldn't deny Probst's claims. That the Phoenix raid had shut down a child cyberporn ring seemed feeble consolation right now. His pride hurt, his fist itched, his blister chafed, and right now his hip tingled.

"Oh," he said out loud. "That's you." He pulled his mobile phone from his belt. "Hello?"

It was Major Elizabeth Lee. "Hello, Mike."

"Whatcha got?"

"Mike, you've got to get over to 2117 Lombard."

Gillette beckoned the departing strike team back to him. "2117 Lombard. Where is that?"

"I think that's…wait a minute," an agent said. "2117 Lombard, that's here! That's this building."

Gillette raised the phone to his ear. "We're already there, Ms. Lee. What's going on?"

"John Hawkwood just sent a message to that address."

"What!"

"Telling them to erase all their files and disappear."

Gillette heard the two search squads coming from the stairwells into the lobby. He pressed the phone to his ear. "That can't be. We've just searched this whole building. It must be another of Hawkwood's tricks."

"I'm telling you, Mr. Gillette," Lee said, "Hawkwood's message was targeted to the building you say you're in. Are you sure you're at the right address, Mike? We've got to hurry. Those boys will have their computers erased in less than ten minutes."

Gillette experienced one of those moments which seem somehow outside of regular time. He watched in crystalline slowness as an FBI agent in a flak jacket placed his hand on something in the stairwell. The man uttered Gillette's own thought, as if Gillette had simply spoken it through another mouth. The words took impossibly long to come out.

What's.

This.

Door?

CHAPTER TWENTY-EIGHT

Patrick Logan was in no mood for a firefight. But the gunman had position on him. Without teammates or even a grenade, there wasn't much Logan could do. The defender had the easier part in this case. All he had to do was watch a spot. He didn't have to gain any ground. And this defender, as Logan's bleeding left shoulder attested, was something of a marksman. That only left cheating.

The concept of the human shield, in its varied forms, was not new. When Saddam Hussein used it in 1991, it was already centuries old. Men at the Battle of Fredericksburg had piled up bodies like sandbags. Archers at Agincourt had stepped over a wall of bodies to fire their arrows. And now Patrick Logan used a human shield against an Algerian terrorist.

He wondered, however briefly, how the gunman must've felt filling his own dead comrade with bullets in an effort to pierce through and strike his enemy.

Seconds later Logan trotted down the hallway after the main objective.

Andy Culbertson hadn't been affected by the fear of Álvarez the way some of the others had, but he'd heard the same voice. It was strange how they'd all heard a man's voice telling them that the spirit of Álvarez was angry with them and was coming to take them to the land of the undead. Andy didn't believe in ghosts, mermaids, or honest car salesmen. Even so, the fact that he'd heard the voice at all energized him to a pitch of action resembling fear.

It explained why now he led the pack in the hunt to find Hamilton. The sooner he discovered the wretch and proved he was not, indeed, in league with Álvarez, the sooner he could relax.

"There he is!" Andy said. He'd led the front-runners to a hallway junction. Now they saw their quarry, hurrying away toward a door to the outside.

"What's he carrying?" one of the other pursuers said.

"Who cares? He's not getting away this time," Andy called behind them. "He's over here! Bring the Arabs."

"He's going outside!"

Hamilton reached the door to the walkway and appeared about to go through.

"He's crazy if he does," Andy said. "The storm's back."

"It's how he got away last time."

"Well, he's not getting away this time." Andy met the other group coming up behind. He pulled one of their two terrorist guards to the front and pointed at Hamilton. "Shoot him!"

The terrorist's shots were wild. Hamilton opened the door and pushed through. They could hear the storm's fury outside.

Andy led them down the hall at a run. The door slammed shut in their faces. The other terrorist elbowed his way to the front of the group.

"Oh, let him go," Andy said.

"What!"

"Look at those waves. He's dead."

They crowded around the small window set in the door. They could see Hamilton on the walkway, struggling to hold on. The treacherous blue monochrome had returned, making Hamilton a blue figure in a blue tempest. He wasn't too far away, no more than twenty feet. He did appear to be clutching something with one arm, though they could only see his back.

The terrorist pushed the door open and wedged into it with his body. He fired into the storm in the general direction of Hamilton, the gunshots oddly muted in the windy howl. Before they could tell if the target had been hit, a massive wave crashed over the walkway. It slammed the door shut and threw the terrorist back.

When they could look out again, the walkway was empty.

Ali al-Fashir hadn't expected people to leave the dining hall. Thus when he rounded a corner and found the hallway thick with them, he was taken aback. Some of the hostages carried assault weapons he recognized. Truly his men were defeated. These peasants were traveling en masse, probably looking for Chehili survivors. Looking for him.

"There's one!" someone shouted.

"That's the leader!"

Without so much as a Stop right there, mister, the former hostages opened fire.

"No! Don't shoot!"

It was Tamara Mack screaming this. She was still around the corner, limping with difficulty, but she heard the gunfire clearly. If bullets were flying around Ali, and one of those canisters was punctured…

"You'll kill us all!"

In the eleventh century, Rainulf Drengo led the Norman mercenary force that fought for Melus of Bari and Duke Sergius IV of Naples. When the Capuan Prince Pandulph seized Naples, it was Rainulf who led the force that recovered the city. For his efforts Duke Sergius awarded him the first fiefdom in Italian history: the town of Aversa.

Rainulf of Aversa's twenty-first-century namesake was a worried young man. He'd been left in charge of the White Company's Indianapolis headquarters in John Hawkwood's absence. But now he'd received orders to destroy the computer files and disappear into the populace.

Count Christoffer ripped the printout from his hands. "You read it wrong."

He had not. Rainulf surveyed the magnificent facility around him. He stood on a raised platform at the axis of four straight radials. The lighting was very low in the wide workspace, except down the radials, which were lit up like convenience stores at midnight. He always felt, on this equipment-packed platform, that he was on the bridge of the *Enterprise*.

If so, the NCC-1701 was operating with a skeleton crew. Most of the White Company had followed Hawkwood out to that island in the Pacific. Rainulf barely had enough people to man the vital systems. Tasks such as maintenance and building security were considered superfluous. The automatic sensors would have to suffice to protect them. And if a lightbulb blew out on someone, he could replace it himself or just move over to the next terminal.

Rainulf had said it was a mistake for Hawkwood to go to Clipperton personally, to say nothing of taking so much of their operation with him. Why expose themselves when from this basement they could touch the world? Now it had proved their undoing.

Count Christoffer wadded the printout up and threw it across the room. Rainulf didn't know if the acne-ridden teenager was really that upset or was just happy to have a performance to deliver. If Christoffer wasn't brownnosing Rainulf he was bad-mouthing him behind his back. Hawkwood loved the kid, but Rainulf would be glad to part company with him.

"You all heard it," Rainulf announced. "We thought the day

might come. Well, now it has. Erase everything. Don't even think about taking anything with you. What you can't delete, burn. If Mr. Hawkwood's assessment was correct, the badges are on their way right now. We've got maybe fifteen minutes to turn and burn. So get deleting, then get lost."

Rainulf set about prepping the main servers for emergency deletion. At first he didn't realize what the new sound was—probably because he'd never heard it before.

Count Christoffer figured it out before he did. "Motion detectors!"

Ali ran back around the corner. He saw the woman geneticist limping after him, and he pushed her down as he passed. A soldier dressed in black rounded the corner at the far end of the hall. The man's gun came up, but Ali had already reached the stairwell.

He went up, huffing with the canisters' extra weight. He was headed for a room he'd been to once before: an observation deck that looked out over the dining hall from the second story. He heard the soldier enter the stairwell behind him. *Let him come,* Ali thought. *He doesn't know where I'm going. And he's too late, even if he knew.*

He found the door and went inside. He closed and locked it softly. He could hear the people below. Many of them, like good sheep, had stayed put. Ali walked past old spotlights and video projection equipment and dropped the canisters at his feet. He set one on the railing and started working on it.

Despite his own imminent demise, he couldn't restrain a smile.

Mike Gillette led the charge personally. This time there was no mistake. No bust. His strike team pulled off a sensational coup, capturing an estimated 93 percent of the White Company's total stored data before it could be deleted. Included were the names of every one of their clients, past and present, along with enough evidence to put all their employees away for many years.

After it was over, Gillette even restrained himself from gloating to Probst. Truly, it was a major victory.

The White Company was shut down. Gillette liked the feel of it. But he knew others would take their place. High-tech terrorists, low-tech terrorists. Like a multiheaded beast—a hydra—it would grow a new head to take the place of the one that was lost. He couldn't shake the foreboding that the twenty-first century was going to be the Age of Terrorism.

Logan had lost him. He'd been chasing the man just because he was the last loose end in the building, but Tamara had shouted to him who the guy was and what he was probably intending. Now he was trying to save himself, Tamara, and all the soft civilians he thought he'd already saved. But he'd lost him.

Logan traversed the second story hallway at a cautious walk. There were too many doors and side passages. This guy could be waiting in ambush for him.

Logan heard gunfire. The civvies shooting each other, probably. He continued down the hall. Then he heard a single crack that stopped him in midstride. He recognized the sound of that weapon. Something crashed in a room he'd already passed. He ran back and found the door locked. He kicked it open.

Inside he found the man he'd been chasing. He was crumpled at the base of a balcony railing. Blood oozed from a hole in the terrorist's chest. Canisters of poison lay around him, intact. He still clutched one in his hands. Logan relieved him of it. Then Logan stood up slowly, hands in the air. On the cafeteria floor he saw what the sound of the gunshot had caused him to expect.

Fourth Platoon, Detachment Echo, SEAL Team Nine.

In 1943, a French naval officer perfected an invention that allowed divers to remain underwater for prolonged periods. It was called the Aqua-Lung. Demolition teams used them throughout World War II to clear away mines and other obstacles before amphibious landings. Later it spawned the sport of scuba diving. The inventor's name was Jacques-Yves Cousteau.

Cousteau—and a booklet called *SCUBA for Beginners*—had just saved Ethan Hamilton's life. Ethan planned to use the scuba gear to sit out the hurricane underwater, preferably in the lagoon. If his tank ran out, he thought he would try to make it to the Rock and climb inside. The wave that had swept him from the walkway had had another plan.

The pursuers had left him only enough time to grab the gear and run. He had just slipped the mask on and swiveled the pressure valve when he'd been forced out onto the walkway. The wave had hit him so unexpectedly that the tank had almost been ripped from his arms. He'd had the sensation of being carried swiftly, but over what distance he had no idea. By the time he'd been able to gather his wits and slip the tank on his back, he'd lost his bearings. And he wasn't going up to find out.

He didn't think he was very deep, but still he couldn't see a thing. The water pressure pressed against his ears uncomfortably. He jutted his chin out the way the pamphlet had suggested, and he found the pressure becoming manageable. Precious little light filtered down from the surface, and whatever benefit it might have bestowed was negated by the murk stirred up by the storm. He was clinging to a sharp coral incline, caring only that it was part of Clipperton Island.

Ethan turned and saw two weak spots of yellow light, like luminous eyes, coming closer. All the sea monsters from all the horror movies he'd ever seen flashed before him. An instant later he realized it wasn't a monster at all.

It was a pair of Navy divers.

Begin transmission:

Clipperton occupation complete. Chehili terrorists eliminated. Hostages recovered. Biological weapons incapacitated. White Company personnel and computers seized. Ethan Hamilton aboard USS *George M. Jackson*. Algerian tanker boarded. SEAL team nine and *Jackson* personnel overseeing occupation and evacuation. Four SEALs MIA, thought lost at sea. Search continuing. French and Mexican warships in vicinity. U.S. Navy warships and aircraft present. Hurricane Flossie safely away.

Operation Sea Fire declared complete success.

End transmission.

CHAPTER TWENTY-NINE

Okay," Ethan said, "which of you is ten times faster than the person covering you?"

Mike Gillette raised his hand. "That would be me."

"You?" Kelly Barnes said. "You didn't even have tennis shoes until today! I'm blowing by my guy."

Ethan looked through his huddle to the other team. They stood around the high school football field, covered with layers of sweat and mud. To his own huddle he said, "Who's Coakley covering?"

"He's on me," the DoE's Hatfield said.

"Is he fast?"

"You'd be surprised."

Commander Dunbar called from across the line of scrimmage. "You guys thinking about running a play maybe?"

"Okay, look," Ethan said to his team, "everybody just go long. This is Hail Mary right. Except you, Giorgio, and you," he said pointing to the shortest player on his team. "You two stay close in case I get in trouble."

"Gotcha," Giorgio Vinzetti, the Treasury agent, said.

"Speaking of getting in trouble," Ethan said, "you blockers try to keep Elizabeth Lee off my case for five seconds, will ya?"

"She's quick!" Sai said.

"Just try. This play's going to take a while to develop. And

I'm so sore I can hardly walk, much less scramble." Ethan **stood**. "On two. Ready, break."

Ethan's Elephants came to the line against Dunbar's Wildcats. Defenders scrambled to square off against their assigned players. Ethan picked up the football and started his mock-quarterback jabber. "Blue twenty-two…"

They'd come back to Virginia for their second debriefing in as many weeks. Safely on the other side of it, they could enjoy hearing how close things had come to disaster. It was Saturday, July 7, at four in the afternoon.

President Connor had made a personal appearance at this morning's debriefing. His words of congratulations were great shots in the arm for the team. Connor also surprised them with some news. The Joint Intelligence Detail, Information Operations and Counter-Cyberterrorism, Provisional team was no longer on trial. On Thursday Connor had instructed Vice President Gwent to propose it to Congress, and on Friday it had been unanimously approved. JIDIOC-P was losing its P. And Ethan Hamilton was offered the directorate on a permanent basis, if he wanted it.

He did.

"Pink thirty-leven, Hut, hut."

Ethan dropped back. His receivers went out. Elizabeth Lee and Commander Dunbar rushed. Sai Cho and Gary Reinke shuffled into their way, hands behind their backs. If Jamar Booker thought passing to four Dallas Cowboys receivers on a single play was tough, he should come try to pick from eleven, all running, all covered, and all screaming at him to throw it to them.

Ethan looked downfield. Just about everybody was headed to the right side of the end zone. He wound up to throw, just as Elizabeth Lee squirted through the pass blockers and came at him with the fanaticism of a guided missile. He rolled out of the pocket, looking short for Vinzetti. He felt every bruise he'd suffered in the hurricane. Out of the corner of his eye he saw Lee slip on the grass. Ethan reached back and heaved the football as far downfield as he could throw it.

It was an ugly, somebody-shoot-that-duck pass, but it covered the distance to the goal line. Forty-four hands went up for it. With that many receivers and the way footballs trounced the rules of physics, it was almost guaranteed to plop to the turf.

It bounced off Mike Gillette's hands, smacked Marine Lieutenant Adam Brosnan in the nose, was knocked up again by a second surge of the pack, balanced comically on State Department Agent Jeffrey Larson's head, then fell into the arms of the smallest player on the field.

Jordan Hamilton.

"Touchdown!"

"Yahoo!"

"The Elephants win fifty-six to forty-two."

"No way! This ain't over."

Ethan approached the clump of players. "It is for me. I'm bushed." He helped Jordan to his feet. "Great catch, dude."

"That's two for me!"

"You were supposed to stay short!"

"Oops."

They headed across to the metal bleachers where wives and children watched. Actually, very few of them were watching the game. The wives were mostly gabbing and the children were chasing each other around.

Ethan walked to the opposing team's captain. "Good game, Mr. Dunbar."

Dunbar slapped Ethan's outstretched hand. "Yeah, right. Fifty-six to forty-two. Next time, let's pick teams."

"I thought it was a good way to do it," Ethan said. He had put one agent from each JIDIOC agency on his team and the other from each agency on Dunbar's.

"What about military versus civilian?" Dunbar said.

The cheers in favor of this idea were drowned out by a chorus of variations on the theme: No way.

"Hey," Ethan said to Dunbar as they all gathered up shirts and watches, "tell me something. You didn't explain this in the briefing. Where did those SEALs come from?"

"You were on the *Jackson,* weren't you? I thought the divers took you aboard."

"But I mean where did they come from after they launched? Logan thought he was alone."

"You mean you thought the whole platoon was history?" Dunbar said skeptically. "Mister, you need to come to So Solly Day."

"Huh?"

"Last day of SEAL training. Make or break day. Makes Hurricane Flossie look like baby spit."

"So why didn't they land when Logan did?"

"You were out in that water, you felt the currents. The rest of the platoon was swept all the way across the island, like you were, and driven out to sea. They had difficulty getting their bearings. A few just swam against the current, hoping to reach land. Others attempted to surface to get a fix on their location. The *Jackson* had tethered dive teams in the water almost from the get-go, checking out every small sonar blip. One by one the SEALs either got picked up or made landfall on their own. Except for the four that are still missing, of course."

"How much longer will they search for them?" Larson asked.

"Not more than another forty-eight hours," Dunbar said. "They're tough. If they're alive, they'll turn up." His eyes dared anyone to contradict him. "Anyway, the team assembled in the designated building, but slowly, piecemeal. Most of them were either injured or completely fatigued, or both. They gathered their strength, then moved on the enemy. I'd say they made it at just the right time."

Ethan nodded. They were almost within earshot of the families. Ethan lingered on the sideline and most of the team members stayed, too.

Dunbar continued. "They finally got the op back in gear and headed over to the right building. When they hit that cafeteria the only gun-toters they were expecting to meet were terrorists. They'd been told they could shoot anything with a weapon. So when they saw all those guns in the hands of what turned out to be hostages, it almost got real bad. But it became clear pretty quick they weren't North African terrorists. They walked inside and found out somebody'd done their job for them. They thought the hostages had, you know, turned on the bad guys. Yeah, right."

"If they had," Brosnan said, "there wouldn't have been just terrorists dead on the floor."

"That's right," Dunbar said. "Logan's the genuine article. I've put him in for the Navy Cross for his actions on Clipperton. Plays his cards right he'll have his own SEAL team in two years."

Ethan almost wished he'd been a fly on the wall when Logan had waded through that cafeteria. He was just glad there were men like Logan on the good guys' side.

"But how did they know to shoot Ali?" Ethan asked. "They couldn't have known who he was or what he was about to do."

"It wasn't too hard to figure out," Dunbar said. "He's the only Arab-looking dude in the place, he's got a black mask on, and he's working on some kind of thing that looked to the men like a gas grenade. You do the math. Then there's half the people in the cafeteria shouting, 'He's their leader, he's their leader!'" Dunbar shrugged. "They popped him like a clay pigeon."

"And they knew not to shoot the canisters…exactly how?"

Dunbar raised a finger and squinted. "Sailor's instinct, Mr. Director, sir."

"What he means," Kelly Barnes said, "is that they got bird-brain lucky."

"Watch your mouth, pencil-neck."

"Hey," Ethan said, "I thought all this was over."

"Yeah, sure," Gary Reinke of the Air Force said. "Two hundred years of it and he thinks it's over."

"Well, it's over in this department," Ethan said, trying out his new authoritative voice. He addressed the whole group. "We've proven ourselves, ladies and gentlemen. We've shown that we're stronger together than we are alone, at least for the jobs this team's charter will catch. So I expect zero clashes from this point forward. Not Army-Navy, not FBI-CIA, not military-civilian, not anything. Am I understood?"

They answered with a few grumbles.

"Am I understood?" he repeated, exactly like Sergeant Carter.

"Sir, yes, sir!"

"Good. Then it's settled."

They stood silently for a while. Barnes grabbed the football from Jordan and they backed off to toss it.

"Hey, I've got a question," Larry Templeton of the National Imagery & Mapping Agency said.

"Shoot, Larry."

"What happened to John Hawkwood? The briefing said he couldn't go to prison yet because he needed counseling. What's that all about?"

Ethan shot a look at Sai and Calvin Coakley. Sai was carefully studying the back of his hand. And Coakley was looking at him innocently. "Well," Ethan said, "it seems Mr. Hawkwood has had…an attack."

"An attack?"

"Yes. Hallucinations, unexplained memory loss, that sort of thing."

"Hmm."

"Yes, it seems poor Mr. Hawkwood is under the impression that he's been abducted by aliens and operated on in their UFO."

"I see."

Ethan nodded grandly. "There's whole chunks of time he can't remember."

"That's too bad," Templeton said.

"That's not the only thing he doesn't remember," Sai said slyly.

"What else?"

Sai looked at Ethan.

"Mr. Hawkwood has inexplicably forgotten one minor detail," Ethan said. "Something he learned but that it was better for him not to know."

"That you're Brainiac," Templeton said.

Ethan lifted his hands. "Did I say that?"

"How did this terrible brain damage happen to poor Mr. Hawkwood?"

"I have no idea," Ethan said. "For that you'll have to ask Sai and Calvin."

"No comment."

"Me neither."

"Anyway," Ethan said, "suffice it to say our secret's safe with Mr. Hawkwood. Even if he ever does get out of prison, which I hope doesn't happen, he'll have trouble explaining that flying saucer episode to potential clients. It's a shame, really. Such a waste of talent." He sighed dramatically.

A female voice drifted out to them. It was Liz Gillette, calling for Mike. Gillette stood up. "Excuse me, y'all."

"Okay, but come back," Elizabeth Lee said. "I want to know how you were already at the Paul Building when I called you."

"Oh, that was nothin', darlin'. All I had to do was solve the murder of a poor ol' street bum. That sparked a lovers' spat, which led to an obstruction of justice, which led to this young kid tellin' us perzactly where the black hats were at." He shrugged. "Simple."

Liz called again.

"You'd better get used to jumping when she calls, Mike," Barnes teased.

"Yeah," Vinzetti said, "especially when the baby comes."

Gillette spun around. "How'd you know about that?"

Vinzetti looked stunned. "What'd I say?"

Realization seeped through the group. "Ooooh, Mike, you dog, you!"

"Shut up, y'all." Gillette scampered over to his wife.

Ethan looked at Vinzetti. "Is she pregnant?"

"How should I know? I was only teasing him."

"You hit it on the head," Coakley said. "That boy's gonna be a daddy."

Ethan watched how Gillette cradled his wife's shoulders. He seemed almost awkward around her, but exceedingly happy. *"You dog" is right.*

"Speaking of families," Elizabeth Lee said to Ethan, "I hear yours became intimately acquainted with the insides of two Mexican jails."

"Ooooh, Ethan!"

Ethan felt his face redden. "It's true. I'm afraid it is. Mr. Hawkwood, may his memory rest in peace, arranged to have my family accused of narcotics smuggling and sent to jail."

"Cheap shot," someone said.

"They're lucky they didn't get executed."

"No kidding," Ethan said. "Of course you all know how I feel about luck." He smiled. "All right, you gangsters, who's for dinner at Cuco's?"

Several people were. Mike Gillette rejoined them, looking sheepish.

"Then let's get cleaned up and meet there at about six." Ethan stood still as his team members walked by. "Oh, one more thing." They turned to look. "You guys don't know how proud I am to serve with you. I... Anyway, thanks. Here's to a bright future together."

They cheered and clapped him on the back. As they walked toward the bleachers, Gillette put his arm around Ethan. "Next time something like this comes up...."

"Yes?"

"Don't go on any vacations, okay?"

"Deal."

Tyler, Texas, had never looked so wonderful. Tall pine trees, orange dirt, and their own private lake. Hal and Penny, their two household computer systems, had tended the place well, but it needed some humans to clutter it up properly.

The day they arrived home they all slept fourteen hours. The next day Ethan and Jordan played in the game room until even they were sick of computer games. Ethan took Kaye out to dinner—"Anything but Mexican food, honey"—and they watched a movie after the kids went to bed.

Now Ethan was up with Katie at two in the morning. "Daddy, I woke up!"

"I see that, sweetie."

"Can I watch Sinnarella?" she asked, nodding happily.

"No, Katie, we're not watching *Cinderella* at two in the morning."

"But I'm not sleepy."

"Tell you what, would you like to read some books?"

"All righty."

Ethan took a stack of books from her shelf and sat on the floor. Katie curled up on his lap. After the fourth book Ethan leaned his head back, just to rest his eyes.

That's how Kaye found them in the morning.

EPILOGUE

he Mexican Navy seized the Algerian tanker. The French got to keep Clipperton. And the Americans got bragging rights.

The French government revoked GeneSys's lease on Clipperton Island. GeneSys was dissolved. Most of the GeneSys specialists were quickly hired by other biotech companies. Mortimer McCall did not escape international law, as he had hoped. His lawyers were still appealing. In the meantime, his assets were frozen.

Tamara Mack was acquitted of all charges related to furthering the efforts of terrorists, as were all the other surviving GeneSys employees. Tamara took a steady, midrange job at the UCLA labs. Two evenings a week, she taught a Bible study in her apartment. John Hawkwood and the White Company went to jail. The names of their clients, present and former, were turned over to the appropriate law enforcement agencies for investigation.

The GeneSys complex on Clipperton was gutted and its equipment sold at auction. The French Navy affixed another brass plaque to the Rock before standing offshore and shelling the GeneSys buildings. Then they sailed for the high seas.

Leaving Clipperton to the crabs.